Behind the Mask

Classical Literature and Society

Series Editor: David Taylor

Classics and the Bible: Hospitality and Recognition
John Taylor

Culture and Philosophy in the Age of Plotinus
Mark Edwards

Homer: The Resonance of Epic
Barbara Graziosi & Johannes Haubold

Juvenal and the Satiric Genre
Frederick Jones

Ovid and His Love Poetry
Rebecca Armstrong

Pastoral Inscriptions: Reading and Writing Virgil's Eclogues
Brian Breed

Pausanias: Travel Writing in Ancient Greece
Maria Pretzler

Propertius: Poet of Love and Leisure
Alison Keith

Silent Eloquence: Lucian and Pantomime Dancing
Ismene Lada-Richards

Statius, Poet Between Rome and Naples
Carole E. Newlands

The Myth of Paganism
Robert Shorrock

The Roman Book
Rex Winsbury

Thucydides and the Shaping of History
Emily Greenwood

Papyrus, third century CE, of the opening of Menander's *Misoumenos*

Behind the Mask

Character and Society in Menander

Angela M. Heap

BLOOMSBURY ACADEMIC
LONDON • NEW YORK • OXFORD • NEW DELHI • SYDNEY

BLOOMSBURY ACADEMIC
Bloomsbury Publishing Plc
50 Bedford Square, London, WC1B 3DP, UK
1385 Broadway, New York, NY 10018, USA

BLOOMSBURY, BLOOMSBURY ACADEMIC and the Diana logo
are trademarks of Bloomsbury Publishing Plc

First published in Great Britain 2019
Paperback edition first published 2021

Cover design: Terry Woodley
Cover image: Relief of a seated poet (Menander) with masks of New Comedy, 1st century
BC – early 1st century AD. Collection of Princeton Art Museum/Wikimedia Commons.

A catalogue record for this book is available from the British Library.

Library of Congress Cataloging-in-Publication Data
Names: Heap, Angela M., author.
Title: Behind the mask: character and society in Menander / by Angela M. Heap.
Description: London: Bloomsbury Academic, 2019. | Series: Classical literature
and society | Includes bibliographical references and index.
Identifiers: LCCN 2018053347 (print) | LCCN 2018054948 (ebook) |
ISBN 9781472528094 (epub) | ISBN 9781472528063 (epdf) | ISBN 9781472534927 (hb)
Subjects: LCSH: Menander, of Athens—Criticism and interpretation. | Menander, of
Athens—Technique. | Classical drama (Comedy)—History and criticism. |
Literature and society—Greece—History—To 146 B.C.
Classification: LCC PA4247 (ebook) | LCC PA4247.H43 2019 (print) | DDC 882/.01—dc23
LC record available at https://lccn.loc.gov/2018053347

ISBN: HB: 978-1-4725-3492-7
      PB: 978-1-3501-9069-6
      ePDF: 978-1-4725-2806-3
      eBook: 978-1-4725-2809-4

Series: Classical Literature and Society

Typeset by RefineCatch Limited, Bungay, Suffolk

To find out more about our authors and books visit
www.bloomsbury.com and sign up for our newsletters.

For John

Contents

Figures

Acknowledgements

I would like to thank the staff of the following libraries: the Faculty of Classics, Cambridge, particularly Lyn Bailey and Judith Waring, Murray Edwards College, Cambridge and its Elizabeth Rawson collection, the University Library and the Central Library in Cambridge, the library of the Institute of Classical Studies in London, and that of the Fondation Hardt, Geneva.

This book could not have been written without the teaching of the marvellous Eric Handley, in particular for his humble observation that critics only frame the painting – they don't paint it. There are no words to thank Pat Easterling for supporting the project with her patient encouragement and mentoring, and her belief that nothing is wasted. The Fellows of Murray Edwards very kindly included me in their number and once granted a sabbatical to me as their Librarian, which was very useful. David Konstan should be thanked for once walking all the way up to Murray Edwards to talk about Menander and for morale-boosting postcards. Thanks also to Lin Foxhall and Graham Shipley.

Paul Cartledge is owed a great debt for wading through my (almost) final draft. Colin Austin also read drafts and shared his love of deciphering Menander papyri; he stayed up all night to find out what happened in the *Samia*. Richard Hunter read an early draft of some of my ideas. Franco Basso answered some rather last-minute linguistic queries. Judith Owen discussed my work and offered helpful suggestions. Paul Millett passed on duplicate articles from Professor Sandbach's private library and Rosanna Omitowoju helped with the historical context. Despina Christodoulou imparted her knowledge of the role of the *hetaira* over tea. I have very much appreciated the moral support of several other members of the Faculty of Classics in Cambridge. Any errors, of course, are my own responsibility.

Various friends from my Oxford days and librarian colleagues from the University of Reading, Emmanuel and Murray Edwards, Cambridge have encouraged me over the years. My Dry Drayton revue friends have also given moral support, practical experience of putting on shows and, most importantly, have made me laugh. Ilektra Devereux helped me decipher Dedoussi's modern Greek commentary on the *Samia*. I am grateful to members of my French conversation class for their friendship; Jenny Bovaird has answered emails giving IT support. Joan Sandford and members of Liz Beardmore's family have even read some of my work.

I would also like to thank Huw Stevenson for sending me a copy of his splendid family history.

Eric and Margaret Heap gave me a love of classics and comedy and, with John and Eileen Patterson, help with young children. My husband John and my daughters Emily and Laura have been wonderful in their belief that the book would one day be finished. 'Team Angela', as they have become, did a great deal to assist in the final stages.

My gratitude is also due to the editors at Bloomsbury, especially David Taylor, for their belief in the project and for their patience. My apologies if I have forgotten anyone else's contribution: the price of enjoying my children's company has been that this book has taken a long time to write.

Approximately one thousand three hundred and fifty (1,350) words are taken from *Menander: Plays and Fragments*, translated with an introduction by Norma Miller (London and New York: Penguin Classics, 1987). Copyright © Norma Miller, 1987. Reproduced by permission of Penguin Books Ltd.

Abbreviations

AAH	Acta Antiqua Academiae Scientiarum Hungaricae
ABSA	Annual of the British School at Athens
AJPh.	American Journal of Philology
AM	Mitteilungen des Deutschen Archäologischen Instituts. Athenische Abteilung
ANT	Antiquity
Ant.K	Antike Kunst
AW	Ancient World
BICS	Bulletin of the Institute of Classical Studies of the University of London
Cl.Ant.	Classical Antiquity
C Phil.	Classical Philology
Class. Med.	Classica et Mediaevalia
CQ	Classical Quarterly
CR	Classical Review
Entretiens Hardt	Entretiens sur l'Antiquité Classique, Fondation Hardt, Vandoeuvres-Geneva
G&R	Greece and Rome
G&R N.S.	Greece and Rome New Surveys in the Classics
GRBS	Greek, Roman and Byzantine Studies
HIR	Harvard International Review
IG	Inscriptiones Graecae
JHS	Journal of Hellenic Studies
JRA	Journal of Roman Archaeology
Kl. Pauly	Der Kleine Pauly: Lexikon der Antike, Stuttgart: Druckenmüller (1964–75)
LCM	Liverpool Classical Monthly

LIMC	*Lexicon Iconographicum Mythologiae Classicae*, Zurich (1981–)
LSJ	H. G. Liddell and R. Scott (eds) (1968), *Greek–English Lexicon* (1925–40), 9th ed. revised and augmented by H. S. Jones; Suppl. by E. A. Barber and others
MNC³	T. B. L. Webster (1995), *Monuments Illustrating New Comedy, 2v.*, 3rd edn revised and enlarged by J. R. Green and A. Seeberg, BICS Supplement 50
OCD	*Oxford Classical Dictionary*, 4th edn, S. Hornblower, A.J. Spawforth and E. Eidinow (eds) OUP (2012)
OCT	*Oxford Classical Texts*
P Oxy.	*Oxyrhynchus Papyri*
PCG	R. Kassel and C. Austin (eds) (1983–), *Poetae Comici Graeci*, v.1, Berlin
PCPS	*Proceedings of the Cambridge Philological Society*
PRIA	*Proceedings of the Royal Irish Academy*
RE	A. Pauly, G. Wissowa and W. Kroll, *Real-Encyclopädie der klassischen Altertumswissenschaft* (1893–)
REG	*Revue des Études Grecques*
RIDA	*Revue Internationale des Droits de l'Antiquité*
SAR	*Scottish Art Review*
TAPhA	*Transactions and Proceedings of the American Philological Association*
Test.	*Testimonium*
ZPE	*Zeitschrift für Papyrologie und Epigraphik*

Introduction

Ancient Greek comedy is often wrongly spoken of as if synonymous with the raucous, boisterous and political humour of Aristophanes. Aristophanes wrote his plays in the fifth century BCE. However, his successor Menander, writing in the fourth century BCE, deserves to be better known. Although famous and admired amongst both the Greeks and the Romans, most of Menander's plays were mysteriously lost, something of a paradox,[1] until recent discoveries on papyrus in the sands of Egypt started to return him to the classical canon. These discoveries continue today and now enough survives of his comedies for him to be examined as an author in his own right.

The lament to Night which opens Menander's play the *Misoumenos*, 'The Man who was Hated', is delivered by Polemon, a soldier lover, by his own front door. This text was completely lost for centuries.[2] Its discovery in the twentieth century helped to overturn certain assumptions that had been made about Menander's use of so-called 'Middle Comedy' stereotypes.[3] Substantially more text exists of Menander than does of Middle Comedy, enough to make viable this study of the plays as social comedies and of the characters as, at least partly, the product of his time. Indeed, new discoveries continue to add to our knowledge of Menander's work.

The Menandrian explosion

The story of Menander's reappearance is a tale worth telling, as scholars struggle to keep pace with new finds. It begins in Egypt, with a fourth-century CE codex[4] found in the library at St Catherine's monastery on Mount Sinai. In 1844 a not altogether reputable adventurer-scholar named Constantin von Tischendorf made an exciting discovery: two parchment leaves glued into the binding, which turned out to contain fragments of *Epitrepontes*, translated often as 'The Arbitration', and *Phasma*, 'The Phantom', by Menander.[5]

Egypt continues to have a very important role in the survival and recovery of ancient Greek literary texts hitherto lost to us, including Menander, due to its dry climate and sand – ideal conditions for the preservation of papyrus, a writing material made by crushing together fibres from the papyrus plant.[6] Large quantities of documentary (as opposed to literary) papyri were found in 1877 and 1887, and in 1895 people started to go to Egypt to look for more.[7] Excavations began in the Fayûm area and at the ancient town of Oxyrhynchus, which was discovered by the Oxford scholars Bernard Grenfell and Arthur Hunt.[8]

In 1905, another manuscript of Menander, on papyrus, turned up stuffing a jar in Aphroditopolis.[9] Gustave Lefebvre had been excavating the house (dating to the sixth century CE) of a lawyer called Flavius Dioskoros. These codex sheets, known now as the Cairo codex, preserved more than 1,500 lines of five of Menander's comedies.

In 1959, thanks to a codex obtained by Martin Bodmer,[10] a Swiss private collector and scholar, the first complete play was published: the *Dyscolus*, 'The Bad-Tempered Man'. An excited Professor Turner exclaimed in the *The Times* of London (6 June) that at last all could share the pleasure of 'direct instead of mediated acquaintance with an exceptionally skilful and elegant playwright'.[11]

Fragments of varying length from other plays had been discovered in the meantime. Perhaps the most remarkable survival has been the manuscript (belonging to the century in which Menander died) of large parts of *Sikyonios*, 'The Man from Sikyon', which was published in 1965, having been skilfully extracted from the wrappings of a mummy by two papyrologists at the Sorbonne, Alain Blanchard and André Bataille.

Since then, new papyri have come to light not only for the *Misoumenos* but also, very significantly, for Menander's *Dis Exapaton*, 'The Double Deceiver', a portion of the Greek text adapted by Plautus for his *Bacchides*, 'The Two Bacchises'.[12] Discoveries continue to be made and published[13] or reported, such as a third-century CE fragment of *Perikeiromene*, 'The Shorn Girl', with three or four different musical settings of the same line (796) written above it each time it is cited (the significance of one of the note-symbols is not known). This could be evidence for later practice in the performance of Menander. The notation may, however, refer to the pitch in spoken delivery, as no other example from comedy is known, and the passage, like others in Menander, imitates tragic style.

Other passages have added significantly to scholars' knowledge of *Epitrepontes*, as well as part of *Titthe*, 'The Wet-Nurse', having been found in the remains of a fourth-century parchment codex of Menander, part of a double palimpsest, in the Vatican Library. There was, then, a medieval tradition for Menander.[14] Erich Segal had referred already, in the preface to his second edition of *Roman Laughter*, to the 'Menandrian Explosion'.[15] A third revised Oxford Classical Text is in preparation to take account of continuing finds. What once was a single Loeb edition volume now fills three.

In spite of his considerable status as an author in ancient times, Menander's work has been dismissed by one scholar as 'puffball plays'[16] and others regularly criticize their conventional plots.[17] Some scholars, however,[18] have been more open to exploring Menander's appeal and that is the aim of this book.

Menander used the theatrical masks of his immediate comic predecessors, whose plays are even more fragmentary. But what kind of plays did he write? His comedies seem at first sight to be concerned with the *oikos*, the 'family' rather than the *polis* or 'city', but that may not be the whole story.

In the past some historians have been tempted to cite Menander as evidence. This was sometimes done without considering which character is speaking and what that character might be like. Here a study such as the second half of this book, which investigates his techniques of characterization, may be very useful. Putting the plays in their historical context will also be key here, since social norms need to be established or at least explored in order to determine what stereotypes may have existed in society at the time as well as in earlier comedy.

The first half of the book covers various important topics relevant to the study of Menander: the theatrical artefacts, the conventions surrounding the performance of his plays and Menander's life and times, together with likely influences on his writing. The opening chapter looks at the terracotta masks and figurines dated to the fourth century BCE found on Lipari, one of the Aeolian islands off the coast of Sicily, miniature versions of those used by Menander and his contemporaries. Masks and costumes would have introduced the characters visually to the audience and suggested to them the various stock types established in earlier comedy, for example, the *hetaira*, the slave, the young man in love and the soldier.

The masks and figurines lead naturally to an investigation of where and how Menander's plays were performed, the subject of Chapter 2. Other artefacts of various kinds, such as mosaics and frescoes showing theatrical scenes, provide further evidence for Menander's continued popularity, both in Roman times and in later antiquity. Theatres became major public buildings all over the Greek world during his lifetime and the acting profession gained significantly in status. Menander was writing for the audiences and the actors of this period.

Chapter 3 attempts to place Menander in a wider context, both from an historical and a literary point of view. The Greek world had expanded and changed since the supremacy of Athens in the fifth century BCE. Most of Menander's own life, as with many ancient authors, is obscure, but he was apparently acquainted with several key figures of the fourth century BCE, such as the philosophers Theophrastus and Epicurus and the leading politician Demetrius of Phalerum. Menander's place in the so-called 'development' of ancient comedy is also examined. Menander's stock characters can be traced in the fragments that remain of his comic predecessors, but more survives of his treatment of these types than does of their original models, making any serious attempt to analyse his debt to them difficult.

The people of Menander's plays can also be recognized, however, as the people of his time: these plays are social comedies. How women, men and slaves of the fourth century BCE actually lived their lives, in so far as such a record can be established, is likely to illuminate Menander's characterization. The second half of the book will investigate this central theme, focusing on the techniques used in the characterization of the women and the slaves in his plays. Both are, in different ways, in the power of freeborn men.

It is, of course, impossible to study the female characters in isolation from their interaction with the men. The men are masters of the family, and thus (in theory at least) masters of their women, their slaves and, by extension, their city. Menander's *Samia* is of particular interest in terms of its concentration on the older lover Demeas, his young, adopted son, Moschion and Chrysis, the *pallake* ('girlfriend' or 'partner' are possible translations). The comic soldier Polemon is the young man in love in Menander's *Perikeiromene*. The male characters in Menander, including the soldiers, will be the main subject of a further study, a kind of sequel to this one.

However, Menander's *Epitrepontes* provides greater scope than these other plays for an exploration of Menander's women, the subject of Chapter 4. The father of a baby does not know that his treatment of what he thinks was another woman (they met in the darkness at a festival) led to his own wife having a baby five months into their marriage. He leaves his young wife, but she defends him to her father. A courtesan who tries to comfort the husband ends up reuniting him and his wife with both their child and each other.

The slaves in *Epitrepontes* are the subject of Chapter 5. Some lament their lot and others seek to rise above it. The *Epitrepontes* presents several different examples of the slave character. One slave finds an abandoned baby and its possessions (recognition tokens) and cannot believe his luck, the other seeks to defend the baby's rights to the man whom the audience knows will turn out to be its grandfather. Another slave recognizes a ring as the one lost by his master on the night of the baby's conception. Particularly important for this study, Habrotonon in the *Epitrepontes* is portrayed as both a woman and a slave and she is perhaps the heroine of this book.

The concluding chapter seeks to draw these various threads together to see how exactly Menander fits into the history of European comedy. A close analysis of the characterization will make clearer what kind of comedy we are dealing with and whether Menander deserved to be so esteemed in antiquity. A central theme will be that Menander does not shy away from serious issues in his plays – the *Epitrepontes* in particular deals with the power that some people can have over others. How can such serious content be reconciled with the simple aim to entertain or with some modern perceptions of the plays as nothing more than 'sit-com' or 'soap'? But first let us travel to sunny Sicily to the exciting archaeology of the wind-swept shores of the island of Lipari and its connection with Menander and his plays.

1

The Treasure on the Rock: Menander and the Masks and Figurines from Lipari

Lipari, the myth of Aiolos and Menander

Menander's story begins, in a way, with Aiolos, god of the winds, and this opening of the tenth book of Homer's *Odyssey*:

> We came next to the Aiolian island, where Aiolos
> lived, Hippotas' son, beloved by the immortal
> gods, on a floating island, the whole enclosed by a rampart
> of bronze, not to be broken, and the sheer of the cliff runs upward
> to it . . .
>
> Homer *Odyssey* X. 1–4, translation by R. Lattimore

Myths of floating islands such as that of Aiolos have been commonplace amongst sailors since time began, and wind sorcerers like Aiolos are to be found in sea-folklore of every period all over the world.[1] However, it does not seem fanciful to turn for the inspiration for Homer's natural fortress on the top of a cliff to the Aeolian island of Lipari. The long association with Aiolos (votive offerings to him were thrown into a sacred pit)[2] and the correspondence of its geography to Homer's description lends credibility to the identification. This tale begins, though, not with the treasure imagined by Odysseus's comrades to be inside the bag of winds which Aiolos gave to him, but with a real treasure to be found today on that very rock.

The Aeolian islands lie about twenty-five miles off the north coast of Sicily and today they may be reached by hydrofoil as well as by boat. Stromboli and Vulcano are volcanic. The latter was known in the fourth century BCE as *Hiera Hephaistoi*, 'sacred to Hephaistos (Vulcan)', the god of the volcano, and he was believed from very ancient times to have a forge there.[3] The volcano would, centuries later, bring one enterprising James Stevenson to the area. It is partly through Stevenson that the 'treasure' on the rock came to light, that is, some archaeological finds of significant relevance to the study of some important ancient plays. The theatrical artefacts date from the fourth century BCE and so are contemporary with the Athenian writer of comedies Menander (344/3–292/1 BCE).

Menander deserves to be better known. He was, apparently, as popular in ancient times as Homer.[4] He came from a distinguished and wealthy family in Cephisia, about

Fig. 1.1 The citadel on Lipari.

eight miles northeast of Athens and is said to have drowned at the age of fifty-two whilst swimming at Piraeus. His tomb was located on the road from Piraeus to Athens. He is said to have written over one hundred plays; the titles of ninety-seven are known; some may, however, be alternative titles for the same play. When exactly Menander produced his first play, the *Orge* or 'Anger', is disputed. His *Dyscolus* ('Old Cantankerous' or 'The Bad-Tempered Man') is recorded, however, as having won a first prize in 317/6 when he was only in his late twenties.

Some traditions suggest that Menander was handsome, but that he was somewhat effeminate in appearance and manner. He is also described as a clever man, mad about women. One credible detail, because there seems no particular reason to invent it, is that he had a squint. A large number of busts and medallions have been identified with Menander which do not support this detail, but the mosaic portrait on the island of Mytilene, together with a miniature bronze bust (Roman, early first century CE, based on the third-century BCE Greek seated statue by the sons of the sculptor Praxiteles) also shows Menander with a squint.[5]

This statue was erected to him in Athens in 293/2 BCE, very soon after his death, in the Theatre of Dionysus. It was placed prominently at one of the main entrances,[6] and Pausanias tells us that Menander's was the only portrait there of a famous comic poet.[7] The pedestal of the statue was found in 1862.[8] Portraits and sculptures of Menander must have been popular private possessions too: at least forty heads, five busts, five herms, three mosaic portraits and one painting survive. There are more copies of his portrait from Roman times than of almost any other person.[9]

All these artefacts constitute evidence for a continued interest in his plays, whether read or staged.[10] Menander became a key figure in the history of European literature:

his comedies were used as models by the Roman playwrights Plautus and Terence and so, indirectly, by Shakespeare and Molière.[11]

James Stevenson[12]

To return to our story, on 3 August 1888, Vulcano, the island immediately next to Lipari, began to erupt. The event was studied by some vulcanologists, and it is they who record that, at that time, the whole of the former island was owned by a shy Presbyterian Scotsman. James Stevenson was a hypochondriac and so rich that his nickname was Croesus, though no-one would have dared use it to his face.

Stevenson owned a chemical works in Glasgow and originally intended to extract sulphur to take back there, but then decided to make use of the natural power available on Vulcano and set up another factory on the spot. His family believed that he was, in a way, responsible for the eruption in 1888, either because he had mined the sulphur or, as the locals thought, he had invited trouble by evicting a Catholic priest from a chapel next to his house.

It was Stevenson's exploitation of Vulcano that brought him into contact with the archaeology of the islands and in particular with the contents of twenty ancient Greek

Fig. 1.2 James Stevenson.

tombs, discovered on Lipari in 1879, which he bought and took back to the Kelvingrove Museum in Glasgow, lending them and eventually donating them.[13] The greater part of his collections was finally bequeathed in 1903.[14] They can still be seen there today.

Bernabò Brea and the treasure on the rock

Someone even more important than Mr Stevenson to Menander, this history of Lipari and its archaeology, however, is Luigi Bernabò Brea, superintendent, when he retired, of Antiquities in Western Sicily. He was a modest, scholarly man.[15] Encouraging tourism and thus helping the island's economy, Brea converted Lipari's citadel on the rock from what had been, in the Second World War, a fascist prison camp, into a fascinating museum, one fit to house the remainder of Lipari's 'treasure'.

This treasure left behind by Stevenson was made up of hundreds of theatrical artefacts which Brea began excavating further in the 1950s. About 3,500 pieces have now been identified, including miniature terracotta theatrical masks and figurines (about 12 cm high) of actors wearing these masks. They are depicted in costume and making lively gestures.[16] The objects were lying where they were originally placed because of the sudden destruction of Lipari by the Romans in 252 BCE: in this way they were frozen in time. Consequently, they provide an exciting starting point for any study of Menander's plays as they date to his lifetime.[17]

The mystery

The importance of the masks and figurines has been established, but not, so far, the reason for their creation and presence such a long way from Athens and on an island so small and remote. It is certain that they were made on Lipari itself, as the scattered moulds used to manufacture them have also been discovered. Production may have been inspired, however, by imported Attic terracottas,[18] since the Glasgow statuettes of an old nurse and a baby and of a man with a pointed beard and cloak bear strong Attic influences.[19]

In fact, Lipari had continued in the fifth and fourth centuries to have an importance greater than its physical size and so the level of culture reflected by the masks and figures is not surprising. Painted ceramics, sculptures, inscribed headstones, bronze objects, coins and imported pottery have all been found. Of particular note for art historians in general is an unusual and beautiful polychrome pottery which developed on Lipari.

By the third century BCE the island had a small, independent town, with a high standard of living. It is puzzling, given the quantity of theatrical artefacts uncovered, that no theatre has yet come to light on the island. It is very likely that one existed by the Roman period at least. It is not just the masks and figurines that suggest a lively interest in drama on the part of the inhabitants: there are five notable vases with theatrical scenes.[20] Similar burial deposits, with masks and figurines of this type, have been found elsewhere in the ancient world, for example, four hundred miles away at Athens, and

Fig. 1.3 Nurse and baby. Terracotta figurine: one of the artefacts brought by Stevenson from Lipari to Glasgow, now housed at the Kelvingrove Museum in Glasgow.

further afield in Greece, Italy, Southern Russia, Egypt, North Africa and Spain, but never so many all together as at Lipari.[21] Indeed, the number found at Lipari demonstrates the degree to which statistics in archaeology can be distorted by the chances of excavation and publication.[22] Initially, terracottas of this type seem to have been more popular than masks, but in the last quarter of the fourth century masks overtake them.[23] The sheer number of the finds makes it difficult to assess them objectively.

The figurines and masks are paralleled, moreover, by representations in other media too across the Greek world at this time. Masks appear on jewellery and stone sculpture and scenes from the plays in mosaics, some deriving, interestingly, from lost works.[24] Some of these theatrical scenes would have been manufactured from materials which have not survived. Wall-painting is a key example. Masks could appear as 'generic references to the theatre' rather than for the sake of the character depicted. Such references were clearly fashionable. Gems, however, had their own iconographic tradition. Many of these objects were costly.[25]

Scholars have tried to unravel the mystery behind the discoveries on Lipari. The masks and figurines could be souvenirs of theatrical productions, particularly as they were found in groups suggestive of the casts of particular plays.[26] Archaeologists are often tempted to suggest some religious explanation. According to such a view, the objects could be offerings to Dionysus, the god of the theatre at Athens at any rate. Over 1,800 tombs have been excavated. The theatrical terracottas were buried in and around thirty-five of these tombs and most in votive ditches.[27] Other gods were worshipped on Lipari, amongst them Aiolos and Hephaestus. Perhaps Dionysus was just one of these gods. The worship of Dionysus is not, however, an explicit element in the extant plays of Menander, with whom the masks have been linked in terms of theatre history.[28] Perhaps the answer may be just that the tombs belonged to actors, but the problem remains of why so many actors retired to Lipari to die.[29]

How, it might also be asked, is it known that the masks found bear any resemblance to those actually worn when performing Menander and other plays from the same period? The originals were made from materials such as linen and so have perished.[30] These objects are fashioned out of terracotta, a fine, hard, brownish-red pottery. Moreover, artistic renderings of the actual masks used in the theatre will, of course, be subject to varied treatment by the artists in question.[31] It does seem a fair assumption, however, that the Lipari masks are closely related to their lost originals.[32]

Pollux's *Onomasticon*

The discoveries on Lipari were classified by Bernabò Brea using a catalogue of masks made by Pollux, who lived during the Roman imperial period. The *Onomasticon* lists forty-four New Comedy masks, but Pollux, from Naucratis in Egypt in the second century CE, was writing much later than the date of the objects he describes. Caution has therefore been urged in the evaluation of this information. However, it is believed to be based on Hellenistic accounts,[33] and this catalogue should be borne in mind when looking at the archaeological evidence.[34] Indeed, correlatives for Pollux's masks are to be found in the remains.[35] Brea himself confidently allocated each of the Lipari masks to one of Pollux's forty-four types, speaking of 'la perfetta rispondenza', 'the perfect correspondence' between the two groups.[36]

It does seem clear that there came to be a standardized collection of stereotypical masks, such as the False Maiden and the Parasite, which could be classified according to a number of types.[37] Many of Pollux's descriptions can convincingly be applied to surviving masks and illustrations and therefore to some of the characters in Menander. On the other hand, his examples for women are very sketchy. Certainly, in spite of Brea's attempts to make the Lipari finds correspond exactly with Pollux,[38] to other scholars they suggest that there was available to Menander a more varied repertory of masks.[39] Whatever the relationship between the artefacts and the catalogue, Menander's comedy does turn on misunderstandings between characters like those represented in the Lipari masks and statuettes.[40]

It therefore seems possible to follow with caution those scholars who have identified amongst the masks those that particular characters in Menander might have worn. There are some who challenge the usefulness of mere archaeological artefacts to the study of the dynamics of the living theatre. However, there should be no doubt as to the importance of the finds for the study of Menander.[41] If the arguments in favour of the importance of the artefacts are accepted, this evidence for New Comedy is earlier in date than almost all comparable data.[42]

Tragic masks are also represented alongside the comic ones. They date from the first half of the fourth century BCE, a period from which we have no other such masks. Twenty different types are preserved. There are also figures representing Homer, Socrates and Lysias. Indeed, among the portrait-masks found on Lipari is possibly the earliest surviving portrait-mask of Menander himself. Although broken, it would appear to derive from a fine and sensitive study, perhaps the same as inspired Menander's statue, one which shows how the poet was imagined in or near to his own lifetime.

The masks and figurines from Lipari bring the ancient Greek theatre alive in a way that is quite remarkable.[43] Although the original masks and costumes have perished, these copies do seem to evoke the actual contemporary performances of Menander's comedies. His contemporaries having been largely lost, Menander is the main playwright associated with this remote and beautiful island and its extraordinary discoveries. The artefacts may therefore be used as a guide to how Menander's men, women and slaves might have looked on stage.[44] How and where were his plays performed?

Further reading

Menander

Balme (Menander 2001) is the most recent Penguin translation of Menander's plays and benefits from an expert introduction by Peter Brown, but Miller (Menander 1987) often gives very well the flavour of the original Greek. Arnott (1975) is still useful for a good overview of this kind of ancient comedy. Goldberg (1980), Hunter (1985) and Walton & Arnott (1996) are very good introductions to any study of Menander's plays. On Menander's statue, see Zanker (1995) and Richter (1965), v.2 on the iconography.

Lipari

On the Lipari finds specifically, see Heap (1994), a brief summary, with colour illustrations in Brea (1981: text in Italian) and Brea (2001), which updates the former with numerous finds (there is some text in English). Stevenson (2009) has more on James Stevenson. Wiles (1991) discusses the Lipari masks in relation to performance.

'Masks for Menander'

As part of the 'Masks for Menander' project (2001–04), University of Glasgow researchers applied cutting-edge 3D imaging techniques to enlarge miniature fourth-century theatre masks from ancient Greece (including Lipari) into life-sized objects. Full-size reconstructions of the masks are now on permanent display in the Kelvingrove Art Gallery and Museum, Glasgow.

2

All the World's a Stage: Menander in Performance

During Menander's lifetime the Athenians may have preferred to watch the plays of his rival Philemon.[1] However, after Menander's death, his plays were frequently staged, both in Greece and abroad. Mosaics or frescoes depicting scenes from them have been found in modern Bulgaria, Ephesus and Pompeii.[2] Of particular note are the scenes from eleven of Menander's plays found in a late third-, fourth- or possibly fifth-century CE house in Mytilene (modern day Lesvos) in which the actors are still wearing masks. At least one of the Mytilene scenes is found in identical form in a mosaic at Pompeii, and there are other close correspondences between mosaics and paintings in Pompeii, Herculaneum and Stabiae. A series of fixed types of composition therefore appears to have been in circulation. The Mytilene mosaics suggest adaptation for text illustrations.[3]

Fig. 2.1 Mytilene mosaic of *Epitrepontes*. 'The Arbitration' with Syros, Smikrines, Daos and Syros's wife holding the baby.

Menander's popularity

Many other kinds of artefacts have been discovered, as has been seen, such as the replica masks and miniature actor figurines from Lipari and other countries too. These finds invite us to imagine how the plays looked on stage. The growth in the number of masks by period may indicate that audiences were increasingly, especially after 325 BCE, interested in character.[4] The volume of all this evidence suggests that Menander was very popular outside Greece. The number of papyrus texts and fragments that have been discovered supports this too.

Menander benefitted of course from the fact that drama had already travelled far from Athens, both in the fifth century BCE[5] and thanks to the patronage of Philip of Macedon and Alexander the Great, of actors, playwrights and performers from many different places. There had been literary exchanges as well as trade beyond Greece well before Alexander's time; for example, Aeschylus had visited the court of Hieron I, producing *Persae* and *Women of Aetna* in Syracuse.[6] The lyric poets also travelled abroad; for example, Pindar had commissions from Macedonia to Africa and Asia Minor, Alcaeus was exiled to Egypt more than once and Simonides was also a guest of Hieron.[7]

Festivals and performances

What was the original context of the performances of Menander's plays? Like those of Aeschylus, Sophocles, Euripides and Aristophanes, they were put on in his lifetime and afterwards at religious festivals which were also competitions. The two major dramatic festivals in Athens were the City Dionysia and the Lenaea. In the fourth century, in any one year, five comedies could be seen at each. 'Old' plays, tragedy, were revived at the Dionysia in 386 BCE, then from 341 to 339, with 'old' comedy known for 339 and perhaps more regularly from 311,[8] and so new and old plays were part of the same great occasion.[9] The date of Menander's first victory at the Lenaea, with *Orge,* 'Anger', was 322/1 or 321/0 BCE, when he was in his early twenties. The only play to survive complete, the *Dyscolus,* won first prize at the Lenaea in 317/6.

The religious elements of these festivals, the procession and the sacrifice at the City Dionysia or festival of Dionysus, for instance, continued in Menander's time: a *phallus* (a pole representing an erect penis) and ox are recorded as being sent for the sacrifice in the fourth century BCE, for instance, and various fifth-century practices, such as the decrees of formal praise of individuals, spread to Dionysia festivals in other cities across the Greek world.[10] By the time of Aeschines' speech *Against Ktesiphon*, dated to 330 BCE (Menander was born in 344/3), war orphans were no longer brought on stage, but other city rituals such as the announcement of honours took place.[11] There were some changes in religious practices in the fourth century which may be reflected in how religion manifests itself in Menander's plays.[12] But how Menander's plays relate to this continuing civic activity which revolved around theatrical performances is as much a question as it is for fifth-century drama. How much were the events purely entertainment, how much were they part of an important civic and religious ritual and how much an opportunity to explore social and political issues?[13]

One important change in theatre practice which took place under Demetrius of Phalerum 317–307 BCE, with whom tradition associates Menander, was that the *choregia* was abolished.[14] An *agonothetes* (an official who organized festivals) was elected annually and given funds,[15] instead of a wealthy individual paying to train the chorus, provide costumes and so on, and the *demos* (people) were now the overall *choregos*,[16] but those elected to be an *agonothetes* were still members of a wealthy élite and the office was of even narrower access than the *choregia* had been.[17]

Since Menander wrote over a hundred comedies, he must therefore have written for festivals further afield than the Dionysia and the Lenaea,[18] which is consistent with the archaeological record described above. As for Athens, our limited records of official Athenian productions might suggest that Menander's *Phasma* was still being performed after his death at the Lenaea festival around 255/4 BCE,[19] and still at the Dionysia in 168/7 BCE, and the *Misogynes* still at the Dionysia in 196/5 BCE.[20] As has been stressed, various theatrical artefacts point to performances of some kind continuing into later centuries.

Theatres

What sort of buildings were used to put on Menander's plays? The theatre of Dionysus, in which a statue of Menander was erected, was located on the south slope of the Acropolis in Athens.[21] There was no roof, reflecting its open and public nature as a central part of the city's life. The three most important elements in Greek theatre design are the *orchestra*, the *theatron* and the *skene*.[22] The theatre of Dionysus underwent structural alterations down to late antiquity which are the subject of scholarly debate; just before the time of Menander the theatre was rebuilt in stone for the first time.

The theatre at Epidaurus in the Peloponnese was designed and built in the late fourth century BCE, that is, roughly in the time of Menander, and was praised by Pausanias above all other theatres. He tells us that its architect was Polykleitos. 'Who', he asks, 'can begin to rival Polykleitos for the beauty . . . of its architecture?'[23] The theatre is located seven kilometres inland from the city, being part of the famous sanctuary of Asclepios, which may be significant for its mathematical proportions.[24] It seats potentially 14,000 and has very fine acoustics.[25] Other Greek theatres were built in many different locations.[26] Having a theatre was one of the things that made a city Greek.[27] Some theatres further afield than Athens, such as Syracuse, predate the fourth century, however, proving that the spread of drama was not just due to Alexander the Great. The theatres in which Menander was performed were not, in fact, all the same. *Orchestra* means, literally, 'dancing place', from (*orcheisthai*, 'to dance'). The *orchestra* in the theatre may have been in the shape of part of an open circle, rectangular or trapezoidal. It seems that a full circle for an orchestra, as is the case at Epidaurus, was unusual.[28] Acoustics and other practical considerations such as visibility played a part in theatre design.[29] The *orchestra*, the flat area where the actors performed, was surrounded by the *theatron*, often bowl-shaped, where the audience sat (the Greek also means 'audience', as well as giving us the word 'theatre'). Later the *orchestra* became smaller.[30]

Fig. 2.2 The Theatre at Epidaurus, fourth century BCE.

The theatre at Athens belonged to the sanctuary of Dionysus of Eleutherai. Dionysus would have been present at performances of Menander in the shape of his statue.[31] The principal human spectator was the priest of Dionysus, who had his seat in the middle of the front row of the *theatron*. Behind him sat other priests and high officials in seats of honour (the *prohedria*).[32] The priest's throne in the stone theatre of Dionysus shows cocks, as symbols of the contest, being urged to fight by winged boys.[33] This has been thought to belong to the fourth century BCE, just before the time of Alexander the

Great, when the first stone theatre there was constructed by Lycurgus,[34] who lived *c.*390–325/4 BCE. It may, however, be a copy of a throne of that date.[35]

The *theatron* in stone was well provided with gangways and radial staircases, to ease the relatively swift entrance and exit of large numbers of spectators, similar numbers to those that could be accommodated at Epidaurus. Ancient audiences were, by modern standards, very large.

Audiences

Spectacle, broad gestures, and probably masks too, would therefore have been important, however good the acoustics, to the production of Menander's plays.[36] The size of Greek theatres was very large, much larger than that of a modern indoor theatre today.[37] However, it is likely that theatres were often built out of civic pride which suggests that they may have been more elaborate than necessary, so the size of a theatre in the fourth century may not be a completely reliable guide to actual audience size.[38]

Who attended these performances? The withdrawal of the theoric fund in Menander's time might have affected in terms of wealth who could afford to be a spectator.[39] The performances were still produced by a wealthy élite too.

Were there women in Menander's audience? There are significant roles for women in tragedy, such as Clytemnestra and Medea, and in Aristophanes, such as Lysistrata. Menander's women characters will be seen to be interesting, but this is not reflected in the amount of time they are on stage. Whether or not women were present in the audience will have had an impact on the reception of female roles. It is now generally believed that women attended tragic performances.[40] What about comedy?

Aristophanes' *Peace* 962–7 may imply that the women were seated at the back where some barleycorns thrown could not reach them. It seems the most natural interpretation of the innuendo.[41] Aristophanes' *Frogs* 1050–1, which concerns the reaction of women to tragic characters, does not prove that they had not just heard about Euripides's plays. But *Peace* 50–3 leaves them out of a list of spectators. These are all fifth-century references.

Later references are more encouraging for their presence but refer to tragedy, such as a story that Aeschylus's *Eumenides* frightened some women into miscarriages. Plato *Laws* vii. 817c, ii.658a-d and *Gorgias* 502b-d suggest that women were there in the fourth century.[42] Despite certain restrictions on their lives no actual ban on the presence of women is mentioned, and their alleged isolation and confinement largely to the house have, in any case, been re-examined.[43] If the question of their presence at performances of comedy were resolved, that would necessitate a similar revaluation of their role in society.[44]

The presence of women at the Great Dionysia has been 'one of the thorniest and most passionately debated issues in theatrical history'.[45] If women were not there, it would then be a departure from their customary inclusion in festivals, but the arguments are largely drawn from these later references, rather than from any conclusive evidence in ancient texts, most of which have been used by scholars on both sides of the debate.[46]

A fragment of Menander, now known to be from Menander's *Synaristosai*, seems to suggest that some women in the fourth century had some opportunity to watch the *pompe* (procession), but not necessarily the performances, themselves. Being a short fragment it lacks a meaningful context. Care is needed also about using the fourth century to illuminate the fifth.[47] In Menander women are not mentioned in the stock formulae for bringing a play to a close (*Dyscolus* 967 is one example: 'young men, boys, gentlemen'), but this may have its origin in an earlier period than the rest of the text. It is therefore difficult to use the formula as evidence for Menander's time. Perhaps one should distinguish here between the 'actual' and the 'notional' audience, as women did not have the same status in society as men.[48] Some allow for the possibility that women were at the theatre outside Athens but this evidence relates to the fifth century rather than the fourth.[49] As for slaves, their presence at the theatre, and therefore at performances of Menander, is suggested by passages in Plato and Theophrastus.[50]

Staging

What about the practical side of putting on Menander's plays? Menander's actors needed somewhere to keep their equipment, their masks and other props, and change of costumes. They used the *skene*, the wooden structure at the back of the orchestra. On either side of it was the *parodos* through which the audience and, later in the proceedings, the chorus entered.[51]

The *skene* was primarily somewhere to change, particularly as actors could take more than one role within any given play.[52] Some of the wooden stands for seating may have been stored there when not in use, as well as props. The front wall of the *skene* doubled up as the back wall of the stage, giving, via the Latin word *scaena*, the English word 'scene'.

The building had a flat roof. This 'house' may have had a second storey, the *theologeion* mentioned by Pollux and the scholiasts as an alternative to the *mechane* (crane) for the appearances of gods as speaking characters.[53] In tragedy at least, other characters may have sometimes appeared here: for example, the watchman at the beginning of Aeschylus's *Agamemnon*. Old Comedy would have required a variety of gadgets. The *mechane* enabled, for instance, Trygaios in Aristophanes' *Peace* to ride a dung beetle into the air in a parody of tragedy. (Aeschylus and Euripides also made use of this device.)[54]

But how did the gods in Menander appear? Pan speaks the prologue in *Dyscolus* and Tyche (Chance) and Agnoia (Misapprehension) deliver the prologues in *Aspis* and *Perikeiromene* respectively. There were others, and where their presence is not confirmed it seems required. The god describes the background to events and sometimes matters of which the characters are unaware. For example, *Epitrepontes* seems to require a divine prologue to explain that the baby in the play is actually Smikrines' grandson in order for the arbitration scene in which he decides its fate to have its full force.[55] For a prologue in Menander, despite the *mechane* used by earlier playwrights, a god would perhaps have been more on the same level as the mortal characters, as in Euripides, that is, not up in the air, whether appearing in the orchestra, on a slightly raised stage or on the *theologeion* (probably the flat roof of the *skene* or later *proskenion*).[56] A fragment of *Theophoroumene* preserves the comment that another character has turned up 'like a god on a crane', which might have worked better as a joke if the gods in Menander did not.[57] The role of the gods in Menander is different from that in tragedy and Aristophanes. There is no human–divine contact on stage, for instance, which contributes to the realism.[58]

From the time of Aeschylus a piece of equipment called the *ekkyklema* may have been used; if so, it was either a sort of chair with wheels or a wheeled platform which sometimes revealed a scene indoors. Use of the *ekkyklema* remains disputed.[59] The evidence concerning the *ekkyklema* is not clear on its exact nature.[60] A wheelbarrow or a bath chair might be successfully used instead to wheel in the injured and subdued Knemon in Menander's *Dyscolus* at line 758.[61]

In the Hellenistic period, perhaps because of changes to the role of the chorus, of which more later, the *orchestra* as a place for acting is replaced by another feature of Hellenistic stages, a raised stage called the *proskenion*, projected in front of the stage-building. This feature can be seen at Oropos in Attica and at Epidaurus.[62] Many classical tragedies must have been performed using a *proskenion*, as they were revived around this period. However, is likely that at Athens in Menander's time the main stage would have been a low platform in front of the *skene* and any *proskenion* would have been just 'a shallow projection' to take scene paintings or hangings.[63]

Setting the scene

There are important, obvious differences between a theatre which is open to the air and the ones more familiar to audiences in the West, at least, today. Lighting would be provided by natural light.[64] The staging of plays might be assumed therefore to be simple in one respect: playwrights relying principally on language to set the scene.[65] An example can be taken from Menander's *Dyscolus*:

> PAN [*addresses audience*]: Imagine, please, that the scene is set in Attica, in fact at Phyle, and that the shrine I'm coming from is the one belonging to that village (Phylaeans are able to farm this stony ground). It's a holy place, and a very famous one. This farm here on my right is where Knemon lives: he's a real hermit of a man, who snarls at everyone and hates company – 'company' isn't the word: he's getting on now, and he's never addressed a civil word to anyone in his life! He's never volunteered a polite greeting to anyone except myself (I'm the god Pan): and that's only because he lives beside me, and can't help passing my door . . .
> Miller (1987), lines 1–12

In fact, the limited technical resources available for the ancient Greek productions had the potential to inspire rather than restrict the dramatist.[66] The description above not only gives a mental picture of the imagined surroundings, but also prepares the audience for the characterization of Knemon, as a man isolated from society, as hostile to it as the rocky land he farms.[67]

Architecture in perspective was represented, however, in a backdrop of painted flat panels which disguised the stage-building, called *skenographia* ('scene-painting').[68] An imitation of such a stage set for tragedy may be found on a fragment of a calyx crater (a kind of mixing bowl) in Würzburg. It is Apulian, painted just before Menander was born, *c.* 350 BCE.[69]

A copy of a backdrop for New Comedy may have been preserved in a bedroom in the Villa of Boscoreale near Vesuvius. It was painted around 50 BCE, but the original may be dated to the Hellenistic period. It is now in the Metropolitan Museum in New York, together with the decoration for the whole room. The stage-building apparently shown no longer has a simple wall disguised, but is divided architecturally as a 'façade', the scenery consisting of several partial views. It may be possible, if one cites Vitruvius 5.6.9, for comic scenes showing private houses, to connect the New Comedy scene from Boscoreale to an actual play by Menander, the *Samia*, as the broken pot on the roof suggests the customs of the festival of Adonis (see *Samia* 38ff). However, a painting which shows perspective need not have its origins in the theatre.[70]

Some of the doors on the *skenographia* may have been false, as the door was a favourite decorative motif in ancient art. A large centre door and two flanking it would have provided a means of entering and exiting for the actors, and for banging or knocking on in farcical scenes in comedy.[71] In fact, the discovery of the *Dyscolus* confirmed the use of three doors in Menander, to represent two houses with a central shrine, already known from Plautus to be standard in New Comedy.[72] A fragment of *Leukadia* shows that the scene could be very different, however: in that case it is a temple on the cliffs.

Actors

The scenery and the theatre itself were the backdrop to the performance of Menander's plays by his actors. Greek actors wore masks, the wider significance of which will be examined later. One practical reason which may be added to that of ease in changing roles could have been in order that the performers might be seen and heard in very large theatres holding large numbers of people.[73] Masks would also have facilitated the sharing of roles.

Addressing the audience is another device which overcomes the distance between the spectators and the actors. Menander made extensive and clever use of the monologue as may be seen, for example, in the long speeches by Demeas and Moschion in his *Samia* and Knemon in the *Dyscolus*. This suggests an increasing importance for the actor by this period of dramatic composition.[74]

This was in fact the case. A prize for comic actors was introduced at the Lenaea in about 442 BCE. Between 329 and 312 BCE another was introduced at the Dionysia.[75] The existence of an actor's prize may have contributed to the economic independence of the actor.[76] Depictions of comic actors on vases may reflect a change in status, since there are none earlier than about 430 BCE, but from then on they become increasingly common.[77] In the past this was, perhaps wrongly, attributed to a diminished role for the chorus.

A significant change of some kind regarding the chorus may have affected the impact of the plays, however. The chorus as a 'character' or 'characters' has already been replaced sometimes in the manuscripts of Aristophanes's *Ecclesiazusae* and *Wealth*. The formal structure of Aristophanes's (and probably some of his contemporaries') plays was altered, to remove the *parabasis*, the point in a play where the chorus addressed the audience. In Menander it is also regularly marked instead by an indication of an interlude, CHOROU (of the chorus), sometimes introduced by a character with a formula such as 'I see a band of drunken youths approaching', although these formulae vary.[78] The words of the chorus or chorus leader have not been preserved. The contribution of such a chorus and the lost music could have been superior to the interludes of the fifth century. The choreography might also have been more developed.[79]

It would be interesting to compare interpretations of how the chorus contributes to tragedy and Aristophanes[80] with Menander and so the impact of its absence from the main body of Menander's plays. One result would be an increased focus on individual actors, with audience perception of the characters proceeding without comments, helpful or otherwise, by a chorus as the play progresses. There may, of course, have been such comment in the lost musical interludes. The characters might, however, be perceived by the audience as more isolated when experiencing problems with their family or sexual relationships without a chorus acting in the main body of the play, for example, to share their pain.

The 'role' of the actor grew to such an extent that by Menander's time famous actors were already touring the Greek world, being used as ambassadors[81] and forming guilds. Celebrity could go hand in hand with being unpopular, however, due to resentment of these newly rich by the élite. The guilds of actors and related theatrical performers came to be called the 'Artists of Dionysus', reflecting that their relationship with Dionysus was a special one.[82] The rise of the guilds coincides with the numbers of theatres 'exploding' all over Greece and the Greek world.[83] A significant number of the leading actors of the fourth century came from other parts of the Greek world than Athens. Already, as has been seen, in the later fifth century in Athens, the period in which Aristophanes was writing his later plays, terracotta figurines of actors in masks and costume had begun to be manufactured. But evidence is growing in the form of the discovery of early theatres outside Athens that the Athenians did not have a monopoly on drama even in the fifth century BCE.[84]

A set of fourteen figurines in all, referred to already and known as the 'New York Group', dating from the end of the fifth century BCE,[85] is said to have been found in a grave in Athens. They are now in the Metropolitan Museum of Art in New York. Others of a similar style, it may be remembered, have been found over a wide geographical spread. The Lipari figurines have been seen to be of a similar kind, but livelier in appearance, and date from Menander's time or before. These terracottas were of inexpensive material and so not for a rich market; they were possibly souvenirs.[86] All would have been brightly painted: red-brown faces and hands for the men and slaves (pink for the women); black, white or red hair, depending on the character; yellow on dresses; blue on cloaks. They have standard masks[87] and are character types found in Menander, such as the slave, old man or nurse.[88]

Costume

The later figurines (there is no mention of or archaeological evidence for tights or artificial *phallus* after the fourth century) we may conclude reflect a new interest in the performers of Menander's plays and those of his contemporaries. The first guide, accurate or otherwise, to the people in Menander's plays would have been the actors' costumes and masks. In this way, the audience would learn or assume certain basic facts about each character.[89] This does not preclude occasional dressing up in deliberate disguise, as with the 'doctor' in *Aspis*, a habit more common in Aristophanes, however.[90] The figurines datable to the period just before Menander was writing, that of the so-called Middle Comedy,[91] show, especially in profile, that there was then heavy padding on the stomach and backside, contained within a body-suit down to the ankles and wrists. On the front was a leather *phallus* (penis), which was normally rolled up, but on some statuettes and vase-paintings hangs loose. Padding was worn by all the actors; the *phallus* was exposed by the short cloaks and tunics worn by the male characters. This kind of costume was still being worn by slaves in Menander's time, when the comic plays had otherwise changed in nature, becoming less bawdy and more 'realistic' in the sense of being situation comedies.[92] For the prologue speakers of Menander's *Dyscolus* and *Aspis*, Pan and Tyche respectively, figurines and statues may be some kind of guide as to how they looked on stage.[93]

The appearance of the *hetairai* characters reflects contemporary fashion. After Menander's time, apparently, no serious attempt was made to bring their costumes up to date.[94] Respectable women, as opposed to courtesans, from the evidence of their replica masks, wore their hair smoothed down.[95] All female parts wore a long *chiton*, coloured shoes and a wrap.[96] Young men wore purple or scarlet, according to Pollux,[97] but white and yellow seem common from the pictorial evidence.[98]

Slaves would have worn a shorter *chiton* than that of citizens, but longer than Aristophanic slaves and with a smaller mantle. Slaves at Athens had no kind of uniform.[99] Some time after 200 CE their dress became long, the costume then acquiring a tasselled belt and a scarf-like mantle.[100] It is interesting that a wide variety of slave figurines survive: running, dancing or holding a baby.[101] Slaves on altars are very common.[102]

As for the soldier character, a statuette of him was found in a set of two, representing two lovers embracing. He wears a short *chiton* and *chlamys*, characteristic of travellers, and a military cloak which Donatus, who wrote about Terence and Menander in the fourth century CE, says was purple. The style was more important than the colour in distinguishing the soldier from other young male characters.[103] An older soldier with hair reaching to his shoulders was found in the Agora at Athens. Another example, now in the British Museum, has a 'plate-like' flat cap.[104] This corresponds with a soldier in a lost painting from Pompeii: he carries a lance.[105] According to Pollux, the parasite, the traditional companion of the comic soldier, wore black or grey, except in Menander's *Sikyonios*, where he wore white: he was about to marry.[106]

For descriptions of the costumes worn, literary evidence from later writers like Pollux and Donatus can be used, but with care, to supplement what can be seen on the terracottas and in theatrical scenes on vases.[107] The vase-paintings present their own problems, as they are not literal reconstructions of the real world.[108] There are various levels of 'reality', between what has been called the 'quasi-photographic', that is, representations of actors acting, through to the recollections of audience or painter of actual performances and the intentions of actors and poets rather than the mechanics of how the scene was put on.[109]

The number of pictures relating to the theatre and to Dionysus as god of drama on vases from S. Italy and Sicily (dating from the first seventy years of the fourth century BCE) distinguishes them from their Athenian contemporaries. Almost all of those which have been discussed in this context were used for funerary purposes. On one vase from Lipari, Dionysus is shown seated on a stage and watching the performance of a female tumbler, while, judging by their masks, a *hetaira* and freeborn girl look on. The scenes on the Paestan vases produced by Asteas and Python (fl. c. 360–330 BCE) show a strong interest in the theatre and theatrical motifs and their later work regularly uses actors as companions of Dionysus.[110]

Masks

Dionysus, as has been noted, could be conceived of as being present at a performance of Menander's plays.[111] Through the theatre he was believed to bring happiness and an escape from the mundane.[112] He also brought happiness through wine: the vases on which theatrical paintings are found were used to hold wine.[113] The mask, whether in vase scenes or on, for example, grave reliefs, comes, by means of its stereotyped appearance, to represent a character,[114] transforming the actor in a kind of metamorphosis. The Lipari masks and figurines were found in graves, provoking speculation, as with the depiction of masks on tomb monuments,[115] about connections with Dionysus as god of the afterlife, a happier world.[116] In the fourth century BCE, Dionysus also becomes associated with love and sex, most noticeably on vases from Apulia:[117] love is always, in some form or other, part of the New Comedy plots that survive, but there may be no particular connection with Dionysus.

The study of the mask, used by Menander's actors, straddles literary criticism and religion 'in a curious limbo'.[118] Worn by the actors in all Greek drama, masks became more stereotyped in appearance after the fourth century and their recognizability seems to have become connected with the practice of leaving them in the sanctuary of Dionysus after a performance, where they stayed visible.[119] The comic masks used in Menander's plays were part of the costume used by his actors, permitting or demanding a range of gestural language,[120] but were also the first hint that the audience had of the characters behind them, Menander's 'people'. These characters will have developed in some way out of the comedy that preceded Menander[121] but also probably out of the people of his time. Masks will make their appearance again in the detailed discussions of characterization and social history to be found later in this book. For now, it is important to remember the dimension of performance in the study of Menander's plays, without which any surviving text is a fragment and the mere notation of what may have been said: without 'a sense of space, the costumes, the audience, and the whole cultural context'.[122]

Further reading

Festivals and performances

For a detailed treatment of performance including Menander's period, with good illustrations in colour, see Dugdale (2008). See Csapo et al. (eds) (2014) for evidence for the fourth century BCE with Pickard-Cambridge, rev. ed. (1988). Peter Wilson and Eric Csapo have begun the process of updating the latter. For the masks and figurines in particular, Green & Handley (1995) has some very fine illustrations. See also Green (1994), Taylor (1999), Goldhill and Osborne (1999) and Hughes (2012). For a variety of essays on Greek and Roman drama, see McDonald and Walton (2007).

On the Great Dionysia and the civic importance of the ceremonies which preceded the theatrical performances, see Goldhill (1990). For the relationship between ritual action and action in the theatre, see Easterling (1993) 7–9. There is a discussion of Menander in this context in the same volume, Scodel (1993): 164, 167 and 174. Roselli (2011) challenges Athenocentric approaches to the Greek theatre audience (7ff): ch. 3 focuses on the *theorika* (festival funds).

Actors

On all aspects of acting in the ancient world, see the very accessible Csapo (2010) with, for a more detailed treatment, Easterling & Hall, eds (2002). On different kinds of monologue, see Gomme and Sandbach (1973), 14–15 and Blundell (1980). On the importance of messenger speeches in this context, see Green (1994), 61: they were 'treasured parts' for actors. See the beginning of *Samia* Act III for an extensive Menandrian example delivered by Demeas, with Sommerstein's commentary (Menander (2013)).

The chorus in the fourth century

See further Sommerstein's introductions to his commentaries (Aristophanes (1998 and 2001)), 23ff. Rothwell (1995) points out that whatever Menander may have done with the chorus, it may not have been the same as his contemporaries (116). There is inscriptional evidence that the chorus continued to be vigorous. See Hunter (1979), 24 with Wilson (2000), 4–5, 267, 301: 'far from moribund', but more investigation is needed for the nature of these dramatic performances.

Lape (2006) argues that the chorus was in Menander a *komos*, 'a revel' or 'mobile, demonstrative celebration with wine', corresponding to other literary and artistic depictions of this, and she believes that it would have taken its character from the specific narrative strand of the play (100), hence the variations in the stock formula for its introduction (see *Dyscolus* 230–2 with the reading 'Pan-worshippers'). She thinks that it anticipated the conventional happy ending with, for example, a wedding (93ff) and agrees with Pöhlmann that it served to emphasize the five act structure (92), which is true, but it would be nice to have more evidence for the chorus's activities. On the importance of music in general in dramatic performance and its demands on the actors, see Hall (2002) and Wilson (2002).

Dionysus

Goldhill (1990), 98 disagrees with what he sees as Taplin's dismissal of the Dionysiac occasion and his concentration on performance. Griffith (2007), 23 argues for the 'domain of Dionysus' as 'a reassuring pretext' to confront the extreme and the disturbing in what is ultimately only a 'play'.

On Dionysus as god of the theatre and the afterlife, see Brea (2001), 276ff. See Green (1994), 78–9 for how, in the fifth century, and probably later, masks were dedicated after a performance. The first evidence of masks in dedicatory reliefs dates, however, from the third quarter of the fourth century (Green (1994), 81). For the vase now in Cleveland and early fourth-century BCE depicting actors with Dionysus (discovering wine), previously the role of satyrs, see 86ff with pl. 3.23–4; see also 89–91. From 330 BCE (Menander was born in 344/3 BCE) the motif develops further. Green notes (92) that a party after a performance has helped relieve the stress for actors of all periods.

Costume

For dress as a means of non-verbal communication in ancient Greece, see Lee (2015), 23ff with 28ff on gender, age, status, ethnicity and social role, *hetairai* being difficult to identify in the visual record. For a more general approach, see Lurie (1981), ch.1, 'Clothing as a sign system': the language of clothes changes at different periods (ix), colours can make statements (xi), different hairstyles can convey different meaning (xiii). Lurie cites Barthes for theatrical dress as a kind of writing (3). The vocabulary of dress includes hair styles, accessories, jewellery and make-up (4).

3

Alexander, Aristophanes and Beyond: Menander in Context

The archaeology and performance of Menander's plays, together with their transmission, have all proved to be important aspects of the study of his work, but what about its further cultural and historical context? In the past, the plays have in fact been used by historians as evidence for the fourth century BCE. However, Menander must be, as he has not always been, treated with caution when seeking to illuminate social history. It will not do to quote from the plays without some analysis of which character is speaking and in what context, which is impossible to determine with the smaller fragments of text.

Moreover, comedy is a notoriously difficult kind of source: are there jokes or irony, and if so where? There will have been visual jokes, choreography and some music, as has been seen, about all of which we have, however, very little information. Similar problems present themselves as for the study of Theophrastus's *Characters*. It is a work which can tell us some things about Athens at the time it was written by correcting certain details of our knowledge, such as, for example, about the separate Women's *Agora* or 'marketplace'. The safest ground, though, is 'the values which the sketches presuppose'.[1] The same is often true for Menander.

Plays are not written in a vacuum, and so it is important to look at what is known about the period in which Menander's plays were written. The replica masks from Lipari represent, in some way, his characters.[2] However, the people of these comedies are derived not only from the stock figures of the comedy that preceded Menander, but also from the social norms of Menander's period. The plays are social comedies. Menander draws not just on a strong literary tradition, but also, somehow, on the women, men and slaves of fourth-century Athens.[3] It appears to have been a rather different world, however, that they inhabited from that familiar to the people of Aristophanes,[4] a world which owed its nature in part to one real character larger than life or fiction – the Macedonian Alexander the Great, the lands he conquered and the many Greek cities he founded far from Greece.

The new Greek world[5]

Was Menander's world significantly different, however, from that of Aristophanes? The extent of Macedonian control at this period, even in Greece itself, is disputed. Athens had lost status and was no longer a major political force. A garrison was installed by the Macedonians at the Piraeus, to ensure that control of the city's port was retained.[6] Yet the city retained a certain degree of military and naval influence and remained the intellectual and cultural capital of this period. She still controlled the largest navy in the Aegean. On the other hand, the constitution was changed under Antipater. His son, Cassander, appointed Demetrius of Phalerum, of whom more later, as Supervisor to rule from 317 to 307 BCE.[7]

There were changes in how things in Athens were run. For example, all political activity, including jury service, was reserved for those with a property qualification of twenty *minae*. This was enough to exclude more than half the citizen population. No more payments were made to citizens from public funds, including the *theoric* payment, as it was called, which had enabled the poor to attend the theatre.[8] Did this social change influence Menander's approach to characterization in any way, for instance, in the people he portrayed? He was aiming to please a different audience from Aristophanes. The withdrawal of the theoric payment did probably make some difference to the kind of people who went to see his plays.[9] However, alongside these restrictions, the Macedonian kings hoped to achieve cultural prestige by gaining control of Athens, and so fostered Athenian drama along with the other arts, as they had done in Macedonia.[10]

With Alexander's death, the 'Hellenistic' period began: a convenient term but rather an 'arbitrary construct'.[11] Some accounts have tended to suggest that there was a single Hellenistic culture of some kind existing in Alexander's new cities and across his new Greek world. It is true that in every state a minority of Greco-Macedonians formed the ruling class. They came from various social backgrounds which could be forgotten in their new environment, but they held on to their memories of their origins and retained their original customs, such as their love of athletics and drama. This is reflected in what remains of their public buildings, which of course included, as has been seen, theatres, the theatres in which Menander's plays were performed. One development already mentioned even before Menander's day was that there was a great increase in the number of professional companies of actors touring the Greek world. These companies would have performed Menander's comedies, and those by other playwrights too.

Menander

According to one story, Menander and Philemon, a contemporary playwright, both received an invitation to Egypt from King Ptolemy I, a follower and then successor of Alexander, an offer which, because of ill health and a desire not to be separated from his girlfriend, Menander turned down. This could be a true account, in some respects at least, since the Ptolemies, acting as patrons, as the Macedonians did with Euripides, and other courts did too, tried to attract leading literary figures.[12]

If true, the account reflects interest in Menander's work far beyond Greece, as the archaeological evidence demonstrates. Alexander's conquests of foreign territory did make it a different Greek world into which Menander (born 344/3 BCE) grew to maturity,[13] from that of his comic predecessor Aristophanes, though there is disagreement in this case too as to exactly how different, partly because Greece had had contact with these other countries long before the 'Hellenistic' age.[14]

There is some evidence, as has already been noted, that Menander's contemporaries preferred Philemon, his main rival in the dramatic contests, to Menander himself.[15] However, in fact, Philemon was less successful in terms of festival victories. Menander had eight victories in all, of which at least two and not more than four were at the Lenaea. Philemon had three Lenaean victories, but his first was later than Menander's first: one of the three was in 307.[16]

Today, even some classicists are vague about Menander's importance, and his name is not as widely known as that of Aristophanes, the latter being studied at school and still, occasionally, performed in the original Greek. Performances of Menander are very rare.[17] Yet, after Menander's death, for more than 800 years, he was very famous. His plays were frequently staged in Greece and abroad as part of the culture of Greeks 'in exile'. The mosaics and frescoes which have survived from various places depicting scenes from Menander's plays provide evidence which supports this fame.

According to another story (all such anecdotes must be treated with caution), Menander had other friends, in addition to his possible support from Ptolemy. He was, it is said, nearly sent to prison merely for being associated with Demetrius of Phalerum.[18] Ancient opinions differed as to whether Demetrius was a restorer of democracy or an autocratic ruler. Trials followed Demetrius's later expulsion from Athens.[19] According to another story, Demetrius was later involved, as an advisor to the king, Ptolemy Soter, with setting up the great Library at Alexandria.[20]

Both Demetrius of Phalerum and Menander are reported to have been pupils of Theophrastus,[21] who was himself a pupil in philosophy of Aristotle. Aristotle was identified with the Macedonian rulers, because at thirteen or fourteen years of age Alexander the Great had been sent by his father to study under him in the 'Gardens of Midas' at Mieza, modern Lefkadia, a village in Macedonia. He subsequently, it is alleged, looked up to Aristotle as a father. Aristotle is said to have given Alexander a copy of the *Iliad*, annotated for him, a treasured possession which went with Alexander all the way to India.[22] Aristotle's Lyceum flourished under Demetrius of Phalerum, but Demetrius was driven out of the city by another Demetrius, Poliorcetes, another Macedonian ruler.

Hellenistic philosophy, incidentally, has in the past received the same treatment as Hellenistic religion from scholars who believed that this was an age of decline. Former certainties were supposed to have been affected by the expansion of the Greek world and Greeks moving far from their homeland. But the fifth century had its own share of uncertainties too and there are ideas in common. For instance, Hellenistic philsosophers also assumed that individuals want to live the best life, that is achieve *eudaimonia*, 'happiness' or 'faring well', just as Aristotle did in his *Nicomachean Ethics* and others before him.[23] But philosophy and religion in Menander are areas that would merit further research than has been possible here.

Theophrastus's *Characters*

Theophrastus wrote a work, as mentioned above, entitled *Characters* whose stock characters live their lives in the Athens of the last few decades of the fourth century BCE. The man who spreads rumours in *Character* 8 has allowed some to date the work to 319 BCE by his reference to the defeat and capture of Cassander. *Character* 23 assumes that the campaigns of Alexander are over, and has also been dated to 319.[24]

Although Theophrastus was a philosopher, his original purpose in writing his *Characters* is puzzling and is still being debated.[25] The work consists of thirty sketches of undesirable types of personality. They are vivid and amusing, and possibly intended for performance at dinner parties. Take, for example, *Character* 18, in which the husband double-checks in bed with his wife that she has locked the cupboard, the money-chest and the front door; he still gets up with nothing on to go and look for himself.

But did Theophrastus's *Characters* influence comedy or comedy Theophrastus? The work does seem to have some relevance to the creation of Menander's characters.[26] Some of the *Characters* have the same names as the titles of Menander's plays; for example, *Kolax* and *Agroikos*. One of Theophrastus's bad characteristics (*Characters* 23) is boastfulness (*Alazoneia*): the *alazon*, 'boastful man', claims to have fought with Alexander. The boastful soldier was a familiar type in fourth-century comedy, but probably also in fourth-century life.[27] The influence of the *Characters* on Menander is unclear. Some may come in general from Theophrastus's philosophy.

Others have explored influences from Aristotle himself, particularly his *Nicomachean Ethics*: there is much vocabulary for character traits in common.[28] Aristotle may have inspired both comedy and Theophrastus's *Characters*. The latter may even have been part of a treatise on comedy.[29]

Epicurus

Theophrastus was an influential figure at the time. Epicurus, also a key philosopher, was said to have been an *ephebe* with Menander and perhaps been his friend.[30] Menander may, of course, have had other friends or acquaintances who were Cynics or Stoics. Demetrius of Phalerum also wrote philosophy, about kindness and fortune, for example. But Epicurus may have had some of his ideas in circulation before he founded his schools of philosophy, ideas of which Menander would, most likely, have been aware.[31]

Epicurus and his followers lived together in his home, called the Garden, which was situated between Athens and the Piraeus. Epicureanism came to be known for hedonism rather than for asceticism, a judgement that was not deserved.[32] Its followers avoided politics and this close community was a group of like minds rather than a centre for research such as the Lycaeum. It included, surprisingly for the time, and interestingly for this study here, women and slaves.[33] Epicureans held that women could be philosophers as well as men, but then so did the Stoics and, in a way, Plato (some very exceptional women). A slave called Mys, however, was one of Epicurus's companions.[34]

Epicureanism held that appearances are never false, only the opinions formed about them by our minds. Similar ideas are explored by Menander in the way the masks of characters sometimes give the audience and the other characters false impressions about them, as will be explored later in relation to an apparently special interest in women and slaves in the plays.[35] The Epicurean ideal sought is freedom from disturbance, and Menander's plays often focus on the distress which is unnecessarily caused by misunderstandings. Of course, this could be argued for comedy in general. In Menander, as will be seen here, although people do not radically change their ways, peace is restored in the end. Epicurean communities were famous even amongst their enemies for the friendships between their members and with Epicurus himself. Friendship is a significant theme in Menander, which will be touched on in the investigation of his characterization that follows.

Against influence from Epicurus in particular, his followers taught that there is no providential god. One character at least in Menander, however, refers to a *daimonion* or 'spirit' that intervenes to correct and make things better (Charisios at *Epitrepontes* 912ff). The god Pan and goddess Tyche, 'Fortune', unless regarded strictly as merely literary devices, exert benevolent influences in *Dyscolus* and *Aspis*. Several characters seem devout in different ways. There may be more interest in religion in Menander's work than in that of Epicurus.[36]

Aristophanes, Middle Comedy, tragedy and Menander[37]

Before looking in more detail, as we shall do, at the social norms of the period, it is important to remember that Menander's comedy was very different from that of Aristophanes and his contemporaries and their immediate successors. Three terms have traditionally been applied since Hellenistic times to periods of ancient comedy: 'Old', for the time of Aristophanes and his contemporaries, that is, the fifth century BCE, 'Middle' for that of his later plays and his successors, c.404–321 BCE and the death of Alexander, and 'New' for plays written from the last quarter of the fourth century BCE to the middle of the third century BCE, which includes those by Menander.[38]

In many ways, calling comedy Old, Middle or New has been unhelpful, because it is likely that the growth in popularity of one kind of comedy at the expense of another was a gradual process and not something that happened suddenly at a particular date. It may also imply, rightly or wrongly, a development of some kind.[39] The term 'New' Comedy has certainly become misleading when used to refer, as it has been in the titles of modern books on ancient comedy, both to Menander's comedies and to Roman comedies which are adaptations of them, as if these two categories were in some way indistinguishable.[40]

Old Comedy

The comic plays of Aristophanes' contemporaries, such as his chief rivals Cratinus and Eupolis, survive now only in fragments, which already makes any study of the development of ancient comedy difficult. The evidence of Aristophanes may distort the picture.[41] However, it does seem that Aristophanes was not alone in being outspoken in his abuse and satire of the famous and powerful. Despite the rise of Macedon and Athens's loss of autonomy, some ridicule of politicians continues. (Already Isocrates complains in 355 BCE, before the conquest by Macedon, that some comedy is irresponsible. Plato echoes this in the *Laws*.[42]) Fourth-century comedy continues to centre on Athens, and this despite the considerable spread of drama beyond the city in this later period.[43]

Covering eight hundred years, the names of nearly 250 playwrights of Greek comedy are known. Their plays date from the sixth century BCE to the second century CE, but almost all of their work has been lost. Only a proportion of the output of the most well-known, Aristophanes, survives (eleven out of forty or so plays). As Menander himself was for many centuries preserved in fragments, the main focus of scholarship on him for a long time was literary context, that is his place in the history of ancient drama and in particular his debt to so-called 'Middle Comedy'.

However, although a character in Athenaeus's *Deipnosophistai*, 'Philosophers at Dinner' (second century BCE), claims at that point to have read over 800 plays,[44] 'Middle Comedy' in particular was either lost completely or survives only as fragments in the form of quotations by other ancient authors, or else on bits of papyrus from Egypt.[45] The corpus of the eighty years or so between Aristophanes's *Frogs* and Menander's *Dyscolus* is 'vast and difficult'. A little can be gleaned about the evolution, standard forms and themes of the genre, but it is good to be cautious, given that little can be known without further discoveries about plot or characterization.[46]

The disappearance of explicit politics from comedy was once used to identify 'Middle' Comedy, but some now regard politics even in Old Comedy as a relatively temporary phenomenon, confined to the end of the fifth century. Mythology provided stories for tragic plots, and some elements from tragedy, especially from Euripides, are to be found in later comedy, such as recognitions of long-lost relatives. Tragedy and comedy had begun to deal with similar issues.[47] It is thought that some of this entered comedy as parody: Aristophanes, for example, parodied a scene from Euripides's *Telephus* in his *Acharnians*. Although ancient opinion regarded Eupolis, Cratinus and Aristophanes as leading exponents of 'Old Comedy', some would attach the label 'Middle Comedy' to the two last plays by Aristophanes, because they mark a transition to a different style of play. They are *Women at the Assembly* (*c*.391 BCE) and *Wealth* (388 BCE, three years before Aristophanes's death).[48]

New Comedy

The leading dramatists of New Comedy wrote from about 320 to 280 BCE and came from different places in the 'new' Greek world. Alexis,[49] who had begun writing about 350 BCE but was still active at this later period, was a native of Thurii in Southern Italy, Menander was from Athens, Diphilus from Sinope on the Black Sea, and Philemon was probably Syracusan. Comedy was being written and performed far beyond Athens.[50] More than sixty playwrights of New Comedy are known from fragments. There were originally several hundred: also known are Philippides, Poseidippos and Apollodorus of Carystus, for example. But the papyri have so far mostly yielded only Menander, although statues were erected to Philemon and Poseidippus as well as to Menander: one of Poseidippus survives.[51]

Philemon (368/60–267/6) wrote 97 plays that have been described both as Middle and New Comedy.[52] In an intriguing anecdote recounted by Aulus Gellius, Menander asks whether Philemon does not blush when he beats him.[53] Philemon satirized Magas, half-brother of Ptolemy II.[54] A number of Philemon's titles suggest mythological themes: for example, *Myrmidons* and *Palamedes*. He wrote about *hetairai*, and some of his plays included recognitions. The tone appears to be that of a caricaturist.[55] Sadly, 24 lines of *Stratiotes*, in which a cook boasts of his skill in Middle Comedy fashion, is the longest excerpt available with which to assess this rival of Menander. The passage is one of those preserved by Athenaeus.[56] Plautus adapted *Mercator* from Philemon's *Emporos*, 'Merchant', *Trinummus* from *Thesauros*, 'Treasure', and perhaps *Mostellaria*, 'Play about a Ghost', from *Phasma*, 'Ghost'.

Alternatively, the latter may be derived from another New Comedy writer, Diphilus (born between 360 and 350 BCE), author of around a hundred plays. Study of how Plautus used Diphilus's plays as models suggests that Diphilus may have written romantic comedies with some mythological themes, involving puns, spectacle, comic routines and some ribaldry. It is known that Plautus adapted *Casina* from Diphilus's *Kleroumenoi* 'Those who Draw Lots', *Rudens*, 'The Rope', from *Pera*, 'Wallet' and the fragmentary *Vidularia*, 'The Suitcase', from *Schedia*, 'Raft'.[57] Terence took a scene from *Synapothnescontes*, 'Those Who Die Together', for his *Adelphoe*, 'The Brothers' (see lines 6–11: Plautus adapted it as *Commorientes*). Diphilus also wrote a play called *Paiderastai*, 'The Lovers of Boys' (usually negative in sense).

Alexis's *Carthaginian* was probably the model for the *Poenulus* of Plautus. Interestingly, Plautus's *Amphitruo* probably had a mythological Middle Comedy model.[58] Apollodorus of Carystus provided the originals for Terence's *Phormio* (from *Epidikazomenos*, 'He who pursues his Claim in the Courts' and *Hecyra*, 'The Mother-in-Law'.[59] Terence otherwise drew extensively on Menander. So did Plautus.[60]

To compare Menander with his rivals, there are very occasional personal jibes in his plays: see *Samia* 603, which mentions Chaerephon, a famous Athenian parasite.[61] His work is not free of politics, although there is little that is explicit. For example, in *Hairnet* (K.-A. fr. 208) Demetrius of Phalerum's *gynaikonomoi* ('regulators of women') were targets for using chefs as informants on excesses at private feasts.[62] In *Sikyonios* Smikrines is called 'oligarchic' and 'vile' (156). But echoes of Euripides' *Orestes* 866–956 in a messenger speech at lines 176ff, in the same act, seem to criticize democracy.[63]

There does appear to be politics of a general and subtle kind in Menander. Some see more.[64] Others comment that Athens as a *polis* is present in New Comedy only in a very much 'dehistoricized and deactualized form'.[65] His plays may not be the apolitical escapism that scholars once took them for. But, as with the examples from *Sikyonios*, it is not clear what the nature of any more specific politics might be. Is there support of Macedonian-imposed oligarchy or of democratic ideology and open political comment? Scholars cannot agree. There is a danger of searching too hard for politics in what is a very different kind of comedy from Aristophanes, for instance, or of taking what is essentially comedy too seriously. Even in Aristophanes the nature of the political content is controversial: whether it backs the *demos*, 'people', or the oligarchs and what its purpose was other than to amuse. If there are any digs at the Macedonians in Menander, they are very subtle indeed. Demeas's heartfelt prayer to Athens at *Samia* 101ff could be one candidate.[66] Comedy can be subversive of the *status quo*, but perhaps, as will be explored, Menander's main target is just a more general one, namely people's behaviour.

There is occasional vulgarity in Menander, but it depends on character and context, as with the soldier's slave Sosias's lewd comments to the *hetaira* ('courtesan') Habrotonon at *Perikeiromene* 482ff. There are no easy answers to questions about changing tastes and the form of those new tastes,[67] although wider contact beyond Greece makes a tempting explanation for the rise of a more 'universal' drama. Whilst Menander's plays are more gentle in flavour than Aristophanes, there can be knockabout comedy such as that at the end of the *Dyscolus*, when Knemon is forced to join the party, or farce, as when just before that Knemon is tortured by people knocking on his door for fun trying to borrow pan after pan from him (914ff), having already asked him at 470ff, or the tussle over the baby between the grandfathers in Act IV (579ff) of the *Samia*.

Extant Menander mostly mentions myths only in passing, but sometimes draws explicitly on mythology for its plots: although it turns to tragedy for situations, language and metre. Gods speak the prologues (there is one human speaker extant).[68] There is realism too in Menander, alongside 'romantic' plots: poverty in his *Farmer* (see line 77) is more poignant than any extant fifth-century treatment,[69] and *Aspis* does not shy away from the horrors of war, employing tragic language in fact to emphasize the presence of a serious motif in a comedy.[70] But fantasy, such as is found in Aristophanes' *Birds*, an avian utopia in the sky, does not feature in what survives.

Menander's texts, as has already been observed, are now extant in sufficient quantity for his techniques of plot construction and characterization to be studied in some of the plays. As yet, this is not possible in the same depth for his predecessors (so-called Middle Comedy) or his contemporaries in New Comedy, due to their still very fragmentary state. To generalize about New Comedy would be as unwise as to do so about the comedy that preceded it, since what evidence there is points to a variety of approaches comparable to that of the later Roman adaptations. Alexander's conquests and the growth in contact with other regions and countries may have created a market for a new kind of comedy, not just with a wider geographical appeal, but also for the kind of gentle characterization that interested Menander.

As has already been observed, in Menander the chorus, although its approach is referred to by the actors, has become partly a device for creating a break in the action, that is, to mark the end of an act. Alexis's *Kouris*, 'Hairdresser', date unknown, has a character announce the arrival of a chorus of revellers in a similar way.[71] (Roman comedy, although frequently derived from Menander, dispensed with the chorus altogether.)[72] It is not known whether the choral interlude had an impact in some way on the action or its interpretation. Certainly the chorus is not interacting with characters on stage during the action, which may sometimes have had the effect of making the characters seem more alone when in distress, or dependent on individual friends.[73]

Old Comedy is seen by some to be the true origin of the stock characters in fourth-century comedy, the comic demagogue in Aristophanes, for instance, being a parasite and flatterer and Lamachus in his *Acharnians* a comic soldier.[74] Eupolis wrote a play called *Kolakes*, 'Parasites' (see fr.172) and there was a parasite in Epicharmus's *Hope or Wealth*. Pherekrates wrote plays about *hetairai*. The slaves Xanthias in *Frogs* and Karion in *Wealth* have substantial roles in Aristophanes. See also Demosthenes the slave in his *Knights*. The characterization is, however, in Aristophanes at least, 'joke-driven'.

Any development in comedy certainly need not be synonymous with a deterioration in quality.[75] There are major unanswered questions anyway surrounding any development as such.[76] But it is important that many plays of what has been termed Middle Comedy in particular, such as those of Alexis (*c*.375–275), do seem to have satirized certain social types, such as the professional soldier and his parasite, the independent courtesan, the cook, and the slave.

These basic characters turn up in more than one play by Menander. Detailed analysis of their use before his recovery on papyrus was based on Roman comedy and its scholarship. The nature of the role of these characters in the plot would be inferred from their appearance, their masks and costumes and from their names.[77] An examination of the extent to which Menander's characters are stereotypes, or rather are based on stereotypes, forms an important part of this book. But it is in the context of what can be known of society and social norms at the time Menander was writing, rather than primarily by considering his debt to his comic predecessors, and without preconceived ideas about them, that Menander's treatment of these stock characters will now be explored in depth, with particular reference to the women and slaves of the *Epitrepontes*.[78]

Further reading

Michael Scott (2009) provides a lively introduction to the fourth century BCE. See also his excellent TV series *Ancient Greece: the Greatest Show on Earth* (2017), which includes a look at Menander's plays in the form of inspired animation. Konstan (2010) examines Menander's place in cultural studies.

Alexander the Great

For very accessible scholarly introductions to Alexander the Great, see Bowden (2014) and (longer) Cartledge (2004) with Shipley (2000), 6–7 on the sources. On problems with the sources, see also Baynham (2003). A vivid sense of the countries through which Alexander travelled and the wider Greek world at this period can be experienced by viewing Michael Wood's *In the Footsteps of Alexander* (1998), Maryland Public Television for the BBC. See Michael Scott's series cited above, episode 2, for pictures of Chaeronea and Aegae (Vergina). Fredricksmeyer (2003) gives a good account of Alexander's attitude to the gods and his own divinity.

Menander and Egypt

The story of Menander's invitation to Egypt is recounted by Alciphron (4.18,19), a sophist from the second or third century CE, who composed his *Letters* as supposedly written by Athenians of the fourth century BCE: 'an unverifiable blending of imaginative fiction and historical fact', as Arnott observes (in his Loeb *Menander* (1997 with corr.), xvi–xvii), though he notes that this story is also in Pliny: HN7.xxx.111 = Test. 10. The Pliny passage does not mention an invitation to Philemon, as Alciphron does, although it does talk about Macedon, a fleet and an embassy, and Menander is said to prefer literary merit to royal fortune, '*regiae fortunae praelata litterarum conscientia*'. Theophrastus, who is said to have taught Menander, could not be persuaded to become tutor to Ptolemy II, Soter's son (El-Abbadi (1990), 82, 85).

Theophrastus's *Characters*

For Theophrastus's importance for the study of Menander and New Comedy, see Fortenbaugh and others (eds) (1992), 2. Lane Fox (1996), 134ff, 138 argues for 310/9 BCE as a date for the *Logopoios*, 'Gossip' and before 323 for the *Alazon*. The name Alexander in *Character* 23 is a corrupted reading, and it is difficult to know how this could have happened to such a well-known name. The alternative, Evander, though, is not known to history (Ussher (1993), 196), and this character would want to have been on campaign with the most famous person he could, that is, Alexander the Great ('surely' Alexander, says Lane Fox (1996), 134). Various allusions to political institutions put at least another eight sketches, together with the Boastful and Oligarchic men in the Athens of Alexander (Lane Fox (1996), 136). But see Theophrastus (2004), 27ff, where Diggle argues on the most natural reading that Alexander is dead; for *Character* 23 he gives a date of about 319. Both Diggle and Lane Fox (141) think that an extended period of composition is likely for the *Characters*: Theophrastus (2004), 37.

Lane Fox goes on to discuss how a high proportion of both Menander's and Theophrastus's characters own slaves, and the possible significance of this for assessing their wealth and position in society. He settles for 'an affinity of outlook' between Theophrastus and Menander (140). 'For all their ethical basis, Theophrastus's sketches ... quite obviously have comic affinities as well' says Rusten (Theophrastus (1993), 15). See further Ussher (1993), 4–5 on how the characters recall Aristophanic types, with 21 on colloquial expressions, and (1977), 78–9: Theophrastus probably never saw these types performed, however (there has unfortunately not been room here to explore the transmission of Aristophanes (see Wilson (2014b) and Taplin (1993)), Aristophanes being ultimately for a long time better known than Menander, or the story of how other Greek authors reached us today.

Demetrius of Phalerum

O'Sullivan (2009) explores what can be known about the rule of Demetrius of Phalerum: see in particular her Conclusion. For the evidence for his life, translated and discussed, see Fortenbaugh and Schütrumpf (eds) (2000).

Epicurus

On Epicurus, see *The Epicurus Reader: Selected Writings and Testimonia* (1994) and Konstan (2003). See Sharples (2006) on Hellenistic philosophy in general, with 226ff on Epicurus in particular. See also 228 and 238 on the rejection of conventional social arrangements by Epicureans and Cynics.

Menander and friendship

On friendship in the classical world, see Konstan (1997), especially 108ff on Epicureanism. For Menander he seems to mention only gnomic phrases for which we do not know the context (57), touching briefly on *Aspis* and *Perikeiromene* at 116. He suggests that New Comedy avoids disloyalty between friends (116). For an exploration of friendship in Menander in more detail, see chs. 4 and 5 here and a study of the male characters which is in preparation.

Menander and religion

Mikalson (2010) is a useful short introduction to ancient Greek religion, with chapters on heroes, cults, the family, the *polis,* 'city-state', and the individual; there are good illustrations. Chapter 8 refers specifically to the Hellenistic period, and there is a new chapter on Greek religion and culture.

For a detailed treatment of Pan, who speaks the prologue in Menander's *Dyscolus*, see Borgeaud (1988). Boardman (1997) is a short but fascinating study of images of Pan down the ages. Pan's worship is found to centre on cave sites rather than temples (Osborne (1987), 191–2). These caves often have wedding *loutophoroi* (a kind of Greek vase) as offerings (Parker (2005), 442); its enthusiasts were city people rather than shepherds. Grooms performed a torch race in honour of Pan, perhaps as a farewell to wild sexuality. Pan could be associated with madness and panic: Larson (2007), 150ff.

Mikalson (1998), 45 refers to 'a rising concern' for the safety of the *demos,* 'people', of the Athenians, linking this to the inauguration and quick growth of the cult of *Agathe Tyche* (Tyche speaks the prologue in Menander's *Aspis*), along with large sacrifices to *Eirene* and *Zeus Soter*, although he does also stress continuity at this stage with the classical period. But see also Shipley (2000). Mikalson observes (63) that there is no evidence for the cult of Agathe Tyche in the third century, the next mention of her being in the last quarter of the first century. He does not assign major importance to her throughout the Hellenistic period, as does, for example, Green (1990), 53, who refers to 'an obsession' with Chance, Fortune. See further on Tyche, Scullion (2014), 351ff.

Aristophanes, Middle Comedy, tragedy and New Comedy

On tragedy and Menander see further Hurst (1990) (in French). Rusten and others (eds) (2011) have opened up the study of the fragments of Greek comedy with their accessible translations based on *PCG*, the standard edition for the Greek. See also Olson (2007) for another selection of translations together with commentary on the fragments organized thematically. The essays in Fontaine and Scafuro (eds) (2014) are wide-ranging and interesting on all aspects of ancient comedy. See also Harvey and

Wilkins (2000) for Old Comedy. On the role of the chorus in Greek drama, see Silk (1998), although there is no mention of its treatment in Menander.

On Eupolis, see Storey (2003). There is an edition of Eubulus by Hunter (1983) and of Alexis by Arnott (1996a). For good overviews of Middle Comedy and New Comedy, see Arnott (2010) and Ireland (2010) respectively. In the same volume, Bowie looks at myth and ritual in ancient comedy and Olson at politics. Biles (2014) puts Aristophanes and Menander in context from what can be known about their rivals. Marshall and Kovacs (2012) have more essays largely focussing on Old Comedy. Sidwell (2014) is an important critical assessment of the problematic evidence for fourth-century comedy before Menander, which questions Arnott (2010) and his more confident view that the genre's development was straightforward. Webster (1970) is still useful.

Menander and politics

For the interpretation of Menander's plays as political in subtle ways and democratic, see Lape (2004), 243 and her ch. 8, discussed in the conclusion to this book. Major (1997) and Owens (2011) see Menander's drama, however, as pro-Macedonian, with Sostratos to Owens (371ff), and rather improbably so, a kind of Demetrius of Phalerum. Olson (2010), 35 and *passim* has a good summary of the debate surrounding politics in Aristophanes.

4

Women in *Epitrepontes*: Habrotonon and Pamphile

Menander's plays give prominent roles to women, although it should be remembered that these characters were played by men.[1] The *Samia* and the *Perikeiromene* both have interesting roles for women, but *Epitrepontes* in particular, with its *hetaira*, Habrotonon, and its young wife, Pamphile, provides an interesting focus. What can a knowledge of the historical background contribute to an appreciation of these female characters, and how do they interact with each other?[2]

Social background

However fascinating ancient sexuality may be,[3] the social history of the women of Ancient Greece remains difficult to write. There are images without precise context, passing references in sources that are not primarily about women, as well as fictional characters or real women who play roles in the work of artists and poets, but roles that bear a loose resemblance to the lives of actual women at any particular period in ancient Greece.[4] Then there is the question of how the lives of women in Athens, the main setting for Menander's plays, may be compared with the lives of their contemporaries in other Greek states.[5]

Because of its subject matter, it has been tempting to use New Comedy as evidence for the social, or even legal, status of women. However, as has already been observed, context and speaker in comedy have received insufficient attention from historians.[6] It is also important to distinguish legal from social status and attitudes. In the case of women the 'evidence' has been recorded by men:[7] thus only a proportion of what might be known survives.

However, fourth-century comedy is, with these provisos, a potentially rich source for the history of its period.[8] Habrotonon in *Epitrepontes* makes one promising case study. She is apparently an *hetaira*, although she is not explicitly described as such.[9] What kind of behaviour might be expected of such a woman?

The *Hetaira*[10]

Hetairai appear in different kinds of literature, especially in the comedy written in the period before Menander, known as Middle Comedy, with the *hetaira* becoming a negative stereotype. For example, in some passages of this earlier comedy as quoted by Athenaeus, an *hetaira* is described as a *symphora*, 'a calamity', to the man who keeps her (literally 'has'), and as *kakon . . . oikoi mega*, 'a great evil to his home'; others are said to 'plot for gain'.[11]

Hetairai appear in the works of speech-writers *c.*420–320 BCE too, as women who were paid for their 'company'. The orators could seem to represent a more 'realistic' source for the ancient world than comedy, but their main aim was to persuade: like actors they had large audiences too, addressing assemblies of some 6,000 citizens or large juries on which as many as 500 men might be selected to serve. The content of the speeches is not therefore unbiased, especially as only male citizens were involved. To gain support for their listeners the orators must have presented *hetairai* with recognizable social norms and moral values; but in turn, these norms may have drawn on literary representations, among them the *hetairai* from comedy as referred to in passages of Athenaeus, which would have drawn on other social norms in the first place, a subtle interplay of influences.

An *hetaira* has been defined by scholars as a 'companion' (its etymological meaning but euphemistic in origin), a 'professional girlfriend' (Handley) as well as as a 'courtesan'. There were *pornai*, women who were paid for sex and of low status, and there were *hetairai*, some of whom had semi-permanent relationships. But the distinction is not always clear, and there is another category sometimes used to describe a woman who had once been an *hetaira*, that is a *pallake*, for which 'live-in-girlfriend', 'partner' and 'concubine' are possible translations, the last being archaic in English but useful in that it conveys a status with possible legal implications.[12]

Some are keen to stress that the *hetaira*, being a 'courtesan', also archaic English, was a kind of prostitute because she offered sex to men outside marriage for gifts or money, although *hetairai* sometimes cohabited. There were slave and free prostitutes[13] and slave and free *hetairai*, but there were *hetairai* who had, as well as physical beauty, intellectual training and artistic talents.[14] Habrotonon, in Menander's *Epitrepontes*, has been hired as a harpist. As noted, *hetairai* may have been euphemistically referred to as companions,[15] but perhaps the term *hetaira* also reflected that men found such women stimulating company intellectually, not just physically. Indeed, some *hetairai* seem to have exerted considerable sexual power over their men.[16] The high-class *hetaira* at least dealt in 'gifts', rather than straightforward money, in what was a gift exchange society, thus avoiding making her relationships with men explicit.[17]

It could therefore be said that *porne* was a coarse term, whereas *hetaira* was a delicate one, but that both kinds of women provided sex for money.[18] Alternatively, there was a Greek distinction between the brothel slave and the free *hetaira*.[19] Habrotonon, however, is an *hetaira* and a slave. Importantly, it will be seen in *Epitrepontes*[20] that *porne* can be used to insult this *hetaira*, so the two terms cannot be synonymous, and the same translation will not do.[21] Yet some *hetairai* (Habrotonon is one of them) would still have been owned by a *pornoboskos*, 'pimp'.[22] There is also no firm line between the *pallake* and the *hetaira*, although a *pallake* might have had children whom the cohabiting father would wish to recognize legally as his.[23]

Against Neaira

Menander's *hetairai* can be compared with at least one famous *hetaira* from 'real life', a woman called Neaira. She was put on trial probably between 343 and 340 BCE, around the time of Menander's birth. The speech *Against Neaira* was attributed to Demosthenes in antiquity but was probably written by Apollodorus, Neaira's main prosecutor, or, technically, the *synegoros*, 'public advocate'. It is the only source for what is known about Neaira, describing her as a woman of many lovers who attended parties with men at which drinking took place, 'being an *hetaira*' (48). At 107, Neaira is said to be '*peporneumene*', 'playing the 'harlot'.[24] A *porne*, it is argued, should not have the liberty to live with whatever man she chooses and name anyone as the father of her child (112). Women of the character of an *hetaira* should not be able to pass for whatever they please (118). Neaira is being prosecuted for living in marriage with Stephanos, despite being a foreigner.[25] She is also an *hetaira* and a *doule*. But he is the real target of Apollodorus: it is he who has passed off a daughter of Neaira as if she were a genuine Athenian.

The speech contains a much quoted and much disputed definition of an *hetaira*'s role:

Hetairai we keep for pleasure, *pallakai*[26] for the daily care of our persons, but wives to bear us legitimate children and to be faithful guardians of our households.

                                                                        59.122

However, Apollodorus is not giving legal definitions but concerned with the offspring of relationships.[27] Neaira is vilified because, it is claimed, attempts were made to pass off liaisons with an *hetaira* as proper marriages, an action which was illegal.

It is important to remember, however, in using this speech, that the evidence from the law-court speeches concerns only that stratum of society which had enough property for legitimacy to be a worry. Moreover, just one person's recorded views should not be taken as representative of a society. There are also dangers in generalization. The particular society and culture must always be borne in mind,[28] and the timing, as this is soon after the *diapsephisis*, 'vote on claims to registration of citizens', of 346/5.[29]

It is also necessary to consider what feelings the orators aimed to arouse in their audiences. It can be concluded, however, from the terms used against Neaira, that to be an *hetaira* was to be socially inferior and to be suspected of exploiting men for financial gain. Yet it seems that to have a relationship with an *hetaira*, as Charisios does with Habrotonon, was not in itself something that would occasion moral condemnation, unless one pretended that she had the rights of a married woman. What was the position of other, socially respected, freeborn women?

Virginity

Against Neaira and Middle Comedy give the impression that the life of a freeborn Greek citizen woman was very different from that of an *hetaira*, setting aside the difficulties of precisely defining the latter. There are, however, also problems associated with the meaning of the Greek word *parthenos*, sometimes translated 'virgin'. The Greek word does not signify unambiguously everything that is implicit in the English noun 'virginity', for example, an intact hymen.[30] *Parthenos* cannot mean 'shuns all sexual activity', because there is a word *parthenios*, meaning 'child of a *parthenos*', but at *Sikyonios* 372 the words *apeiros andros*, 'without experience of a man', are added to 'still a *parthenos*'.

Parthenos sometimes had active rather than passive connotations: in myth the *parthenos* is often not only beautiful but courageous, intelligent or physically strong and so attractive to male gods and heroes. Nausicaa in Homer's *Odyssey* is one example, Antigone another, from Greek tragedy. There is no particular reference to sexuality, although to describe a young woman as a *parthenos* is to emphasize that she is at a transitional point, nubile – ready and able to become a wife and mother.[31]

A text about Artemisian ritual contains an unambiguous formulation: the *parthenoi* must serve as *kanephoroi* before marrying in order to satisfy the goddess, for otherwise Artemis would have been offended by the loss of their virginity.[32] It is not clear whether virginity was a physical state or not. But that there were myths in which *parthenoi* were tested suggests that virginity was for the Greeks a sexual not a sociological matter.[33]

The protection of virginity was one likely intention behind the seclusion of women, the ideal conveyed by Lysias 1.9 and 3.6 with their references to the women's quarters of the speakers' houses. Respectable women were apparently expected to avoid being seen even by relatives. In Xenophon's *Oeconomicus* Ischomachos's wife had lived carefully supervised and had seen, heard and said as little as possible.[34] Thus the integrity of the *oikos* was preserved, which would be threatened by lost virginity and illegitimate children. But ancient ideals about seclusion have sometimes been reinforced by male scholars in their interpretation of the evidence.[35]

Against the view that women in ancient Greece led secluded, protected or repressed lives, comparisons have been made with some modern Mediterranean societies deemed to be similar, using established methods for anthropological study which suggest that ideals are often contradicted by what happens in practice, with women having their own spheres of influence and social networks.[36] Poor women would have had to go out into public spaces to work, for example, selling goods in the market.[37] There are also the women of literature, with larger than life characters like Clytemnestra (Aeschylus's *Agamemnon*) and Lysistrata (in Aristophanes's play of that name). They may represent male anxieties about loss of control, but to be believable and either frightening or funny, they must be somehow grounded in social norms which included assertive, angry women. It will be interesting to see how Menander's women compare with those of tragedy and Aristophanes.

Opinions are divided, then, as to how restricted the lives of freeborn women were. In reality, they may have had a certain freedom, since they were able to attend festivals, even taking roles in their own organizations, and at liberty to shop and fetch water.[38] These may have been opportunities to meet men, though with sometimes undesirable consequences. Ideals of seclusion may have been dependent on the financial means of the head of the household[39] to employ chaperones. However, whatever the degree of seclusion or segregation, a freeborn woman did not sell herself for sex unless she had become an *hetaira*.[40]

Rape[41] and seduction

But what happened if a freeborn girl was raped? Scholars are wary of anachronisms in moral judgements, but, given the way that a rape or seduction is sometimes the 'peg' on which the plot of a play by Menander hangs, what would the reaction of a fourth-century Athenian audience have been to this plot motif and did it make a difference if the girl was raped rather than seduced?

The differences in ancient attitudes to rape have been vigorously debated.[42] Evidence has been cited in the past that an unmarried man who had raped or seduced a girl could, in certain circumstances, be forced to marry her. But this evidence is almost entirely from Roman comedy.[43] It does seem that no particular duty of fidelity was legally owed by a husband to his wife, but a man was liable, in various ways, for misconduct with the wife or recognized *pallake* of another man. The wife owed fidelity to her husband, because otherwise a bastard might be introduced into the family.[44]

With regard to norms for male sexual behaviour, Lysias 1.32–3 appears to suggest that rape was less seriously regarded than seduction: the former excused as a young man's ardour, the latter seen as gaining power over a woman's mind and thus damaging her as a desirable property for her husband or prospective suitors. The seducer was liable to be put to death; the rapist merely paid a fine.[45]

This interpretation has been challenged, however.[46] Rape or seduction could hardly be proved on the spot by someone taking the law into his own hands and the speaker's words in Lysias I cannot be taken at face value, since he himself has recently confessed to being the killer of an alleged adulterer.[47] The speaker argues for seduction, but his wife arranged the encounter.[48] The larger picture is important here:[49] the statement is part of an attempt to exaggerate a dead man's offence as an excuse for his homicide. But, as with the question of women's seclusion,[50] when different attitudes to rape at different times and periods are compared, modern Mediterranean cultures can be found in which it is hard for a raped woman to find a husband.[51]

The woman and her chastity are hardly protected in their own right, but only as the humble but necessary vehicle for carrying on the *oikos*. The victim of rape was apparently liable to the same treatment as a willing partner in adultery, that is, she was deterred from taking part in any public cult ceremonies.[52] It has been supposed that a raped wife must be divorced under the same terms as a woman taken in adultery, but there is no direct evidence.[53] Women who served in brothels or who openly offered themselves for hire certainly could not, however, seek any of the redress that might be available to others.[54]

Whatever the law, social attitudes may differ; the law is often made by men, but social attitudes can, of course, be shaped by both men and women. Rape does seem to have been condoned by the Athenian law-makers to some extent. But nothing in the evidence for Athens suggests that it was not possible to feel sorry for the victim, even if in reality it was accepted that the woman should expect to suffer further indignities.[55]

It is still the case, and important, given traditional descriptions of New Comedy plots as concerning rapes and seductions, that in both the Greek and Roman plays of New Comedy the distinction between rape and seduction is often left unclear.[56] It may be that there is often deliberate ambiguity in Menander because there is concern with the reputation of a freeborn girl.[57]

Moichos, often translated 'adulterer', and its derivations probably originally referred to the violation of the marriage tie; but by extension it was applied to the rape or seduction of an unmarried or widowed woman or *pallake* from whom the husband had intended to rear free children. Sexual acts of males outside matrimony are punished only if committed with freeborn Athenians.[58]

Marriage

What was the position of a woman once she married? The evidence is again selective. Menander's plays are usually set in Athens and amongst the more wealthy citizens. The law-court speeches concern only a certain section of society and were written to win a case.

There are documentary papyri from a period close in time to Menander which mention marriage, but they are mostly from Hellenistic Egypt.[59] Marriage contracts among the papyri specify financial arrangements, but also reciprocal moral obligations of the spouses. The husband undertakes to support the wife economically (implicit in the Greek conception of the dowry which was repaid if the wife returns to her family); the husband also undertakes not to have children by another woman or keep alternative sexual partners in the marital home.[60] The woman in the papyri marriage contracts promises in more vague terms to do nothing to shame her husband.[61] Disputes over alleged breaches of contract were put to (male) arbitrators, agreed on by both parties.

As with the *hetaira*, the *parthenos*, words for rape, such as *biasmos*, 'sexual violence', and the *moichos*, no single Greek word translates the English word 'marriage', although *aner* and *gyne* are the usual translations for 'husband' and 'wife'. The principal terms used in connexion with 'marriage' are *engye* and *gamos*. When the verb *engyan* is used in this context, the bride's father pledges his daughter to the future bridegroom – a transaction between the two men. *Gamos* has the same basic sense as 'pairing'. It is used of the physically consummated marriage and is a fully solemnized union. A married woman is sometimes called *gyne gamete* as opposed to being a *pallake*. There were few, if any, formal requirements to secure the validity of a solemn marriage and so it has been called in this context 'a social process'. But, although it had no legal definition, marriage was regarded as important to Athenian democratic ideology as it produced the citizens needed to participate in that democracy.[62]

Brides (the Greek word is *nymphe*) were normally quite young.[63] The expression is found, 'when she had attained the age', which indicates that there was an age when girls were regarded as suitable for marriage. A man expects applause for having arranged an early marriage for his daughter or sister, and a guardian may be rebuked for any delay in arranging the wedding of his female ward.[64]

Thirty is too old for a woman to *synoikein* 'live together', probably because pregnancy became more risky to mother and child beyond that age. The verb *synoikein* could be used from the mid-fourth century of a union between a citizen and an alien; it was subject to prosecution.[65] It is not certain whether it came to mean not just cohabitation but also the accepted term for living together in legal union.[66] But, again, complicating any attempt to illuminate their social background, Menander's plays have themselves sometimes been used as evidence for the study of Athenian marriage, as they have for other aspects of the social history of the period.[67]

Divorce

What about when marriages failed?[68] Plutarch's account concerning Pericles suggests that a voluntary dissolution of a marriage might arise from an agreement between a husband and a wife to separate, but Plutarch is far removed in time from the fifth and the fourth century. Papyri from Hellenistic Egypt indicate that both partners in a marriage had equal rights to initiate divorce.[69]

Divorce at Athens, to judge from the basis of references to it in the law-court speeches, was not common.[70] *Apopempein*, literally 'send away' is used of the husband (also *ekpempein*, 'send out', *ekballein*, 'throw out'), and *apoleipein*, 'abandon' or 'desert', used of the wife.[71] The husband could dismiss the wife, but she was not necessarily immediately compliant.[72] It seems that witnesses were not necessary, but that if the woman wished to initiate the divorce, she had to notify the eponymous archon.[73] Divorce for a woman taken in adultery was compulsory, if the man chose to enforce it.[74] There is an account in Demosthenes of a father taking his daughter away when he quarrelled with his son-in-law.[75] In all cases, a woman's dowry had to be repaid to her *kyrios*. The dowry was never legally required but its provision meant that marriage was a kind of 'fusion' of two estates, that of the husband and that of the wife's *oikos* of origin.[76] The wife's father or other male guardian could take her back, it has been suggested, but not if there was a child.[77]

Exposure

Would an action such as exposing a child have been commonplace in Menander's day and accepted by all without much emotion, including the mother?[78] Although the exposure of offspring was not unknown at the end of the fourth century, the historical evidence seems insufficient: for example, the full number of members of a family listed in the orators is seldom beyond question, yet some have used the greater number of sons listed in proportion to daughters as an argument for the exposure of girls.[79] How much exposure was practised and with what attitude has been very controversial.[80]

Moreover, a variety of sources could suggest that in late fifth and early fourth-century Athens the ethics of exposure had become a subject of controversy. Sophocles's *Oedipus* and Euripides's *Ion* are examples of literature which explores the issues, and to these can be added Menander's *Perikeiromene* and *Epitrepontes*.[81] However, the fact that recognition tokens were a necessary plot device for stories involving abandoned infants, as talismans against evil, suggesting a desire to have the child returned when older, does not prove they were used in real life.[82]

Exposure had already been a literary motif in Aristophanes[83] and in tragedy and mythology, but there are passages in other authors which appear to be evidence that it could, to some extent, happen in reality.[84] Plato's *Theaetetus* 151 A–D[85] has been seen as strongly suggesting that examination of newborn babies was done by midwives to determine whether they were worthy of rearing.[86] The *Republic* 460c includes children born of inferior parents with deformed ones as candidates for exposure. Adoption was restricted, which may have influenced decision-making about unwanted babies.[87] *Laws* 740c, however, perhaps part of the possible controversy mentioned above, shows Plato less keen to adopt exposure as a means of population control, advocating instead marrying girls off, and Aristotle *Politics* 7.14.10 (1335b) indicates that there was some feeling against exposure in his day.[88] Terence *Heauton Timoroumenos* 626–7 shows exposure of a girl to be a credible action for a sympathetic character, but it may not be a literal translation of the original Menander.[89]

Menander's women

It is time, in the light of this brief historical survey, to turn to an analysis of the female characters in Menander. The *Samia* and *Perikeiromene* will be examined briefly first. Most attention will be devoted, however, to the *Epitrepontes*.

Samia

> **Chrysis** (a *pallake,* speaking to her partner's adopted son, Moschion)   He'll cool down again. For he's in love, too, my dear, desperately in love, just as much as you. And that brings even the angriest man to terms pretty fast. And I'd put up with anything, myself, before I'd let a wet-nurse bring up Baby here in some slum.
>
> *Samia* 80–5 (Miller)

Samia has a prologue spoken by Moschion, which introduces the characters, including Chrysis. Moschion tells us (21) that his father, Demeas, fell in love with a Samian *hetaira*, a fact that might mislead. Demeas has, then, for his part, entered into more than a business relationship.[90]

Chrysis is seen largely through her dealings with other characters. The audience do not get to know her well, but she seems to be likeable, although she is rather misunderstood. She is shown as involved in interesting relationships, with Demeas and Moschion, but these are ones which are ultimately subordinated to another which receives more central treatment, that between the father and his son. Chrysis is portrayed as experienced with men (82ff) and close to Moschion. Demeas and Chrysis appear strikingly on stage together (Act III, lines 369ff) in an extremely emotional exchange. It is at line 509 that Nikeratos, Demeas's neighbour, calls Chrysis a *pallake*. What exactly is her status and why does Demeas, according to Moschion, feel shame at his involvement with her (23)? At 36–8, the audience learns that, once Demeas started living with Chrysis, she was quite accepted by their freeborn neighbours. She willingly goes along with the deception about the baby, without fuss or thought of the cost to herself (79), although it is relevant here whether or not Chrysis lost a baby of her own.[91]

Chrysis is perceptive, kind-hearted, altruistic and maternal in her words to Moschion at 80ff. She says that Demeas is in love and that makes men angry and that she could not bear to see the baby treated badly. There may also, however, be a little complacency in her confidence that she can bring Demeas round. In the end, though, at line 577, Demeas reproves Nikeratos for his angry behaviour towards Chrysis, calling her a free woman.

Perikeiromene

> **Glykera**   Even so, you can go back and tell him to find some other girl to insult in
> future.
> **Pataikos** (her father)   It wasn't so very dreadful, what he did.
> **Glykera**   It was abominable! ...
>
> > *Perikeiromene* 722–4 (Miller)

Glykera of *Perikeiromene* is freeborn and has not been an *hetaira*; she is treated as one, however, when she is 'given' to a soldier, according to the prologue (130), spoken by Agnoia.[92] Act IV begins with a dialogue between Glykera and her father. Their relationship is not yet known but a recognition scene between the two of them is a possibility later realized. Glykera is a very memorable female figure.[93]

Although the audience knows that Glykera is free, Glykera, Polemon and Moschion do not. Moschion treats her as she might expect, Polemon as she apparently cannot hope to be treated, but would be if her circumstances were known, that is, as a wife. Indeed it is striking that he says at 489: 'I think of her as my wedded wife.'

Epitrepontes

> ([... **Habrotonon** *enters from Chairestratos's house, carrying the baby.*])
> **Habrotonon**   I'll just take him outside. Poor dear, he's been crying for ages. I don't
> know what's wrong with him.
> **Pamphile** [*not seeing her*]   God pity me, I'm so unhappy!
>
> > *Epitrepontes* 852–5 (Miller)

An *hetaira* and a married woman meet on stage in Athens, four centuries before the birth of Christ. The audience has been watching Menander's *Epitrepontes*, and the problems of the play are approaching resolution. What sort of people are Habrotonon and Pamphile? How has Menander led us up to this moment, when the *hetaira* recognises Pamphile as the girl who was raped at a festival they both attended, and as the supposedly unfaithful (and so rejected) wife of the man by whom she herself has been hired?

Habrotonon

Habrotonon the *hetaira* is first mentioned in a fragment which reports the opinions of some other characters: the prologue to *Epitrepontes* does not survive. In what were the

Fig. 4.1 Mask: *Hetaira*.[94] Third century BCE and so later than Menander, but part of a continuing tradition of images: (Green and Handley (1995) pl. 45).

opening lines of the play,[95] a cook, Karion, asks Onesimos, a slave, if it is true that his *trophimos*, 'young master', is now keeping their friend Habrotonon[96] the *psaltria*, 'harp-girl', and if he married not all that long ago. Onesimos replies that it is. A *psaltria*, as Habrotonon is, was of higher status than a flute girl.[97] A passage of Themistios (quoted by Sandbach) mentions Karion as a lover of gossip; the fact that a harp-girl is with the newly married Charisios occasions comment and a hint of criticism, perhaps.[98] From Smikrines, we learn that Charisios is drinking with Habrotonon (127ff), and giving twelve drachmas[99] a day to a *pornoboskos*, 'pimp'.[100]

So is Charisios with a 'prostitute'? As has been seen, whilst *psaltria* and *porne* are not synonymous terms, they are not mutually exclusive either, and both kinds of girl were paid for, so there was probably room for speculation. It is significant who is speaking. Smikrines seems to be a miser, since he goes on to call wine costing an obol a *kotyle* or 'cup' expensive (130),[101] and he appears more concerned with his daughter's dowry than with her feelings (134).[102] Smikrines does at 136 refer to a pimp, but there is no further allusion to such a person in the extant play.[103] Chairestratos, who is eavesdropping, confirms the sum of money being spent on Habrotonon, at least (137), but makes a joke about how Smikrines has managed to calculate the daily payment being made.[104]

(From Act I) **Habrotonon** [*entering from Chairestratos's house*]   Charisios is waiting for you, Chairestratos. Who's that, darling?

Chairestratos   The bride's father.

Habrotonon   Why does he look like a miserable old schoolmaster?

Some verses are missing and the rest of the act is damaged. The general sense is clear,
but allocation of lines to speakers is not, nor is the interpretation of details.

Habrotonon   Bless you, don't speak like that.

Smikrines   You go to hell! You'll pay for this and pay dearly. I'm going in now, and
when I know how my daughter's fixed, I'll work out how I'm going to launch my
attack on Charisios. [*He goes into Charisios' house*].

Habrotonon   We'd better warn Charisios that he's here, hadn't we?

Chairestratos   Yes, we had. What a nuisance he is, turns a house upside down.[105]

Epitrepontes 142–66 (Miller)

Habrotonon has been the subject of conversation, but when does the *hetaira* first
appear? It seems likely that it is Habrotonon who enters at 142 with '*glykytate*', 'darling'
'sweetheart'.[106] If so, there is a chance very early on in the play to judge her from what
she herself says, rather than from the comments of others in her absence. Charisios's
wife Pamphile appears to be referred to for the first time in what survives: Smikrines is
father of Charisios's *nymphe*, his 'wife'.[107] If it is Habrotonon who has asked who
Smikrines is, her response that he looks 'miserable' (144) is not altogether a sympathetic
one. Care is needed with the interpretation of what follows.[108] The presence of
Chairestratos, a friend of Charisos, from 127 should be noted.

It is probably Smikrines who speaks harshly to Habrotonon at 160ff (this from
a character who has not so far been presented to us as particularly likeable). If it
is Habrotonon who speaks earlier the lines quoted above, she appears uninhibited
with men, lively and quick-witted: at 164 she suggests warning Charisios of Smikrines's
arrival.

In what survives of Act II (that is, all but 34 lines at the beginning), Habrotonon is
not referred to at all. The focus is entirely on the dispute between the two slaves over
the baby. The audience is all the more interested when Habrotonon makes her entrance
to see the woman Charisios is allegedly preferring to his wife, as the misunderstanding
over the baby threatens its future and the future of Charisios and Pamphile's *oikos*,
'household'.

Habrotonon alone 430ff (from Act III)

[*Enter* **Habrotonon** *from Chairestratos's house, speaking back over her shoulder*
(and failing to see Onesimos at first)]

Habrotonon   Let me go, please (especially you)! Leave me alone (all of you)!
[*Shuts door.*] Oh, dear! I think I've made a fool of myself. How was I to know? I
expected a spot of loving, but the man positively hates me: it's uncanny. He
won't even let me sit beside him at table, but keeps me at a distance.

Epitrepontes 430–5 (Miller with my additions in the round brackets)

Habrotonon would have been recognized as an *hetaira* (although it is not known that
that word has been used of her yet) first of all by her mask and costume. So far, we have

heard of money changing hands between Charisios and a *pornoboskos*, 'a pimp',[109] but this from Smikrines, a 'miser' who, as the original giver of his daughter's dowry, thinks he has reason to dislike the arrangement over Habrotonon.

Her words at lines 430–5 are a little surprising. She says, 'Leave me alone, I beg you – stop pestering me', as she comes out of the house. This could be spoken to some young male companions of Charisios who are molesting her, one in particular being singled out.[110] Could she be upset, and this be reflected in the change suddenly from plural to singular? Or are her words ungrammatical in order to give a hint of lack of general education? In any case, a woman who is 'used to' men tells them to 'get lost': a chaste *hetaira* is not to be chased – unusual. Next she complains that she has made a fool of herself ('myself' is emphasized, as it begins a sentence). It appears that her pride is hurt, but she blames herself not Charisios: 'love' (she thought he would feel that) is the first word in the next sentence, again for emphasis. The Greek word here, *erasthai*, is used of sexual love,[111] that is sex involving a warmth of feeling, and this Habrotonon expected. At 433, she is very vehement indeed (Arnott's translation imitates the alliteration in the Greek: 'loathes me with a loathing'; more literally, 'the man hates (me) with hatred that is amazing').[112] Charisios is angrily referred to in an impersonal way as the *anthropos*, 'guy', and not by name.[113]

In this way, Habrotonon's description of Charisios's behaviour serves at the same time to characterize herself. He does not even let her sit beside him at table, but keeps her at a distance and this has upset her. But her words also serve to arouse our curiosity about Charisios, who has still to appear, and his feelings for his estranged and, he supposes, unfaithful wife. Interestingly, his wife is not referred to at all by Habrotonon here.

If Habrotonon is just doing a day's work as an *hetaira*, why should Charisios's behaviour bother her? Vanity and professional pride perhaps? If so, the strength of her language is rather surprising – why 'hatred', the antithesis of 'love', in the same sentence? Menander seems to hint here that there is more than 'business' involved in Habrotonon's eyes. There are no humorously distracting asides from the slave Onesimos, who is present, but deep in thought, and who has not noticed her. She neither thinks she is overheard by Onesimos, nor is she – he is too self-absorbed; so these words voice her inner thoughts. She does not use the audience address *andres*, 'gentlemen', which is used often by other Menandrian characters when emotional.[114] Habrotonon's speech is short and addressed to herself, rather than explicitly to the audience; this leaves them still unsure about her feelings, and intrigued.

This is a harp-girl, then, who appears to expect more than payment for musical entertainment. Does Habrotonon just want sex, or seek social advancement through a more permanent sexual relationship with Charisios? Or does she perhaps love him?

Habrotonon is in Chairestratos's house, drinking with Charisios, and money appears to have changed hands. He has fallen out with his wife, but not into bed with the *hetaira*,[115] according to Habrotonon when alone, whom the audience may presumably believe. Is any moral condemnation of either suggested? There are ancient sources which seem to show that Charisios would have been regarded as wrong to bring Habrotonon into their home if Pamphile were there: Alcibiades's wife walked out on him because he regularly did the same thing, and Lysias's client was ashamed to bring an *hetaira* home because of his wife and old mother.[116] It is not suggested by these authors that a relationship with an *hetaira* was wrong in itself, nor that a settled married man should not have an *hetaira* outside his home.[117]

Although Habrotonon confirms emphatically that the arrangement could have involved sexual intercourse, she says that for all Charisios has done, she could be a virgin (438–40). What she actually says is that she could carry the goddess's basket: this is an allusion to the great procession of the Panathenaic festival. The girls who carried the sacred baskets, the *kanephoroi*, had to be virgins.[118] The phrase *hagne gamon*, 'pure of (sexual) union', may come from legal language concerning festivals[119] but calls to mind 'marriage', which is interesting for her comparison and contrast with Pamphile later. For another mention of virginity by Habrotonon, see on lines 478–9 below: taken with that remark and 432ff, it could at least be argued that there may be serious affection behind what could, at face value, be interpreted as a joke from a stereotypical *hetaira*.

Habrotonon's words often seem to be somewhat enigmatic and the overall picture of her contrary to expectation of her type. The mention of money at 437 rather echoes Smikrines' criticism of Charisios. Money and sex do bring to mind Habrotonon's main concerns as a hired *hetaira*. But however much money was involved, this does not seem to be a very mercenary *hetaira*, despite her stereotype.

Habrotonon uses *talas*, 'poor dear',[120] at 434, 436, 439, 466, 547 and 853: it is a favourite of hers. Compare *o theoi*, 'o gods', at 484, 489, 548. These repeated phrases are used to characterize her speech.[121] Onesimos and Habrotonon speak alone in parallel from 419 to 441. This invites us to contrast how they feel about Charisios. How would members of the audience start to feel? When will Charisios appear so that they can then judge for themselves? Into the reflections of these characters bursts another slave, Syros (mid-line). It is not clear what Habrotonon does while he and Onesimos discuss the ring: there is nothing resembling a stage direction in the Greek. Her words at 464ff show that she has overheard the exchange, however, and has successfully put two and two together.

Habrotonon was complaining of Charisios's coldness and the audience was wondering why, apart from vanity, this should bother her, as long as she got paid. Onesimos does not notice her, and continues to dither about the ring he took from Syros, which he recognized as Charisios's; both at 435–6 and at 441–2 he speaks still to himself. So Habrotonon's words at 436–41 are not overheard, but it should be borne in mind that she perhaps fears that she may be, if she has seen Onesimos. No indication is given, however, that she does fear this, any more than we can surmise that Onesimos hears her.[122] Onesimos appears self-centred: what are the implications of his new knowledge for him? Habrotonon, on the other hand, now switches to a certain sympathy for Charisios: 'Poor guy. Why is he wasting so much money?' (436–7).

Dialogue 464ff

Habrotonon and Onesimos now have a conversation. Each reveals a little more of the other. Both are slaves. It will be seen that various categories of characters overlap in this way, Habrotonon being presented as a slave as well as a woman. This works against the acceptance of stereotypes which seem to have dominated the comedy before Menander.

Both know Charisios: how do they view the situation that has developed? Firstly, and very importantly, the way in which they speak of the baby differs. Onesimos is matter-of-fact: a girl had 'this baby' (454); showing Charisios the ring will as good as make him father of 'the child' (448). Habrotonon, however, calls the baby *to paidarion* (464), a diminutive indicative of affection, and says 'Dear me, how cute!'[123] (466), 'Ah, poor thing!' (468) in sympathy, and refers to him as a person with rights:

> **Habrotonon**   Then, if he really is your master's son, can you stand by and watch
> him being brought up as a slave? That would be a capital crime.
>
> *Epitrepontes* 468–70 (Miller)

Compare Syros and Daos in Act II: the baby is again used to characterize two slaves in terms of how they relate to it – as an object or as a person.[124]

Habrotonon's attitude to the baby is not only sympathetic but in a sense rather contrary to expectation. An *hetaira*, who moves from man to man, is moved by the sight of a baby. Yet might not such a woman want a baby of her own some day, if not now? That something of the sort is intended is one possible explanation of her tender reaction to the baby, again making Habrotonon a somewhat enigmatic character. Against this it could be argued that one can feel sympathy for a baby without wanting one oneself. But both interpretations are possible.[125]

Some members of the audience might now wonder about Pamphile's relationship with her own baby. As the question arises 'who is the mother?' (a fact the audience probably knew from the lost prologue, if the irony of the arbitration scene was to be fully appreciated), one might wonder how she felt on exposing the child. Habrotonon's tenderness towards the baby, whatever her reasons, certainly evokes sympathy for it, but it also, perhaps, arouses curiosity about its mother who abandoned it. She is a character of whom as yet little is known.[126]

Habrotonon has challenged Onesimos that it would be wrong to stand by and allow a freeborn baby to be brought up as a slave. There is pathos here, as she and he are slaves themselves. But she appears generous-hearted, with a sense of justice, in that she does not want her own lot to befall another. She also points out sharply that he would deserve to die if he did nothing[127] and is quick to connect Onesimos's statement that Charisios lost the ring at the Tauropolia (451) with the incident she witnessed then.[128] She describes (477–8) how she played for some young girls,[129] and how Pamphile, as she turns out to be, was with them.

Dialogue 478ff

> **Habrotonon**   He lost the ring, you say, at the Tauropolia?
> **Onesimos**   Yes, he was drunk and disorderly, so I was told by the boy who was
> attending him.
> **Habrotonon**   I suppose he came across the woman when they were celebrating
> and unprotected. *[Thoughtfully]* You know, something very like that actually
> happened. I saw it.
> **Onesimos**   *You* saw it?

Habrotonon   Yes, last year at the very same festival. I was playing for some young ladies, and this girl was dancing with them. I was still a virgin myself then.
Onesimos   Oh yeah?
Habrotonon   Take my oath on it.

Epitrepontes 471–80 (Miller)

Balme's translation of lines 478–9 ('I did not know then what a man is like') is closer to the Greek. Is virginity, if virginity is strictly meant here, commended as such in Menander? It is certain that in the *Dyscolus* Sostratos, who is a pleasant young man, praises the following in Knemon's daughter, that she has been brought up:

Sostratos   ... pretty properly brought up by a fierce father who's naturally against all vice ...

Dyscolus 387–9 (Miller)

And at 58ff Chaireas contrasts how one may treat an *hetaira* with how one should approach a freeborn girl – passion must wait where the latter is concerned.[130]

There are no stage directions to tell us how Habrotonon delivers her claim to virginity at that time. Her tone might conceivably be wistful; another instance of Menander's paradox, a (relatively) chaste *hetaira*. Onesimos's 'Oh, yes!' at 479 would then sound unkind and rude, thus winning sympathy for her and antipathy for himself. That Habrotonon is not just explaining that she was able to be present because she was still a virgin is suggested by her protest in reply (literally): "I didn't, by Aphrodite!"[131]

In fact, these lines could be played in a number of ways, with Habrotonon indignant, upset, playful or enigmatic.[132] Whichever is preferred, it is interesting to have a picture of Habrotonon, hired for free girls but in company with them rather than with men, and possibly still a virgin. It could connect her in a way with Pamphile, and her sympathy for Pamphile elicit sympathy for herself,[133] especially when she tenderly describes the freeborn girl's state after the rape:

Habrotonon   ... on her own, crying and tearing her hair. And her silky wrap, very thin and pretty, was quite ruined, all torn to pieces.[134]

Epitrepontes 487–90 (Miller)

Critics have differed as to how we are to view Habrotonon's attitude here; some think that she emphasizes more the loss of Pamphile's dress than anything else.[135] It would work well to have her upset, or, alternatively, her protests enigmatic; both interpretations would be more subtle, and so less like her stereotype, as an *hetaira*, of a 'loose' woman. Rape as a plot motif is one of New Comedy's conventions, but that does not mean that characters cannot care about a girl's misfortune. For example, it could be argued that the alliteration of 't' sounds in line 488 of the Greek draws attention to the roughness suffered by the girl and thus evokes our pity.[136]

Habrotonon's words at 488–90 show us that, whatever the attitude of society may have been to a girl who has been raped, this *hetaira* is compassionate. They also serve to prepare us for Pamphile's appearance: Habrotonon tells us that she is 'pretty/ beautiful' (484) and rich (485). Jealousy of her status might have caused some girls to be less generous about Pamphile's looks.

Pamphile did not show to Habrotonon the ring she may have been given by the young man (491–2). It can perhaps be deduced from the words of the *hetaira* at 495–6 (Charisios should know if the mother is of good family) that he has not confided in Habrotonon either, since otherwise her quick wit would put two and two together. Again, Charisios has kept her at a distance (lines 434–5), and Habrotonon's words characterize him in his absence, keep him in mind and prepare for his entrance. His and Pamphile's reticence in this respect may link them together, and, with the knowledge gained from the lost prologue, that he, her husband, was her rapist at the festival, arouse curiosity as to how this broken relationship will be healed.

In the course of this scene, Habrotonon and Onesimos are strongly compared and contrasted. Both are slaves; both are in a position to help bring the action to its conclusion. Onesimos is seen as selfish and cynical with regard to Habrotonon, who is shown to be shrewd and sensitive, with a strong sense of justice. She also comes across as sensibly cautious, out of consideration to others, but also decisive: at 493ff, she allows that what Onesimos does is up to him, but suggests that he tell Charisios the whole story. He is afraid to do so, presumably in case Charisios is angry at what he knows. So, despite his rudeness to her, he asks for Habrotonon's help, which she gives willingly, but in her way, in case false accusations cause upset, she says. A more conventional presentation of an *hetaira* comes to the fore again, to make her proposed plan credible: her words at 499ff characterize her as used to seeing men gambling and drinking. *Hetairai* are used to performing for men:[137]

Onesimos   First let's find out who she *is*, Habrotonon. Help me with this now, do.
Habrotonon   Oh no, I couldn't, not until I know the name of her attacker. I'm
   scared of telling a tale to the ladies I mentioned, and putting them on the wrong
   track. After all, another man in his set could have accepted the ring from him as
   security, and then lost it; perhaps he was gambling, and put it in to guarantee his
   contribution to the jackpot; or he may have been under pressure in some deal,
   and handed it over. Thousands of things like that happen every day, when men
   get drinking. Until I know the guilty man's name, I'm not going to start a search
   for the girl, or breathe one word of anything like this.

Epitrepontes 497–510 (Miller)

But again, Menander cheats expectation. She is excited at thinking up the scheme, suggested at 511 by her use of the emphatic imperative *theas'*, 'see!' in place of the more usual verbs for 'looking', as she asks Onesimos to 'see' if he likes it – a use unparalleled in New Comedy.[138] She develops an imaginative and lengthy description of how she intends to re-enact the rape, open perhaps to the interpretation that she wishes it had been her. This would at the same time raise common misconceptions, ancient and modern, about rape victims' feelings. See lines 433ff for hints that her feelings about Charisios are more than just professional.[139] Against this background, Onesimos's words at 557ff sound callous:

Onesimos   ... No sooner sees that the love game's no road to freedom, but only to heartache, than off she goes on the other track.

Epitrepontes 557–60 (Miller)

especially as gaining her freedom does not appear to have been Habrotonon's main motive in thinking up the plan: 'I don't know' (541) she says to Onesimos's sneer that Charisios will free her at once, if he thinks she is the baby's mother.

Habrotonon's self-quotation (517ff), as she imagines the scene, serves two purposes. Firstly, it reinforces Menander's characterization of her as a lively girl.[140] Secondly, it makes vivid the description of action important to the plot, which will therefore not need to be seen repeated on stage. This economy of composition is a favourite ploy of Menander's; compare the messenger speech in *Sikyonios* and Demeas's monologue at the opening of Act III of *Samia*. Here we have a clever variation on the technique: Habrotonon reports what will be rather than what has been said, at the same time demonstrating that she has a vivid imagination.

At the beginning of the play, Habrotonon is presented, thanks to comments by Smikrines, in a poor light, as helping to keep Pamphile and Charisios apart. Now she seeks, with good motives, though unaware of Pamphile's identity, to bring them together. She also uses words which are critical of Charisios (*ton adikounta*, 'the one who has wronged (her)/culprit/attacker/guilty man' (499)[141] and again at 508), despite Onesimos's report at 472 that Charisios was 'drunk' (often offered as an excuse for such behaviour).[142] This prepares us for Charisios's self-condemnation later.

Habrotonon's dialogue with Onesimos shows him to be indecisive: he offers no ideas at all. He is selfish: 'do I get anything (*charis*, 'thanks') out of this?' (542), he asks, to which she playfully replies:

Habrotonon   Oh *yes*. You get my eternal gratitude for all my blessings.

Epitrepontes 543–4 (Miller)

meaning that, rather than sharing any reward if the trick works, she could get him to share the blame if things go wrong, thus showing a sense of humour that he lacks.

Onesimos's relationship with his master is not, in his view at least, good, since he fears punishment for knowing too much. Not only can he not trust Charisios, he cannot trust Habrotonon either, despite her offer to help him: what will happen if she reveals the truth, he asks (544–6)? He compliments her only on 'acting craftily/being a minx/up to anything', *panourgos* – and 'naughty/clever/sly', *kakoethos* (535),[143] and being *topastikon ton gunaikon*, 'a wizard/smart, that girl' (557), not on her goodwill. He is clearly a bad judge of character. At 549, he manages to say 'may you get it', with regard to her freedom, but he seems to be either not very effusive or just wishing a schemer luck. He comes out of the exchange in a bad light, something to which scholars[144] could have paid more attention in their differing interpretations of Habrotonon. But Onesimos may, of course, be subject to his own prejudices based on the stereotype of an *hetaira*.

Habrotonon comes across as warm-hearted, despite Onesimos's suspicious pessimism, and, whilst liking the thrill of the intrigue, not selfish in her motives. And yet, again, a few of her words are enigmatic, especially as very little of her has been seen here from monologue, whereas Onesimos is given several such speeches showing something of the workings of his mind.[145] At 547, she says 'do I look to you like I want children?', which is a reminder to Onesimos that there would be no point in her pretending for ever to be the baby's mother. But in the light of hints about her feelings for Charisios, the fact that she is an *hetaira* and not a *gyne*, 'wife', and indications that she does like babies (at 466 she says that baby is 'cute', at 530, she will kiss the baby, at 833, she shows concern for it when she believes herself alone),[146] the comment is an interesting one. Sometimes a vehement denial is a proud way of concealing the truth.[147] At 548, she exclaims, 'May I just get free!' and emphasizes this with another characteristic oath by the goddesses, continuing: 'That's the reward I hope for from this.'[148]

Why then did she say, less emphatically, when Onesimos assumed she would get her freedom by pretending to be the baby's mother (541), 'I don't know – it's what I'd like'? The picture is a complex one of affection for Charisios, willingness to find the woman he wronged, but criticism of him, of compassion for Pamphile, but a desire to be free like her, and of a willingness to help Onesimos too, in spite of an awareness of his faults.

Habrotonon's prayer to Peitho (Persuasion) 555–6

Habrotonon   Sweet Persuasion, be my friend! May the words I speak do the trick.

Epitrepontes 555–6 (Miller)

Habrotonon wants to see justice done. She prays, 'dear Persuasion,'[149] that her words will 'bring success, put to rights'.[150] The elevated style wins sympathy for Habrotonon, a style which reinforces her desire for freedom expressed at 541 and 548–9 and its likely importance for her.[151] *Peitho* was the goddess of *hetairai* as well as of rhetorical persuasion.[152] It is also worth noting that Athenian law found it necessary to provide that the persuasion of a woman was a cause sufficient to invalidate a man's legal acts, along with senility, drugs, disease or constraint.[153] Persuasion gave a woman power over a man – at least that was a male anxiety.

The prayer therefore reminds us that Habrotonon is an *hetaira*, with more complex nuances.[154] Both sexual love and convincing speech must be taken into account.[155] The prayer certainly encourages reflection on some of the noble qualities Habrotonon has displayed. Charisios stood up well to her charms, which she soon intends, ironically, to use to unite him with another woman, not herself. Her action is thus made credible and contrary to expectation at the same time. How much harsher, then, does Smikrines's description of Habrotonon later appear when he refers to her at line 794 as a *porne*.[156] Earlier at 691ff, Habrotonon is sarcastically called (by Smikrines?) the 'beautiful lady' (*gyne*), with whom Charisios is drinking and ruining his life 'in a brothel'.[157] In the light of what has been shown of both Smikrines and now Habrotonon, these words seem not only exaggerated but unfair.

Character of Habrotonon: summary

So the beginning of Act IV is reached – the dialogue with which this analysis of the women in *Epitrepontes* opened. Habrotonon has been characterized as a *porne*, 'a common prostitute, whore', but only by people whose opinions are 'suspect', namely, Onesimos and Smikrines. However, her behaviour suggests that she is not what might be expected from the stereotype of a comic *hetaira*,[158] in the sense that her own personal gain does not seem more important to her than other people's happiness, and that love seems to matter to her, not just sex. In other fourth-century comedy an *hetaira* could, by contrast, as has been noted, be a scheming and greedy woman.[159]

Until her encounter with Pamphile, Habrotonon is seen largely through her exchanges with Onesimos, whose fear and self-absorption throw into relief her lively sense of adventure and concern for others. She appears only briefly alone, but just enough to hint at deeper feelings than she is willing to reveal in the company of others. However, she is not wholly the modest *hetaira* introduced by Antiphanes and Euboulos either,[160] having some practical motives to improve her lot (or so it seems). Preconceived ideas about *hetairai* are exploited and then subverted by being shown from a different perspective.[161] Habrotonon's character is deliberately left a little enigmatic,[162] one technique for arousing, and keeping, the interest of the audience, whilst achieving a certain effect of reality, since it is difficult in real life too to know what people are really like.

Pamphile[163]

The audience has a little background knowledge about Habrotonon by the time it witnesses her conversation with Pamphile in Act IV. However, what has been seen of Pamphile so far does not tell the audience how to interpret her reactions to the *hetaira* there. Pamphile's character so far, in what is extant, has been a mere sketch.

It is known that Charisios has not been married long (fragment 1). Pamphile is referred to first in what survives as *gyne*, 'wife' (Smikrines at 135) and as *nymphe*, 'bride' (if this is the correct reading) by Chairestratos at 143. At 162, she is *thygater*, 'my daughter' (Smikrines). In Act II Pamphile is not spoken of at all. All that can be plausibly inferred about her is that she is quite young. Impersonal references and silence: there is no sense of her personality. At the opening of Act III, Onesimos is afraid that Charisios will be reconciled with 'his wife' (impersonal again). At 453, he guesses that a girl (*parthenos*) got raped. At 478, Habrotonon recounts how she played for some 'young girls' and that the girl who was raped then was one of them. Habrotonon emphasizes Pamphile's previous virginity by referring to her own. Onesimos asks about her using the word *pais*, 'child' (480). She is 'beautiful' and 'rich' (484–5).

Smikrines, her father, has, in his own way, expressed concern on her behalf, but also an equal amount, if not more, of consternation at her wasted dowry. Charisios has left home, but not laid a finger on the woman who has supposedly taken his wife's place. The latter, Habrotonon, has referred to her rape sympathetically, and to her good looks and wealth without jealousy.

As has been observed, no prologue survives which might either have prepared the way or misled, as is the case with characters in other plays by Menander. For example, Knemon in Pan's prologue in the *Dyscolus* is said (line 10) to speak to no-one but is later revealed to be close to his daughter. In what is extant, Pamphile is talked about only by the other characters: no special insight is yet known to have been given to the audience by any early speech and tension builds as her actual appearance is awaited.

Smikrines

Lines 583–602 appear to be a monologue by Smikrines reviewing what he has discovered. He is angry at his son-in-law's drinking (588) and hiring of a harp-girl (589, 600). A conversation with the cook, Karion, follows and then one with Chairestratos.

Smikrines now thinks, having probably heard it from Karion, that Charisios has had an illegitimate child by a *porne*, 'prostitute' (646), a word which, as has been discussed, insults Habrotonon; he uses its diminutive, *pornidion*, at 667. At 664–8 and 680–8 there are further tirades by Smikrines. Chairestratos tries to interject.[164]

At 693 Smikrines uses the Greek word *epeisagein*, which described bringing a second woman into one's home.[165] This would have been criticized by contemporary society (Karion finds it a subject for gossip in fragment 1) and many would therefore feel inclined to take Pamphile's side against Habrotonon, especially as the former, Charisios's wife, has been victim of a sexual assault. Habrotonon, by contrast with Pamphile, has been frequently seen, has been portrayed sympathetically and has shared her feelings with the audience. Moreover, Smikrines has misrepresented the facts by his choice of word at 693, as it seems it is Charisios who has moved out: Smikrines himself referred to this at line 136. So as Act IV begins, some audience sympathy is probably with Habrotonon and perhaps Charisios, but still some with Pamphile too. Pamphile's entrance is awaited with anticipation. How does she feel about everything that has happened and how will she deal with such an angry father?

The new fragments: Act IV and the argument between Pamphile and her father

Half of the papyri which preserve Menander's *Epitrepontes* have been published in recent years and yet it remains very fragmentary.[166] The new discoveries are extremely important for understanding this particular section of the play and, therefore, for the characters of Smikrines and Pamphile. The new fragments show for the first time the precise end of the third act, that is, that it closes with Smikrines's exit, as well as the beginning of Act IV, where he is the first speaker and again attacks Charisios's behaviour.[167]

Strikingly, it is in an argument with her father that Pamphile is now seen for the first time on stage. He tells her (gently or vehemently, depending on the tone adopted by the actor) to leave Charisios. Smikrines is not certain of his power, because *apoleipsis* would be divorce initiated by the wife, rather than *aphairesis*, divorce initiated by the wife's father.[168]

Pamphile's words at lines 714–15 are arresting. She says:

> But if, in seeking to protect me, you don't try to persuade me about this – then you'd be judged not a father, but a master.[169]

There are of course no stage directions for how this was spoken although the new fragments have supplied the words exchanged before this. Perhaps there are clues in the text to Pamphile's mood. The new fragments show us that Smikrines had an exceptionally long speech in reply. A substantial number of lines of Pamphile's reply to that survive, but still incompletely. So she does not give up easily her disagreement with her father.[170]

Another similar speech of 44 lines survives as Pap. Didot I and is interesting in this context. The lines were previously attributed to Menander, even by some to Pamphile in this very play.[171] The speech is also delivered by a wife who defends her husband to her father, and its links with the one here in *Epitrepontes* suggest that this was the sort of exchange that was popular with audiences.[172] Both wives urge their fathers not to exercise their power to take them away from their husbands. The new fragments now confirm, however, that this speech cannot be from *Epitrepontes*.

Although preparation has been made for Pamphile's entrance in Act IV, she has still not been referred to by name, although it should be noted that such avoidance is realistic in alluding to a freeborn woman anyway.[173] Pamphile is 'unknown' to Onesimos and Habrotonon; she has not appeared on stage yet until this point in the extant play and so has not expressed herself or been seen reacting to other characters. However, the curiosity of the audience has been aroused.

Habrotonon's compassionate description of Pamphile's rape at the Tauropolia has elicited sympathy and interest. Habrotonon was critical of Charisios (499, 508), despite her society's apparently casual attitude to rape as a characteristic form of young male behaviour.[174] The expectation that has been created is of a weak young woman of defiled innocence, wronged by the man who later became her husband.

Yet, for those who are alert, there is a hint that there is more to Pamphile than the deflowered *parthenos*,[175] or (now) the wronged *gyne*. She did not show Habrotonon and the other girls the ring (Charisios has not confided in the *hetaira* either; indeed; as has been noted, he has kept her at a distance.) Through Habrotonon, it is suspected that Pamphile and Charisios are reticent with others; it has been clear for some time that they do not confide in each other either. There is interest in meeting both characters and in how they will be reconciled, something even the pessimistic Onesimos regards as a possibility (425–6).

References to Pamphile continued to be impersonal. There will be plenty of time to look for the *kore*, 'the young girl', once Charisios is shown to be the baby's father (Habrotonon at 537); the position of 'my *kektemene*', my 'mistress' is not safe (Onesimos at 567); 'I have the right to take my *thygater*, my daughter' (Smikrines at 657). The problems grow for Pamphile, but the audience does not as yet really know what she is like. This makes her entrance at the beginning of Act IV a powerful one.[176]

Pamphile's language is strong in the dialogue with Smikrines which opens Act IV. Both what survived before, and the new evidence discussed above, show that she is able to stand up for herself to her father and that she goes on to have a long speech during which the attention of the audience would have been focused on her. Despite her youth she is able to hint that her father can be domineering: note that she uses the word 'master', although she is careful and respectful enough not to call him one directly. She recognizes that he wishes to 'protect', 'rescue' her too (714). Subtly, she asserts a right to choose, although legally she may have none,[177] saying that he seeks to 'persuade' her (714). She wishes to be treated as an adult. By means of the word 'master', she also reminds Smikrines that she is a free woman, no slave.[178]

Her words come out in an antithetical, reasoning manner. This suggests control of emotion, rather than lack of feeling for her father, taken with the stylistic evidence above. Even allowing for the fact that much of what she says is lost, her manner of speech contrasts with Habrotonon's spontaneity. In fact, 'persuade' at 714 particularly invites comparison and contrast with Habrotonon: the latter intends to exercise persuasion on a young man, and makes an emotional appeal to Persuasion, but Pamphile asks for it from her father, rather than the enforcement of his will, and seeks to persuade him herself.

What is Pamphile's actual situation? Firstly, Charisios has left her and gone next door, to Chairestratos's house. He still has her dowry, as Smikrines complains (134), as, in a sense, he is spending it on Habrotonon. So he has neither divorced Pamphile, although that would have been expected, nor set up house alone with an *hetaira*, nor brought an *hetaira* home with Pamphile still there, something on which it appears society would frown. Nor has he even touched Habrotonon (440). Charisios has found some fault with Pamphile. She was clearly no virgin when they married; at 1116, Onesimos reveals that she gave birth after only five months. An investigation of Greek ideas about virginity has suggested how Charisios might feel on finding out soon after marriage that his bride had not been a virgin. It is likely that the virginity of his bride mattered to an Athenian husband.

Perhaps Pamphile was rejected by Charisios on the grounds that she had committed adultery. She has had pre-marital sex, though, as the audience knows but Charisios does not yet, with himself, the man who is now her husband; this was without her consent, however. Divorce may have been compulsory for a woman taken in adultery, yet he has left her, not expelled her. Apparently it was not unusual for victims of rape to suffer the same treatment as willing partners in adultery. Would Pamphile's rapist have been considered to be a *moichos*, a word sometimes translated as 'adulterer'?[179] Whatever the case, it is likely that Charisios has left because Pamphile turned out not to be pure or because she produced a *nothos*, 'illegitimate child'[180] for his *oikos*, 'household'.

Some fourth-century audience sympathy could, despite the law, have been with Pamphile, in having suffered rape, however. It has been seen that Habrotonon, a likeable character, feels for her, even if Charisios was socially, even legally, within his rights to leave her and to expose[181] the child of the rape. The fact that he himself was her rapist and is the father of the child, as the audience probably knew from the lost prologue, adds an extra dimension to our reactions to the characters.

Charisios's behaviour is understandable, in terms of the probable attitudes of a fourth-century Athenian male, given his ignorance of the true facts. Members of a modern secular Western audience might sympathize with Pamphile more than fourth-century or even Victorian spectators would have done. Some would sympathize with Charisios too, as he has not divorced Pamphile, although he could have done so. If he has acted harshly it has only been through ignorance. But it might be argued that, in ancient terms, any sympathy is allayed by the important knowledge that only Pamphile's husband was involved after all, and that her exposed child is alive and well. Thus social norms would be ultimately reinforced after a 'what if' situation regarding confusion of roles has been explored. Another view would allow for 'possible' world interpretations and a more 'bitter aftertaste' at the end of Menander's plays.[182] But a play could explore situations and expectations without necessarily supporting the *status quo*.

To return to the exchange between Pamphile and her father: it is now known that both had speeches of a substantial length. This would have revealed a considerable amount about their characters. Pamphile shows control and determination, appeals to natural justice and fatherly love, and displays tact in the midst of her distress.[183] Her loyalty to Charisios and refusal to give up on the marriage are also clear.[184] There may be further hints concerning the content of her lost speech. Look at what Smikrines says to her (716):

Is argument or persuasion necessary in this matter?

Rhetorical speech was a common way of speaking, but not expected from women, who were debarred from the public places where it was generally used.[185] Certainly, one might expect Pamphile to be distraught and emotional, and her father to be pleading with her to see sense. Instead, she appears calm, and he is the one forced to find arguments.

Is this a comic reversal of expectation, juggled with a serious subject matter? Praxagora, in drag, that is, men's clothes, makes an assembly speech in Aristophanes's *Ecclesiazousae*, motivated at the end by the excuse that she had listened to the men on the Pnyx (lines 243–4). But for the possible effect here in Menander, compare Getas's account of Thrasonides's (in his case a lover, not a father) and Krateia's encounter at *Misoumenos* 705ff, where she turns her back on him.[186] Krateia, however, has lived as an *hetaira* before her identity is discovered, whereas Pamphile is freeborn from the outset and has been raped. Other kinds of drama such as tragedy or Old Comedy allow women to be rhetorical without seeking to imitate real life, but this is a different kind of comedy, making it difficult to be certain of the effect.

At 717, Smikrines uses his daughter's name,[187] giving a hint of affection behind his words. But his bluntness is brutal: Charisios will be unable to keep two women and will be ruined financially; Pamphile will wait around for him while he spends his time drinking with Habrotonon. It is probable, though not certain,[188] that after his petty reference to Charisios's double expense, he becomes more blunt, indeed (though perhaps unintentionally) cruel, at the end of his long speech; certainly he uses frequent and harsh alliteration, together with assonance, anaphora and asyndeton in the Greek to emphasize his point.

It's difficult, Pamphile, for a lady to fight a tart. *She* fights unfairly, knows more tricks, has no shame, coaxes him more.

Epitrepontes 793–6 (Miller)

Sympathy for Pamphile is likely to be doubled by this outburst, although the manner in which the actor playing Smikrines delivered this speech might soften its tone.

His repetition of Pamphile's name (717, 793) suggests emotion. *Porne* (794) is again an unfair description of Habrotonon as she has been portrayed. Smikrines, whether sorrowfully or angrily, taunts Pamphile with a dismal picture of her future. From her forthright speech so far and his knowledge of her as a daughter it must be clear that she could not tolerate such treatment. His words pit Pamphile against Habrotonon as her rival: note the emphasis on fighting at the end of line 794. Very ironically, although Habrotonon does not yet know that it was Pamphile who was wronged by Charisios, the *hetaira* was acting in Pamphile's best interests to achieve a reconciliation.

Smikrines has spoken sarcastically of Habrotonon (692–3) as 'this fine woman' with whom Charisios has been living, having ruined his life in a brothel, for which place Smikrines emphatically uses a rare word. This unkindness, after Habrotonon's concern for Pamphile, would elicit some sympathy for her, but the mention of her in this impersonal way also makes her seem distant; sympathy would switch imperceptibly to Pamphile. Habrotonon is at Charisios's friend's not his own house, as Smikrines implies. At 694 he refers to his, Smikrines', and Pamphile's feelings about all this in the same breath ('we'),[189] indicating that he does indeed feel for his daughter.

It seems likely that Smikrines has expressed an intention to remove his daughter now that, as he supposes, her husband has produced a child by the *hetaira* he is keeping. But a father's right to withdraw his daughter from her marriage possibly ended as soon as she had become the mother of a son.[190]

At 641 Smikrines may use *parakalein,* the technical word in Greek for calling witnesses, in one of its senses. Did Smikrines threaten to bring a complaint before the *archon*, demanding a divorce and the return of his daughter's dowry? He would call Charisios's friends as witnesses for his misconduct. An Athenian wife would have needed the co-operation of some male citizen to go through the proceedings before the *archon*.[191]

Smikrines, ignorant of the existence of his grandchild, would have had no doubts about the legality of his proposed actions, and expresses his feelings through sarcasm:

> But perhaps you think I'm meddling beyond what should concern me? Yet I've every reason to take my daughter home.
>
> 655–8

It is clear, anyway, that divorce is his aim.

At 719, picking up her rhetorical device that he should exercise persuasion, he spoke of three points he would put to her. The first would be financial ruin, the second the likelihood of divorce, and the third the expected behaviour of the other woman.

Pamphile shows herself philosophical, independent and still loyal to Charisios: her words 'throw me out' (829) presumably pick up her father's. She seems to allude at 833 to being 'inferior'. If she compares herself with Habrotonon there, she seems to be concerned with loyalty and love, rather than social standing, or skill in bed, or the right to enjoy Charisios's money, the arguments her father has used. The audience will also remember, however, that there were hints earlier that Habrotonon has feelings for Charisios too, rather than being the kind of companion Smikrines describes.

To conclude this discussion: the new fragments continue to extend our knowledge as to the nature of the exchange between Pamphile and Smikrines. Pamphile is given a great deal to say, and more than holds her own. However, she is also tactful[192] in the face of her father's insensitivity, recognizing that he cares for her and is affectionate, apparently addressing him as 'Father' (801, 833) and even 'Dad' (806).[193]

Through her discussion with Smikrines, Pamphile is shown to be loyal and courageous. Up to this point, there has been no opportunity for her to be directly seen or heard. As he argues with his daughter Smikrines expresses paternal feeling, albeit in a gauche, indeed hurtful, way. He is concerned for her happiness, not just the dowry.[194] In addition, suspense is created in anticipation of the meeting between the two female rivals that is to follow.

What happens next? The scholiast on Eur. *Phoenissae* 1154 quotes:

I was completely burned out with crying.

The fragment may come from a soliloquy uttered by Pamphile after Smikrines has left to return to the town. If so, her reasoned arguments with her father have taken their toll and she allows her emotions to take over once alone. She may speak of her distress at parting with her child. But, for now at least, this can only be conjecture.[195]

The recognition scene 853ff

All this has led up to Habrotonon appearing with the baby, the point at which this analysis of *Epitrepontes* began. The *hetaira* tells us that the child has been crying for ages, which adds to the pathos. Pamphile continues to speak to herself:

Which of the gods will take pity on me, wretch that I am?!

855

Often in Menandrian scenes the serious mood is defused by the presence of another person making asides whilst eavesdropping. The young man Moschion is on stage in the recognition scene at *Perikeiromene* 779ff, and the cook intervenes in Chrysis's ejection in *Samia* at 375ff. Some overhearings are reported: in this case, it has seemed from what survives that no-one else was present whilst Pamphile argued with her father at the beginning of Act IV of the *Epitrepontes*, but Onesimos's words at 883ff and Charisios's at 920 tell us that Charisios was listening. Pamphile says (817–18)[196] that she came to share Charisios's happiness. Charisios repeats Pamphile's words at line 920: 'I'm his wife', she said, 'his life's partner'. There is no sign that Charisios overheard anything but dialogue.[197]

There seems, however, to be no humorously distracting third presence actually on stage with Habrotonon and Pamphile. Perhaps some humour then, comes from Pamphile's lament above (855), as it is usually the sort of stock phrase uttered by the thwarted young man in New Comedy; compare *Perikeiromene* 532–6 (Moschion) and the opening lines of the *Misoumenos* (the soldier Thrasonides).

Menander continues to delay the discovery of Pamphile's identity and her reunion with her child, adding to the suspense: Habrotonon asks when he will see his mother, and Pamphile, presumably not noticing her, announces she is going indoors.[198] This creates a subtle blend of irony and emotional tension. The two women of Smikrines' speech just now are compared and contrasted in person, the freeborn woman and the supposed *porne*:

Habrotonon [*to baby*]   Poor darling, when will you see your mother?
Pamphile   I'll go in.
Habrotonon [*seeing her and recognizing her*]   Just a minute, please, madam.
Pamphile   Are you addressing me?
Habrotonon   Yes I am. Turn and face me.
Pamphle   Do you know me, madam?
Habrotonon   It's the girl I saw. Hello, darling.
Pamphile   And who are *you*?

Epitrepontes 856–60 (Miller)

It is not known how a freeborn woman and an *hetaira* might have behaved on meeting in real-life fourth-century Athens. Such meetings would, perhaps, not have been frequent. Pamphile would have recognized Habrotonon's profession by her dress, as the contemporary audience would have already done also by her mask,[199] and Habrotonon would in the same way have noted Pamphile's status. Any *hetaira* would probably have reminded Pamphile of the one who has been with her (still loved but estranged) husband, adding to the coldness with which she might treat such a woman anyway.[200] Has she not seen the *hetaira* when she announces she is going in or is she avoiding her deliberately?[201] At first both women may think they are alone. At 858 Habrotonon uses the polite *gynai*, 'madam', to address her,[202] but Pamphile responds only with a surprised 'Are you calling me?' At 859, however, she interestingly addresses Habrotonon herself with 'Madam'. Recognition may be dawning.[203] Pamphile's reserve could partly result from resentment of any woman who has a baby when she no longer has hers. Alternatively, she is just extremely upset and in no mood to converse with anyone.

Habrotonon   Give me your hand! Tell me, sweetheart, did you go to watch the Tauropolia last year?
Pamphile   Madam, where did you get the baby you're carrying? Tell me!
Habrotonon   Recognize something it's wearing, love? [*Pamphile starts back*] No need to be afraid of me, madam.
Pamphile   Is this not your own child?
Habrotonon   I pretended it was, not to do down his real mother but to give me time to find her. And found her I have! You're the girl I saw before.
Pamphile   But who's the father?
Habrotonon   Charisios.
Pampile   Are you sure, my dear?
Habrotonon   Quite sure. But – aren't you his wife from next door?
Pamphile [*happily*]   Oh, yes!
Habrotonon   Dear madam, some power (literally 'god') above has looked with pity on you both. Oh, there's the neighbour's door, someone's coming out. Take me into your house, and I'll tell you the whole story, from beginning to end.

Epitrepontes 861–77 (Miller)

At 860, Habrotonon cannot help but become characteristically warm: compare *philtate*, 'darling' with *glykytate*, 'sweetheart' at 143, and with *talas,* 'poor thing', used frequently by her. Pamphile, however, apparently continues formal and distant with 'and who are you?' Habrotonon voices her recognition only to herself at 860; she is gentle in revealing herself gradually to Pamphile. At 862 she asks sensitively for her hand, calling her *glykeia*, 'sweet one' at 863. Pamphile is polite but startled, responding again with 'madam' at 864[204] and her first gradual recognition[205] is of her child.

There may be a hint of suspicion when she asks how Habrotonon came by the baby. Habrotonon seeks to reassure again with 'darling' at 865, and 'you have nothing to fear from me', reverting to the polite 'madam' at the end of 866. Does she suddenly remember her place?[206] Pamphile asks whether the child is not hers, then? Habrotonon then defends herself: she pretended the baby was hers in order to find its mother. There seems to be pathos in Pamphile's failure to return her obvious affection and Habrotonon could be hurt. Pamphile can only utter cautious questions again (870) – who then is the father? Habrotonon's one-word answer, "It's Charisios", finally breaks down the other woman's reserve and she cries:

Are you absolutely sure of that, dearest lady?[207]

at last responding in kind.[208] The motif of the recognition scene, common in tragedy as well as New Comedy, is given a new turn with a freeborn woman and an *hetaira* given the main roles.

Habrotonon at 873–4 teasing, maybe, but polite (*makaria*, 'happy lady'[209]), picks up Pamphile's slightly (and unwittingly) humorous declaration of misery, and need of the pity of the gods, at 855 with: 'One of the gods has pitied you both'. Or she too could be being unwittingly humorous, if she did not overhear Pamphile earlier. There is, at the same time, more pathos in her unselfish joy at Pamphile's happiness, when this other woman, especially now, has so much more in life than she does, including a baby by the man she perhaps came to love (432ff).[210]

Pamphile appears to hold back her emotions, suggested partly by her rather impersonal references to the baby, whereas it has been very obviously in Habrotonon's thoughts. For example the *hetaira*'s 'me' at 854 is an ('ethical') dative expressing concern;[211] its mother has, by contrast, seemed, perhaps wrongly so, more absorbed in herself.

Syros and Daos's behaviour in Act II might be compared here: Pamphile and Daos refer to the baby thus: 'that child' (864) and 'this baby' (867) (Pamphile), 'with this baby' (276) and 'Finders Keepers' (the Greek equivalent) at 284 (Daos); Syros refers warmly to its things as 'Baby's' (403). Habrotonon, however, even more warmly, addresses it directly – 'darling (child)!' (at 856).[212]

Does Pamphile at any stage recognize Habrotonon as the *hetaira* keeping company with her husband? She expresses no surprise that Habrotonon seems to know Charisios and refers to him by name (871). If Pamphile does not, it adds to the irony; if she does, it adds to the poignancy, especially when Habrotonon asks to be taken into her house[213] so that she can tell her the whole story (876–7).

For a rich, freeborn woman and an *hetaira* to meet on stage, a fictitious meeting, but one deliberately presented to the audience, as they do in *Epitrepontes* Act IV, would be a meeting of very different worlds. Both women have been characterized in some depth, compared and contrasted implicitly and explicitly, though their psychology, characteristically of Menander, is left to be deduced from what they say. Some background knowledge of social conditions at the period, however, has helped to illuminate their relationships with the other characters and with each other.

This is nearly, in what is extant at least, the last word on the two women. But not quite. Pamphile continues to be kept in mind through references to her by other characters such as Onesimos and Charisios; though absent, she thus helps the audience to understand them. Habrotonon appears again, but also becomes a reflector of other people's feelings rather than being prominent on stage.

So Onesimos now rushes out and announces, to our surprise (883ff) that Charisios has overheard the whole conversation between father and daughter. This immediately defuses the serious mood: all will be well, as would have been expected from the prologue,[214] since Charisios is reported to be full of remorse. Far from enjoying himself with a *porne*, he is 'quite mad ... mad ... really crazy ... mad'. The repetition emphasizes humorously how much. Some might feel an empathy with Charisios at this point and sense his relationship with Pamphile healing already, despite the fact that the two of them have never been seen together on stage. Onesimos, however, just shows his selfishness. He is not brimming with joy at recent events. No – (902–3) he is afraid that Charisios will murder him for having brought him the news about Pamphile in the first place.[215]

Unable to appreciate that she can be trusted, Onesimos begs Habrotonon not to desert him (934). At 951 it looks as though he accuses her to Charisios of persuading him into the trick, which does not demonstrate much loyalty to someone, who, as we have seen, deserves more. Still she does not retaliate but just reproves him with:

No need to squabble, darling.

Miller 952–3

To Charisios, Habrotonon gently delivers the welcome truth on which happiness depends: that the baby is his, stressing the solemnity of his relationship with Pamphile, his 'wedded wife' (953). It is surprising, perhaps, to hear a fourth-century *hetaira* speaking respectfully of the marriage bond. Again, she has to protest that she can be trusted, when Charisios asks what tale she is telling and she retorts that it is the truth (956).

Habrotonon probably does not appear again. How Act V began is disputed.[216] One plausible suggestion is that it opened with a monologue by Chairestratos, in which he revealed that he loved Habrotonon, enough to find it hard to remain 'faithful' to his friend Charisios who, he thinks, is having an affair with her. Chairestratos seems to have known all along what the audience has realized only gradually, that

She's not a common tart, who's available to anyone.

Miller 984–5

Lines 986–7 have seemed to some to show that he thinks Habrotonon is fond of Charisios, already hinted at by her at 433. She may have given up a great deal personally in bringing about a reconciliation with Pamphile.

There may also have been further talk of Habrotonon gaining her freedom. This could be too romantic a view, but Charisios might have shown his gratitude in that way, and it would have provided one part of the necessary satisfactory happy ending. The text as it stands is inconclusive.[217] Whatever happened, Habrotonon is a slave as well as an *hetaira*, which leads us neatly to an analysis of the slave characters in *Epitrepontes*.

Further reading

For good translations of Menander's plays, see the Further Reading to chapter 1. Arnott's Loeb, 3v. (1997 with corr.-2000) has parallel text and translation, but there have been subsequent discoveries of Menander papyri, for which see *ZPE*. Konstan (1995) is excellent on culture and characterization: 'the texts as vehicles of social or ideological tensions', as Konstan says in his preface. The book includes Aristophanes and is intended as a companion to the author's *Roman Comedy*. It revises several articles published elsewhere. Zagagi (1994) is a good general study of Menander. Webster (1974) is still useful.

Texts and commentaries on *Epitrepontes*

See Bibliography at Menander (1997–2000, 2010), Bathrellou (2009), Furley (2009) and Sisti (1991).

Epitrepontes: Fragments

See Furley (2013), Römer (2012a, 2012b) and Petrides (2014), 28ff for the latest papyrus readings of Act IV. See also Austin (2008) on lines 785/6–835 and Arnott (2004a, 2004b) with Austin (2006). Contributors to Bastianini & Casanova (eds) (2004) such as Nünlist discuss finds relevant to all the plays. The published and edited text to date is being revised for the forthcoming OCT (substantial pieces can now be added to Sandbach's (1990) *OCT* Appendix, 347ff, that is, lines 680–835.) For a fuller description of the Michigan papyrus, Inv. no. 4733, see Gronewald (1986), 3.

Women in Menander

Essential reading (also for the male characters) is the excellent book by Traill (2008). See Lape (2004) for a more historical approach but with a good understanding of the plays as literature.

Images

See Cameron & Kuhrt (1993) and Lewis (2002) for images of women on vases. Lewis discusses (7, 72ff) vases which depict women at fountain houses, with regard to the status of the women and whether they are images designed to be read as part of a male discourse about women or as part of a gender-specific range of themes for the afterlife.

Ferrari (2003 with corr.) discusses the difficulties of interpreting all images on Greek vases.

See Green & Handley (1995) and Brea (1981) for some colour pictures of replica masks and figurines of women and a pimp, including finds from Lipari (for which see ch.1 of this book). See Wiles (1991) on the possible contributions of masks and costumes to performances.

Feminist approaches

See Simone De Beauvoir (1953), 445–6; 578 for a seminal discussion of women's roles in society. (The 2009 edition in French is the basis of the 2010 English translation.) See also Skinner (2005) on women in Greek and Roman culture.

Women in antiquity

Lin Foxhall (2013) is of key importance on gender. Hubbard (ed.) (2014) is a collection of essays on Greek and Roman sexualities. Just (1989) is a good general study; see also Fantham and others (1994). See further Richlin (2009), Steel (2009) and Gagarin (2000) and (2001) with Patterson (1998), especially ch. 6, on Menander. Omitowoju (2002) discusses rape in Menander in its historical context. Davidson (1997) is lively and advocates using comedy, but wisely warns that it is 'slippery' as a source (xx). Golden & Toohey (eds) (2003) is also useful, with Skinner (2005), introduction. Lefkowitz (1982) is a sourcebook. See also Pomeroy (1975).

The *hetaira*

Christodoulou (1997) is very important. See also Davidson (1997) for the *hetaira*: he concludes that her life was 'a highly compromised form of independence' (105). See also McClure (2003). Brown (1990) looks at the differences between *pornai*, *hetairai* and *pallakai*. See also Wiles (1989). Henry (1985) discusses Menander. Use with caution also her book on Aspasia (1995). On Neaira, see Hamel (2003), especially 4ff. *Against Neaira* has been edited by Carey (Apollodorus (1992)): see Kapparis's introduction to Apollodorus (1999), 5–7 on other *hetairai* and 1ff on the reliability of the speech as a source ('very important'). Also relevant here is Sommerstein (2014), primarily on the *pallake*.

Virginity

For ancient Greek attitudes to virginity, see Sissa (1990a, 1990b). On the *parthenos* in myth and tragedy, see Lefkowitz (1995), 32–3, 36–7. Arguing for seclusion, see Just (1989), 66, Garland (1990), 209 and Carey (Apollodorus (1992)), 98 on 24. Putting the counter-argument, see Taylor (2011) and Foxhall (2003). For the orators, see Todd on Lysias (2007). For possible evidence for the women's quarters, see Nevett (1999) and Morgan (1982) on Lysias's house. Dover (1989), 149 and Halperin (1990) use the seclusion of women as an argument for the prevalence of male homosexuality due to frustration: homosexuality is absent, for whatever reason, from Menander's plays (see the forthcoming study by Heap of the male characters).

Ogden (1996) looks at illegitimate children and also at 'the ideology of seclusion' (136). Cohen (1989), 3, 6, 9 and (1990), esp. 151 also notes practice might differ from ideology and might entail only separation. Ogden cites *Dysc.*189–201 (Knemon's daughter at the well) as an example of what could happen instead (136–7). Is Knemon's daughter in *Dyscolus* at the well unguarded because he is not rich, or because he is a recluse?

Patterson (1998), 2, feels that the study of women has emphasized too much their separation from the political (and historical) world. Taylor (2011) and Foxhall (2003), 182 also believe that a refusal 'to hear alternative discourses' has left women 'passive and compliant': they had their kind of autonomy, with their own networks and places to be powerful. On 'open' relations between men and women as depicted on pottery, supporting the arguments for seclusion as only the ideal, see Lewis (2002). *Sikyonios* 372, to which reference was made above on Virginity, strongly implies that a value was placed by at least some ancient Greeks on virginity: a father asks his slave whether his daughter is 'really safe … or just alive' (Miller (1987)), and is assured that she is 'still a virgin', that is, at least, a '*parthenos*'.

The Tauropolia

For more about this festival, see Bathrellou (2012) and (2009) Pt.II.3, 'The Tauropolia and its significance for the *Epitrepontes*'. On Habrotonon's presence at the Tauropolia and Chrysis's involvement in the Adonia in the *Samia* (perhaps part of a future study of that play), see Todd (1993), 188 with n.37, where he notes that there were several festivals from which slaves were banned by law, but others in which they could play a full part. The Thesmophoria may have excluded them, but the Kronia and the Rural Dionysia allowed them to participate and they were given special roles. He does not mention the Tauropolia, however.

The Tauropolia was a festival in honour of Artemis Tauropolos: Arnott (1997 with corr.), 443n.1 and Bathrellou (2012), 155. Very few things are known about this Tauropolia: the existing ancient evidence is scarce and the historical importance of the evidence a matter for debate: Rangos (1995), 114. The 'scattered evidence' has been discussed at length in an account of excavations at Artemida near Athens, and the conclusion is that the precise nature of the festival is not certain. The evidence points to a chief concern with young men and their transition to adulthood, but the transition of girls seems to be a feature too: Bathrellou (2009), 236ff, 267, updated by Bathrellou (2012). See further on the Tauropolia the conclusion to this book.

Peitho

Buxton (1982), 29–30 with 38 cautions that the translation of *Peitho* as 'Persuasion' will not always do. She is a goddess of love as well as of rhetoric. Ireland (1992), 74 wonders whether 'Persuasion' spoke the lost prologue in the *Epitrepontes*. This is possible, given the oath to her by Habrotonon later. Against the suggestion of a prologue by Persuasion is the presence of an address to *Penia* at *Dysk*. 209 when it is in fact Pan who speaks the prologue to that play.

Peitho certainly had a place in the 'mythology of love' in erotic poetry from early lyric to the Hellenistic epigram. Buxton also notes that *Peitho* is opposed to *bia*, 'force', in Plato's *Krito* (see Buxton (1982), 58). It was *bia* that Charisios used in the *Epitrepontes*, *bia* being regarded as morally reprehensible; *peitho* is also often contrasted with *dolos*, but sometimes identical: Buxton (1982), 63ff. The scheming *hetaira* of bad character would use the latter.

Marriage

See Oakley and Sinos (1993) on marriage in Greek society. Patterson (1998) and Omitowoju (2002) in particular stress the importance of private marriage to the *polis* in terms of the production of citizens, Omitowoju seeing marriage as a key motif in Menander (205), but emphasizing the dangers of anachronism in relation to rape (233). See also Lape (2004), 42 on how 'the emergence of comic narratives celebrating the democratic marriage system ... contributed to the robustness of democratic and *polis* culture'. These are possibly over-politicizations of Menander. For a contrasting, more literary view, see the conclusion to this book.

Xenophon's *Oeconomicus*

Xenophon's *Oeconomicus* was written rather earlier than Menander (Xenophon was born *c*.430 BCE, Menander 344/3: most of Xenophon's extant works belong to the 360s or 350s). The treatise is the earliest extant Greek didactic work to focus on the *oikos* and, interestingly, it is the marital relationship which is viewed as fundamental to its success, that is, the involvement of the *gyne* 'wife', in running it. Xenophon seems to discuss, more than was usual for classical authors, the relationship between men and women in the private sphere. See Pomeroy in her introduction to her commentary (1994), viii and 31ff, who regards this work as one of the richest primary sources for the social, economic and intellectual history of classical Athens. Too (2001), 65 rightly urges more caution in dealing with a complicated author, one that is neither simply misogynistic nor feminist. The work may reflect only one man's view and it is not clear how representative that view was of his society. However, Aristotle does also emphasize marriage as fundamental to the *oikos*: *Politics* 1253 b1–18. However, he mentions the master and slave relationship in the same context. See Garnsey (1996), 23–4. Garnsey thinks that, in his discussion of the household as a whole, Aristotle gives prominence to slavery. Plato *Republic* 458e refers to marriage as sacred (my thanks to M. Langford for this). See further Ferrari (2003 with corr.), n.15 to ch.8.

Divorce

Cohn-Haft (1995), 3 in discussing *Epitrepontes* notes that Smikrines's power is unclear. The text is fragmentary, but it seems that the father would prefer his daughter to initiate the divorce. Perhaps, if she did not, it might affect her reputation (7 n.27). He assumes a responsibility to protect, rather than arbitrarily asserting a legal right of ownership or control (6). Rosivach (1984) concludes, but with too much reference to Roman Comedy, that a father had no legal right to take his daughter away from her husband, but that he could bring psychological pressure to bear (223).

Women's speech

Bain (1984), 29 discusses the possibility that *theion* at *Epitr.* 433 is characteristic of female speech. See further Traill (2008), 227 on Habrotonon's 'chatty informal style', and, on women's speech generally, Bain (1984), Sommerstein (1995) with Dickey (1996), other relevant essays in De Martino & Sommerstein (eds) (1995) and Gagarin (2001).

Sandbach (Gromme & Sandbach (1973), 328) on 434 reports that *talan*, originally the vocative of *talas*, is used in comedy exclusively by women. See further Bain (1984), 33ff. Dickey (1996), however, is cautious (246): she finds little evidence for elements of 'women's language'.

Rape and seduction

There has not been room here to discuss these issues in full in relation to Menander. James (2014) is good but cautious: the viewpoint of the female victim is present, however (34–5). For a general introduction, see Deacy and Pierce (eds) (1997). Cohen (1990) and Harris (1990) are important articles. See further on Menander, Brown (1991), Ogden (1997) and Pierce (1998). Omitowoju (2002) is a key study but (181) she is sure Menander's plays conform to social norms in the end: Heap (1998a, 1998b) already sees a challenging of these norms. See rather Traill (2008), 235–6 with n.123 on Habrotonon's word at 499 for Charisios as 'culprit'. Sommerstein (1998), 112, n.14 is right, however, to point out that premarital sex may sometimes have been disguised as 'rape'. Khan (1993) discusses the *Dyscolus* in this context.

Exposure

Complex feelings are probably involved in 'exposing' a child, whatever the period or culture, among them anxiety for the child to have its identity. At *Epitr.* 403 the child's ownership of its tokens is stressed. The same trinkets are buried with dead babies: the exposed child is 'dead' to the natural parents. Golden (2011a), 263 notes, however, that the goods left in a grave by the parents of a dead child are sometimes a statement about their standing in society rather than appropriate to the youth of the deceased. Dasen (2011), 291 observes that the interpretation of grave goods along with votive and domestic objects is often debated.

Cantarella (2011), 344 notes that an Athenian father could decide whether a newborn child was raised or abandoned, but this was not the case in some other Greek cities, for instance, Sparta. Golden (2015) concludes (80ff) that there is nothing to suggest that societies which permit exposure necessarily care less for their children; it seems to him, however, that daughters were valued less at birth than sons in Ancient

Greece (81). Kapparis (2002), 4 lists Menander as one of several potential sources for the practice of exposure, but warns (5) against treating the ancient world as 'one unit with a single system of values'. See further Kapparis (2002), 154–62: the book as a whole is about abortion, but summarizes well the scholarly debate on exposure in the ancient world.

On exposure generally, see Riddle (1992). The same term is used in ancient Greek for the new-born child as for a foetus (see further Dasen (2011), 292 on vocabulary): it seems that exposing such a child was different legally, morally and terminologically from killing a child who was a recognized and named member of a family. But *ektithenai*, 'to put out' in Greek, a euphemism (see, for instance, Menander *Perikeiromene* 801) was not necessarily neutral in moral import, nor free from religious pollution or personal feelings of responsibility; take, for example, Oedipus's condemnation of his parents' knowing act of exposure at Sophocles's *Oedipus at Colonus* 272 (Patterson (1985), 105ff). Garland (1990), 92 comments on exposure in drama and concludes that the evidence is problematic.

Pomeroy (1993) notes the lack of census data for Greece (208). Patterson (1985) believes in combining the evidence from drama (which she reviews) with that from demography and other sources (111–12), noting that if a totally coherent or unambiguous picture fails to emerge it may be because Greek attitudes differed regarding the morality of exposing children (113). She does not regard the practice as widespread. Some ancient Greeks were capable of selling the children of other Greeks into slavery (Golden (2011), 265); there was corporal punishment, there were underage partners and paederastic relationships and surrogates such as wet-nurses and *paidagogoi*, 'slave tutors', were used to raise children, perhaps as a distancing strategy to reduce emotional investment in a child that might die.

Boswell (1988), 6 makes the important point that a motif can be introduced by an author because its improbability is fascinating. He stresses the problems with exposure (9–10), using abortion today as an analogy: although commonly practised, it does not feature as a common theme in literature or film, because the problems it raises are too troubling.

On Menander's influence on Oscar Wilde, as the inspiration for, among others, the exposure motif in *The Importance of Being Earnest*, see Witzke (2014). *Perikeiromene*, lines 800–12 may be added to the *Epitrepontes* as interesting in the context of exposure; Pataikos exposed his twins because his wife died after they were born and he lost his ship, his only source of income. It would have been, he says, the action of someone 'ill-advised/unfeeling' to have tried to bring them up. More knowledge of real-life attitudes to exposure, with careful attention to period and culture, would help illuminate whether Pataikos here justifies himself or admits a mistake, and how the audience would have viewed his decision. Did he leave the trinkets with the babies because he hoped they would be found, never imagining that he himself would find them?

5

Slaves in *Epitrepontes*: Habrotonon, Onesimos, Syros and Daos

There is another significant group of characters in Menander, one which includes both males and females – the slaves.[1] Menander's treatment of his female characters as women has already been explored.[2] Here the slave characters will be approached primarily as a group distinct from freeborn men and women. However, the question of the nature of power in general, for example, the power held by men over women in many societies and at different periods, overlaps with discussions of freedom and slavery.

Slavery was a universal phenomenon of ancient society. It is, therefore, part of daily life as reflected in the literature. Anxieties, fears and thoughts expressed in the literary texts are what remains from the daily contact of exploiter and exploited.[3] Menander's plays provide some of that literary evidence, but they may also in turn be illuminated by historical sources. *Epitrepontes* in particular has four significant slave roles: Daos, Syros, Onesimus and Habrotonon. What is known about the real lives of slaves like these? How does this knowledge contribute to an understanding of Menander's slaves and how they behave to one another and to the other characters? Once again, for the social background to Menander, the focus is on fourth-century Athens.

Social background

In case a study of ancient (or Atlantic) slavery seems too remote, it should be noted that there are still many slaves around the world today.[4] Statistics are hard to gather, as slavery is illegal now in nearly every country and is often disguised.[5] Sadly, slavery has always existed in all kinds of societies and at all periods. Not far from Cambridge, England, and its beautiful ancient seat of learning may be found a plaque commemorating the death of a former Atlantic slave's little girl,[6] whilst the figure for people currently enslaved around the world has been estimated at around 27 million, or even ten times that number.[7]

It has perhaps been conveniently forgotten that the amazing achievements of the cultures of ancient Greece and Rome were built, often literally, on the backs of suffering slaves, although the Greeks realized this themselves.[8] Setting the record straight, partly by the inclusion of literary evidence, could help illuminate exactly how easily some attractively priced food, fashion and even sex is enjoyed by people in the West now, in spite of the questionable ways in which these commodities are produced or sold, and demonstrate in the process some similarly uncomfortable truths today.

Slaves in Menander's time could be found around the Greek world standing, probably in shackles, in busy slave markets, on sale with other 'things', such as oil, pottery and food, the sort of scene described, as we shall see, in Menander's *Sikyonios* (lines 3–15). They might be surrounded by the sophisticated buildings that made up any 'civilized' Greek city. Slaves had been typically taken from their non-Greek native lands and deliberately forced to forget their former lives and cultures. Slaves were essentially afforded no rights and no dignity and usually went to their graves as slaves.

How did people become slaves? Slavery has been well defined as 'the permanent, violent domination of natally alienated and generally dishonoured persons.' Slavery was also one of the earliest objects of trade with other countries. How did these people lose their liberty?

War and piracy

A major means was by being made a prisoner of war, the situation for the crowd of captives at the beginning of Menander's *Aspis*. However, becoming slaves was not the usual fate of the population when a city was overcome. A conquering group does not often enslave in this way. There are practical reasons for this. Natal alienation could not be achieved by one's new masters, that is, effective separation from one's previous life: the 'social death' of the person, where one no longer had any birth rights or membership of any legitimate social order.[9] For this there would need to be cultural isolation from any potential source of rescue. For any master, enslaving one's own people also makes no sense, as at home slaves would know the terrain and be more successful at running away. They would be more likely to find refuge too.[10]

Sometimes, however, the whole population of a Greek city was deported or sold away into slavery and new colonists brought in who already had their own slaves. Acquiring slaves to trade may have been one of the main motives of colonization, with war as a mere pretext.[11] Alexander the Great, as punishment for defying him, had enslaved 30,000 Greeks: these Thebans, men, women and children, were sold, reportedly at an insulting price.[12]

Slaves were and still are also acquired by means of kidnapping and piracy, as is the case in Menander's *Sikyonios*.[13] No state had the naval strength to police the seas, and piracy became a profession; the inhabitants of Lipari are one example. Every city involved in trade had to maintain its own fleet, partly against commercial rivals engaged in piracy themselves. Being captured by pirates was a motif of some ancient comedy.[14]

Debt and exposure

People might also be sold to pay a debt,[15] or poverty might force even a relative to sell someone[16] or have them given away, as happens to the twins in Menander's *Heros*.

Prisoners might be used as slaves rather than sold on, or unwanted children 'rescued' from exposure, a method of population control which may have been common in the ancient world.[17] People might escape in return for a ransom, if they could raise the money.[18] All this is part of the reality behind the fictional portrayal of slavery in Menander.

Transport and trade

Slaves were probably transported with other 'goods', the routes depending on where they were acquired or bought.[19] Daos in Menander's *Aspis* (37ff) was originally to have travelled to Rhodes from Lycia with his prisoners of war. The Greek world expanded under Alexander the Great, with new cities being founded and ever wider markets for trade, including slaves. Increased trade led to bigger ports (Alexandria with its lighthouse and Rhodes with its Colossus statue) and bigger ships.[20]

Ancient roads were not satisfactory (mainland Greece itself is very mountainous, making journeys difficult) and slaves may often have been brought instead by sea[21] or river, although, unlike oil or silver, they could be self-transporting, that is, made to march, or could be made to carry the other goods being taken to market.[22] The advantages of this would have had to be weighed against the costs of feeding and watching them, or losing them to illness and death from exhaustion.[23]

Andrapodistai ('slave dealers/kidnappers') and *andrapodokapeloi* ('slave dealers/ thieves') (*andrapoda* means literally 'man-footed creatures'), including pimps, *pornoboskoi*,[24] will have sold slaves on to other slave dealers to sell at market alongside other 'produce'. There were markets at Athens, Aegina and Crete and many other places.[25] There may have been specialized markets for industrial slaves, such as those unfortunate enough to work in the grim conditions of the mines at Laurium or sex workers. Others were purchased as domestic slaves.

Prices and skills, homes and punishments

The prices of slaves depended very much on their skills. An overseer bought by Nicias, for example, cost 6,000 drachmas, reflecting his experience in the mines in Thrace. One could produce one's own slaves by breeding them, but they would have to be housed, fed and kept fit. The absolute power of owners entailed the right to prevent slaves from entering family relationships.[26] Not all women slaves were destined to be sex-workers: some might be nurses or some might sew. A woman mentioned by Aeschines was a slave acquired by one Timarchos through an inheritance, but she made fine textiles and sold them too. Some slave women and poor free women will have had to perform hard labour in, for instance, the fields.[27] It may be assumed that the Greeks selected carefully any slaves who were going to work in their homes, as Simiche, for example, does for Knemon in Menander's *Dyscolus*. Some of those buying the slaves would have been slaves themselves, entrusted with the task by their masters.[28]

The process of natal alienation would be continued for domestic slaves even by kind masters, in terms of rituals for entering service and establishing fictive kinship.[29]

Branding was not uncommon[30] and rebelliousness (this could be mere mistakes) punished. For whatever reason, Greek slave revolts, to judge by surviving accounts, were rare.[31] Slaves were usually assigned new names, further obliterating their original identity and reinforcing stereotypes.[32] The slave names Syros and Daos in Menander's *Epitrepontes* are ethnic words given to slaves.[33] Being uprooted from their home countries may have resulted in linguistic isolation, particularly for women, who were likely to be less educated. Such isolation would have increased their dependency on their new masters.[34]

A slave voice?

It is important to note that the same evidence does not exist in every form for ancient slavery as it does for the Atlantic slave trade. Photographs of some of those slaves survive from the latter period[35] as well as some slave narratives, that is, first-hand accounts by ex-slaves, which bring home the terrible reality of how they were treated: for example, those by Olaudah Equiano (published in 1789) and Frederick Douglass (1845, 1855). For the slaves of Greece and Rome, remote from their suffering, it is necessary to rely on inscriptions, reliefs, administrative documents and letters and references in the literature, comedy being the most problematic source.[36]

It has been observed that for ancient Greece and Rome the slave's voice is just the voice of his or her master.[37] A slave does speak in Plato's *Meno*; he possesses reason and achieves understanding, answering questions put to him with his own opinions; he is even represented as having a soul.[38] Others would therefore regard there being no slave 'voice' as an oversimplification, pointing in particular to drama. Tragedy has examples of slave characters, though there are more in Euripides than Aeschylus and Sophocles.[39] Comedy should also be studied, albeit carefully, in this context. In Aristophanes at least, slaves are given substantial roles, and masters can be mocked. Xanthias in *Frogs*, for instance, has a role unprecedented in its development and authority.[40]

Moreover, it should also not be assumed that everyone in a slave-owning society agrees with the enslavement of others. For example, although Aristotle defended the acquiring of slaves as justified, being like the science of war or animal-hunting,[41] in the process he refers to some opponents of slavery,[42] although nothing is known about them. It is common to find Greek authors skirting around mention of the slave trade itself,[43] suggesting perhaps some suppressed guilt at the way people were being treated, as it necessarily involved violence. However, when scruples are expressed, it is about the enslavement of other Greeks, rather than non-Greeks who were termed 'barbarians'.

Slaves are often mentioned by the ancient historians, whether as a large section of the population, such as those employed in agriculture or in the mines, or as individuals, such as Pasion the banker. However, their role, for instance, in warfare is glossed over, as if it is impossible to recognize that those stereotyped as supposedly cowardly could possibly have contributed to the security of the state. Stereotyping slaves as cowardly helped masters not to fear that these servants might one day rise up against them.[44]

Terminology

It seems it was not that easy to become a slave. Surprisingly, perhaps, short of large-scale military operations (leading to mass slavery) it would have been unusual, and a personal disaster, for an ordinary citizen to have become enslaved. Failure to pay a public debt could lead to personal enslavement for an Athenian citizen (and sale abroad). However, though there was no legal bar to enslaving another Greek,[45] most slaves were barbarian.[46]

There were a dozen different words that could be translated 'slave':[47] for example, *doulos* should be distinguished from *oiketes*, the latter being used for free men too, depending on the context. There is a fourth-century BCE tendency to talk of *doulos* when stressing the personal rather than the property aspect of slavery.[48] *Andrapodon*[49] was neuter in gender and impersonal in tone: 'a thing'. There is an ambiguity in the terminology of slavery, partly derived from the use of slavery as a metaphor to describe the position of free men, but also from the terminology being constituted from terms borrowed from traditional ways of being dependent.[50]

There were other, privileged groups of slaves, such as *demosioi*, 'public slaves' and *choris oikountes*, 'slaves living apart', who paid a rent to their masters, but who were otherwise more or less independent: they could, for example, go to law on their own behalf. The *anthrakeus*, 'charcoal burner', Syros in Menander's *Epitrepontes* appears to be one of these (lines 380, 408).[51] It is known that in the fifth century, a slave could normally give evidence only under torture, the assumption being that he would otherwise be likely to lie.[52] However, torture was not used very frequently in this way[53] and the *choris oikountes* could appear as parties in court.[54] This may have some bearing on the arbitration between two slaves that gives *Epitrepontes* its name.

There is, corresponding to that for slaves, a terminology used for their masters. In New Comedy *despotes* is used of the master and *trophimos*, from *trophe*, 'sustenance', of his son.[55] Charisios in *Epitrepontes* is Onesimos's *despotes* and the baby Onesimos's *trophimos* (lines 420 and 468, for example).

Manumission and freedom[56]

For a slave to work and be happy, and not, perhaps, contemplate suicide, there had to be hope, which took the form of manumission, the process by which a slave could be freed. Slaves might save up to buy this or be rewarded with it, but it seems it was easier to come by and easier to integrate with society afterwards in ancient Rome than in ancient Greece.[57] Manumitted slaves in Greece did not become citizens of the state as they did in Roman Italy, if duly freed by a Roman citizen owner.[58] There were exceptions, however, like the father of the minor politician Apollodoros, Pasion, who rose as a banker to become very wealthy and finally attain his freedom, indeed, citizenship, which he 'earned' by public economic benefaction.[59] The English word manumission derives from the Latin, but Greek practice with regard to freeing slaves usually differed from that of the Romans. The Greek word for a freedman, *apeleutheros*, is far less common in sources than the Latin word *libertus*. However, it is not clear whether this reflects the infrequency of manumission in Greece, or a less well-developed terminology, or both.[60]

The hope for freedom is expressed by some literary slaves. Habrotonon the slave *hetaira* yearns for it, for instance, in Menander's *Epitrepontes* (548). There is a literary example in Menander: Demeas in the *Samia* freed the nurse.[61] But Ischomachus in Xenophon's *Oeconomicus* never mentions manumission, despite what one scholar at least finds to be a 'liberal, or even radical' approach in Xenophon's attitude.[62]

In practice, slaves may have had more freedom of movement at least than might be supposed. In relation to contractual status, for instance, it has been pointed out that a master's permission to act will often have been assumed by all concerned, because it would be very inconvenient to restrict your slave to acting only when you yourself were present: for example, doing the shopping, which would require decision-making on the master's behalf. Such situations would have arisen particularly in the case of a *choris oikon*, 'a slave living apart'. However, Sostratos in the *Dyscolus* realizes he has gone too far perhaps when he sends his slave Parmenon to meet the grumpy Knemon on his behalf (75–6).

Slaves may have been able to attend the theatre.[63] A slave could earn manumission as a witness or, in a homicide case, as informer against wrongdoers.[64] It was also quite common for a slave to purchase his freedom out of accumulated earnings. But there were still restrictions on ex-slaves; for instance, a freedman could not own land in Attica and, which was part of the reason, only had the status of a *metic*.[65] Moreover, there was a strong stigma attached to having once been a slave.[66] Some Greeks asserted that freedmen continued to be 'natural' slaves.[67] True freedom was, therefore, an impossible goal, as Menander's slave Onesimos laments at *Epitr.* 560ff.

It is interesting, given that this was the period when Menander was writing, that some scholars believe in the second half of the fourth century BCE there was an 'evolution' in commercial law in ancient Greece, especially in Athens, whereby the 'legal personality' of the slave began to emerge, although property acquired by a *choris oikon* remained in law that of the master, whatever independent rights of ownership public slaves may have had. Slaves were also now allowed to give evidence like free men.[68] The *Epitrepontes* has been thought by some to be a product of Menander's later years;[69] slaves' new rights, in commercial law at least, could then have been topical.[70] It should be added that since the privileges of citizenship in a democracy had disappeared, the status of the poorest citizens and that of the best-off slaves could be more closely compared. Sadly, debt-bondage seems to have reappeared.[71]

There are, of course, similar problems to be faced when studying slaves in ancient Greece as there are with the lives of women, in terms both of the historical evidence for literary interpretation, and of literature as historical evidence: those writing about women and slaves were freeborn men. Moreover, the nature of the genre is important: there will be some basis for slave types in Greek and Roman comedy in real life, but there are also the prejudices of the citizen audience to be considered. Slaves seem often expected to be lazy, sex-crazed, or gluttonous, and therefore to be beaten.[72]

This last assumption about them must be too much of a generalization, however. It is more likely that there was a 'spectrum of responses' in any 'real-life' slaves to their condition and their owners, from 'working the system' through passive acquiescence,

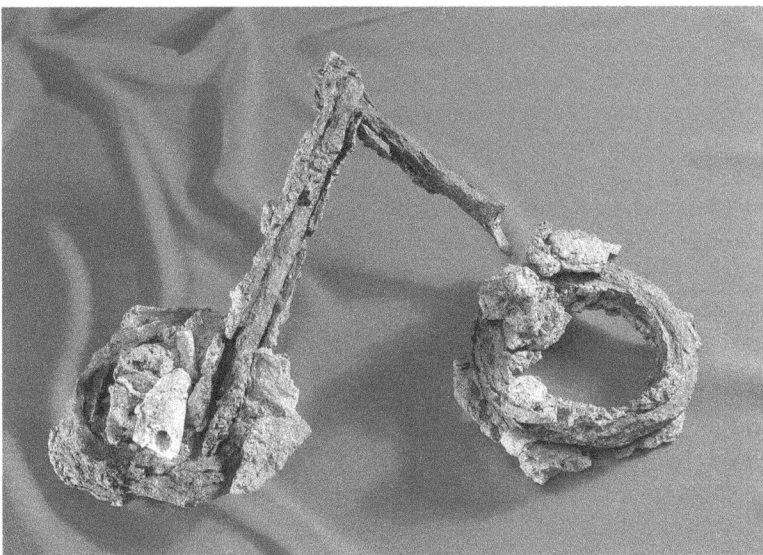

Fig. 5.1 Slave Shackles. Dating from the fourth century BCE, found in the Laurium area, S. Attica. (They were probably made from poor quality iron which would have rusted away with any skeletons if slaves were lost at sea with other cargo on their way to market.)

non-cooperation to active resistance.[73] Slaves could be stereotyped as good, that is, loyal, devoted and willing to sacrifice themselves for their masters, albeit as an antidote to the fear of rebellion. It is certainly unwise, as with the other characters, to comment on slaves in Greek and Roman comedy as if they were products of the same societies.

Menander's slaves

It will be interesting to see how Menander's treatment of his slave characters compares with this sketch of the lives of real slaves at the time the plays were written.

Aspis

In Menander's *Aspis*, the long-serving slave Daos returns from war with his master's booty – gold and silver, textiles, and the slaves and animals carrying it all (see lines 35–7).[74] The word used for the people is *aichmalotoi*, 'prisoners of war': they were captured so that they could be enslaved. They are later referred to as *andrapodia*, 'little slaves',[75] when, at *Aspis* 54–5, Daos seems to be recounting how he stood guard over them.

Daos's speech recounts his experiences in battle as a soldier's slave, but refers to his being an established domestic slave too. There is a contrast of status here with the war captives. Yet this slave himself seems to have no problem with their enslavement (32ff):

he is escorting new slaves, despite the insights which his opening speech gives into slavery as an institution.[76] He was once his lost master's tutor (*paidagogos*, line 14) and seems close to him (the metre is tragic as he laments what he believes has happened).[77] However, he had hopes of rest from labour in old age (probably manumission, that is, gaining his freedom) and these do seem to have been dashed by his belief that his master is dead (11–12).[78]

Some stereotyping is to be found in the mouth of the waiter[79] at Menander's *Aspis* 242ff, probably a slave himself; for example, the claim that Phrygians like Daos, the *paidogogos*, 'tutor', are effeminate, but Thracians like himself are 'real men'. The slaves' masks may have drawn attention to certain ethnic features.[80]

Sikyonios

Menander's *Sikyonios* opens[81] with a slave sale (7ff) in the *agora* or 'market' at Mylasa.[82] (The soldier in Menander's *Misoumenos* (line 37) buys his beloved Krateia at one.) The prologue to *Sikyonios* tells us that three people (here the Greek word *somata*,[83] 'bodies' is used, which came standardly to mean 'slaves') were captured,[84] perhaps at Halai Araphenides on the coast of Attica.[85] An old woman, probably a nurse, was thought to be worth nothing, but the child and slave, Philoumene and Dromon, were taken to be sold.[86] The rejection of the old woman leaves behind a witness to the kidnap.[87] Here is the passage:

> PROLOGUE: (The pirates), having overpowered three people, decided it wasn't worth taking the old woman, but took the child and the slave to Mylasa in Caria, where they made use of the market. The slave sat with an arm round his young mistress.[88] An army officer came up to them as they were on sale. He asked, 'How much are these?' He was told the price, he agreed to it, he bought them. Another local man, on sale again with them nearby, said to the slave 'Cheer up, sir! The Sikyonian who has bought you is a good man and rich too ...'
>
> *Sik.* 3–15

Misoumenos

The soldier in *Misoumenos* buys the girl rather than capturing her in war.[89] He then, paradoxically, becomes a prisoner himself, of love, outside his own house. This is made plain by his opening serenade[90] to Night. His slave comes out and questions him:

> **Getas**   What's upsetting you?
> **Thrasonides**   I'm being abused,[91] sadly.
> **Getas**   [Who by?]
> **Thrasonides**   By the girl prisoner. I bought her,
> I promised her her freedom (*eleutheria*), made her mistress[92] of my house,
> Gave her servants, jewellery and clothes, thought of her as my wife.
>
> *Mis.* 37–40

This is an interesting reversal of roles for master and female slave.

Epitrepontes

The *Epitrepontes* has three slave characters – four, if Habrotonon the *hetaira* is looked at from this point of view, as she certainly can be – and is therefore likely to be particularly interesting for a study of Menander's slaves. Again, the first that the audience would see of any slave character would be his or her mask, which would have been very distinctively that of a slave – even different kinds of slave, including the slave *hetaira*.

The *Epitrepontes* has already shown Menander's female characters to be engaging, with major roles to play in the action despite their comparatively limited time on stage and the traditionally somewhat restricted lives of their counterparts in real life. If women's lives were restricted, how much more so were those of slaves, so how does Menander incorporate four slaves into his play and why?

Act I is incomplete, but it is thought that it opened with a dialogue between the cook, Karion, and the slave Onesimos, 'Useful'/ 'Helpful'.[93] Little survives of this, but it is clear Onesimos was called *periergos*, 'a busybody/nosy' and commended for this (fr. 2). The comment is, however, probably made by Karion, who is a cook and a gossip himself: (Themistios *Or.* xxi 262C).[94] Karion reveals that Onesimos's master has taken up with an *hetaira*, although he has only recently married. A prologue which does not survive must have revealed that the child produced by the master's wife, which he assumes is illegitimate, was actually his own. Onesimos then disappears from the action for two whole scenes, the longer of these being the famous Arbitration Scene, after which the play is named and in which two slaves dominate the stage.

The Arbitration Scene: Daos and Syros

Onesimos appears in the extant fragments only briefly in Acts I and II – just long enough for the impression that he is inquisitive to be reinforced (he is curious at 386 about the tokens belonging to the baby). He is also observant: he recognizes the ring which his master lost (392). At present it is not known how Act II began; Sandbach thinks Onesimos was on stage[95] for a monologue and then had a dialogue with Smikrines. At the beginning of what survives, it is the slaves Daos and Syros who enter arguing.

Daos[96]

Daos accuses Syros at 218 of 'blackmailing' him (*sykophantein*).[97] At 236 he feels at a disadvantage: 'I have got entangled with rather a good orator,' he says. (The verb in the Greek is thought by Sandbach to be a metaphor from wrestling.[98]) The line is spoken aside, a brief sharing of his thoughts, which could encourage some spectators to sympathize with him.[99]

At 243 we learn that Daos is a shepherd, and at 257 he tells us that Syros is a charcoal burner.[100] These are details which immediately serve to distinguish the two slaves. Daos's speech is lively: he quotes his own thoughts and Syros's words[101] and he uses asyndeton to convey what he now regards as hastiness in rescuing the baby[102] he found:

Well, I picked up the child and took it home with its trinkets; thought I'd bring it up.

                                                          250–1, Miller

But he shows himself selfish: others[103] have noted that he repeatedly refers to himself in lines 253 and 255, both references emphatically placed at the end of the line. He equates 'childcare' and 'trouble' (254) and, by his own admission, grumbled about the expense and the worry in store, having proverbially thought it over at night (252). Of course Daos was probably quite poor – Smikrines comments on the 'jerkins/overalls' (229) that both slaves are wearing.[104] So it is possible, to some extent, to sympathize with his second thoughts about the cost and responsibility involved. Nevertheless he reveals his thoughts to have been self-centred, rather than centred on the baby.

Daos himself begins, perhaps unintentionally, to characterize Syros favourably when he quotes his words on finding him in such a state – he asks Daos tactfully what is wrong (261). Daos goes on to report their conversation at that moment in some more lively direct speech. His own reply, that, having been curious about the child, he, Daos, is a 'busybody' (262), recalls by means of the same Greek word, *periergos*, the description of Onesimos by Karion in fr. 1 and demonstrates that he is to some extent aware of his faults; on the other hand, concern for himself and the trouble he has brought on himself is uppermost in his mind.

At 270, to his own detriment, he states himself that Syros had to plead with him all day, even though Syros had explained that his wife and therefore Syros himself had in fact lost a baby. So it would have been particularly fitting and kind if Daos had let Syros relieve him of his anxiety. Despite having known Syros a long time (259), Daos was not easily persuaded; if correctly read, his use of the diminutive form of Syros's name at 270, which would normally be affectionate, is obviously ironical.[105] He recounts with satisfaction Syros's extreme gratitude to him when he finally agreed to give him the baby (272–4).

Daos really shows his true colours at 276–7, when he refers to the child's trinkets as:

trashy bits and pieces they are, not worth anything.

                                                                  Miller

He has already passed over them hurriedly at 246–7, retorting to Syros's comment that they are the cause of the whole quarrel and that Syros is interrupting. If the necklace and other items are so worthless, why is Daos making all this fuss? At 280, he speaks in terms of having shared the find – that is, he got the trinkets and Syros the baby. He goes on in the same vein:

No need to put me in the dock for not giving him the lot.

                                                          281–2, Miller

speaking at 284 of 'finders keepers': the Greek version of this proverb to which he refers first relates to sharing anything found, but Daos goes on to point out that he was alone at the time. The structure of his sentence at 275ff, with its parenthesis about the mere trinkets quoted above 276–7, conveys his indignation.[106] He emphasizes his position at 287, with a colloquial word for 'finally', speaking of the baby again, materialistically, as a thing – one of his things.

At 354 Daos is interested in the baby only when it is made clear by Smikrines, who has been asked to judge the matter, that the child and his property, that is the trinkets found with him, must go together. He is unmoved by Syros's plea for justice (293–352), accepting Smikrines' decision in Syros's favour with very bad grace:

> That's a terrible verdict, by God it is.
>
> Miller

repeating again (362–3):

> That's a terrible verdict, be damned if it isn't.
>
> Miller

He stresses (360) that no good has come out of it for himself. He continues whining as he is made to hand the baby's things over and argues with Syros after Smikrines has left. Nor does it sound as if he has given up hope; he utters a veiled threat, under the pretence of concern for the baby's welfare, that Syros had better look after the baby's things, as he, Daos will be watching him day and night (375).[107]

To sum up, Daos is given a lively manner of speech, often quoting his own words and those of other people. He also shows himself to be materialistic and selfish.[108] How does his opponent's character compare?

Syros

Syros is a 'slave living apart';[109] at 380 he says to his wife:

> We'll stay tonight, and get back to work tomorrow, after we've paid our dues.
>
> Miller

Syros's first words in the arbitration scene are a serious charge against Daos, but at the same time constitute typical stereotyping of slave behaviour: 'You're running away from the right thing to do' (218). The Greek word could also be translated 'a lawful claim'. In the face of Daos's accusation of blackmail, he remains calm and rational, proposing that they find someone to arbitrate the matter. He politely seeks Daos's agreement as to who this should be. He is equally polite to Smikrines, addressing him as 'sir' (224)[110] and asking if he could spare a little time. He does not seek to prejudice Smikrines at this stage, replying only to his question as to what this is all about:

> We're at loggerheads about something.
>
> Miller

He is too wise to cast aspersions on Daos. Indeed he stresses that their 'judge' should be 'impartial'. Again, at 227, he is courteous to Smikrines:

If it's not inconveniencing you.

Miller

As he did not allow Daos to provoke him to anger, so he does not rise to Smikrines' taunt about presenting legal cases in 'overalls'. He says simply 'all the same ...' and continues to be polite, using the Greek form of address, *pater* ('father') (231), and *O pater* at 296, with *pater* again at 301, 320, 340;[111] he uses 'sir' again at 308, and at 370, where he does not actually need to be polite, since he has by this point won.

Syros widens the issue at the outset, presenting what is at stake as something much more important than a quarrel between two slaves: justice should 'triumph the whole world over' (233), and we all have an obligation to ensure this. If Daos's aside at 236–7 is supposed to be audible,[112] Syros ignores it; thus, Daos's attempt to ridicule Syros contrasts with Syros's dignified approach to the matter. If Daos's words are spoken instead directly to him, it throws into relief the contrasting attitudes of the slaves towards the nature of justice.

At 247, Syros cannot contain himself at Daos's passing reference to the trinkets: 'They're what the quarrel's about', he says (Miller). But he is quick to admit his error in interrupting: 'And serve me right too' (250, Miller), he replies, when Smikrines threatens imperiously to beat him with his stick. Whether he does so through genuine regret, or in recognition that it is in the interests of his case, is not clear. Interruptions are characteristic of comic (as opposed to tragic) set confrontations.[113] From then on he only speaks when addressed (as he is rudely, and ironically, by Daos (270, 274)) and confines himself, despite provocation, to one-word answers. Finally, at 293, he gets his chance to reply, having politely (but coolly) ascertained that Daos has finished.

His speech is a long one (293–352), full, as has been noted, of appeals to the judge, and with no break in its reasoned, persuasive argument.[114] He even begins by giving Daos credit for those parts of his story which were true. Indeed he emphasizes that, in saying he found the child on his own, Daos spoke the truth, as he did too about Syros begging for it from him:

He did find this child on his own, and his account is quite correct . . . quite true.

Miller

There is emphatic repetition and placing of 'he says' in the Greek, again stressing that Daos spoke the truth. But when he goes on to reveal that he, Syros, only heard about the jewellery from a shepherd friend of Daos, and not from Daos himself, Daos's omission appears more of an act of commission, a deceit, in fact. The delayed attack on Daos has great effect. This manipulation of language shows that Syros, as Daos half-feared at the outset (236–7), understands the art of rhetoric.

Next he shows a sense of the dramatic, and how to win sympathy, using a rhetorical ploy standard in forensic oratory. Either by luck or by design he has brought his wife and the baby with him. Presumably he could not have foreseen the arbitration; nevertheless, he instinctively uses the most powerful means of persuasion at his disposal.[115] He takes the baby from his wife (302–3): her presence adds to the sense of surrogate family – something that Daos is not represented as being able to offer the child – and holds it up. Unlike Daos, he treats the baby as a person, not just a 'lucky find', and speaks of him as claiming what is his. To give himself authority, he uses the official-sounding word *kyrios* (306), the term for a legal guardian. To add to the strength of the plea, he addresses Daos by name (304). His accusation is a subtle one, put in the form of a strong antithesis:

> This child claims his necklace and his tokens of recognition, Daos. He points out that they were put there for his adornment, not to keep you in food.
>
> Miller 303–5

The Greek word *gnorismata,* 'recognition tokens', emphasizes the importance of the trinkets to the child in establishing his parentage and looks forward to their later role in the play.[116]

Syros claims that Daos himself made him, Syros, *kyrios,* 'guardian' of the child by giving it to him (307). He proceeds to blacken his character by his use of the word 'robber' (312); such a criminal was 'liable to summary arrest and execution if he admitted the crime'.[117] Pathos is created by Syros's argument that he could not stand up for the child before because he was not then its *kyrios*.[118]

Syros again shows that he is clever with words at 317, where he implies that Daos claimed that (284) the baby was *koinos Hermes,* a Greek idiom meaning 'a common find'. In fact, what he said was that he found the baby not whilst with Syros, but on his own – 'finders keepers' – selfish, but not exactly sharing the right to it as Syros insinuates. He reinforces his point with neat antithesis and assonance in the Greek: 'That's not "finding", it's robbing' (319, Ireland). This forceful sense of outraged indignation is expressed mainly through the (Greek) words *heuresis* and *aphairesis,* rather strange and unusual abstract words, that occur mostly in the philosophers.[119]

The tone continues to become elevated. The Greek word for 'rise' (to his own level – Miller) restored in the Greek (323) belongs to epic and tragedy.[120] It lends emphasis to the importance of *eleutheron,* 'befitting a free man': this baby is perhaps freeborn. A poignant plea, spoken as it is by a slave.[121] At 324 in the Greek, with *hopla,* 'weapons', unusual scansion may be due to the atmosphere of tragedy,[122] *bastazein,* 'bear' in the sense of 'carrying' being a word from poetry. The footrace, with which he ends the list of activities which the child may grow up to perform, was the most prestigious of the athletic events at the great festivals.[123]

At 325–6 Syros flatters Smikrines:

> You've been to the theatre (seen tragic plays), I'm sure, and know all the stories.
>
> Miller

There is perhaps, too, an implicit audience address and flattery of them, since they would be familiar with tragedy too; it was still popular in Menander's day.[124]

It would seem that Syros has at least heard the stories of the plots of these plays.[125] He goes on confidently to compare himself to the goatherd who found Neleus and Pelias, in the sense that that man was, he says (328), 'dressed in a jerkin just as I am now'. This, on its own, would give him an air of dignity;[126] it may at the same time be a gentle riposte to Smikrines' rudeness about 'overalls' at 229–30. His tone remains humble, however, as he recounts that this goatherd realized that the babies concerned were of noble birth,[127] unlike himself.

He then brings his listener sharply back to earth at 334 – what would have happened if Daos in this case had kept the tokens? The princes would have remained 'unknown' all their lives. The Greek word *agnotes* (336) is found only here in comedy[128] and is thus emphatic. At 339–40, he makes his meaning clear: Daos seeks, in taking the recognition tokens, to steal the baby's 'hope' (also emphatic at the beginning of 340) of *soteria*, 'rescue/salvation'; this word surely arouses sympathy for his own situation as well as the baby's, perhaps with a touch of humour, given the nature of his grand language.

Fig. 5.2 Slave holding a baby. Terracotta figurine (325–250 BCE), probably from Boeotia (MNC³ 1AT13a).

Again he appeals to tragedy, with more examples of how such tokens helped to avert disasters;[129] at 342, he uses a word (*errusato*, 'whisked her away') from epic and tragedy rather than comedy. He finishes with a solemn saying:

> Nature, sir, makes human life precarious: we must make provision to protect it, carefully calculating all possible means of doing so.
>
> Miller 343–5

but then switches dramatically back to the matter in hand with direct reference to Daos's taunt at 289, that he, Syros, should give the baby back. He appeals at the end of his speech (348, and again at 352), as he did in his first words (at 218), to what is *dikaion*, 'just'.

Daos and Syros, then, are characterized and distinguished as people, rather than as slaves. For example, neither reflects explicitly on his own status as a slave, as Habrotonon and Onesimos, by contrast, will share sentiments later; only Syros spells out the danger of enslavement for the baby. Nor are they distinguished from free people by means of any (detectable at present) different kind of speech peculiar to slaves. One is, on the interpretation here, a good man with good motives for wanting the baby, and the other mercenary, although they might, according to stereotypes at the time, both be expected to be selfish simply because they are slaves, or in a reasonable attempt to improve their lot.[130]

Effect and purpose of the Arbitration Scene

Since the majority of scholars have believed that Menander took the idea for this arbitration straight from Euripides's *Alope*,[131] how 'real' a legal scene is it? It is interesting that slaves are perhaps behaving like free men. The appeal of trans-status behaviour of women in Aristophanes can be compared; there may be underlying serious elements, that comment on arguments for greater independence.[132] But the attitudes of comic poets need not be, and often are not, one-sided in such matters. There are also different kinds of comedy.

The degree of humour would be determined by such factors as whether there was such a procedure as private arbitration in Menander's Athens, and if so, whether the judge of such an arbitration could be a willing passer-by;[133] also whether a slave would ever speak on such an occasion on his own behalf. The comic effect of the scene is hard to pin down. Without stage directions, much depends on the interpretation by the actors, whose importance had grown by Menander's time, but there is also, whatever the slaves are saying, the presence of the stereotypical slave masks to be considered.

The Arbitration Scene has been very thoroughly analyzed in terms of identifying rhetorical devices and their effect. More should be said about characterization and the possible effect and purpose of the scene.[134] It has been interpreted as the portrayal of 'an informal private case', without evidence that such a scene would have been credible to a fourth-century audience.[135] The use of rhetorical devices has been taken as an indication that the audience would think immediately of the law courts, rather than questioning whether slaves would have been allowed to 'go to court' on their own behalf, although what is depicted is an arbitration, not a court scene as such.

Being in metre, however, the speeches would immediately sound different from prose speeches. Tragic metre, together with poetic diction, followed by comic metre are used to produce a subtle effect, as Syros refers to tragic motifs and then returns audience attention to the 'real' world.[136] There is also here a single judge, whereas the Attic orators delivered their speeches before at least 200 judges/jury members, but there was of course a large audience in the theatre watching the arbitration scene. Slaves may have been in the audience and have enjoyed seeing themselves depicted, depending on the tone of this scene.[137] A certain metatheatricality, a play within a play, in other words, parallels a later monologue at lines 516ff by Habrotonon, the slave *hetaira*, in which she acts out a scheme she has in mind. On the other hand, the references by Syros to the tragic motif of exposed children paradoxically draws attention to the 'reality' of the scene.[138] That a child's guardians were called *epitropoi*, 'those entrusted' with its well-being, recalls the verb *epitrepein*, 'refer to arbitration', and suggests that the scene is of central significance to the main plot.[139]

Parody

The Arbitration Scene needs to be placed in context, as a scene at a certain point in a comedy and containing rhetorical language between two characters representing fourth-century Athenian slaves. It is not clear whether the audience are intended to laugh at them or sympathize with them, or both. The scene could be a farce, or a traditional exchange between slaves or some more subtle effect may have been sought and achieved.

A legal dispute of some kind is clearly being imitated. Smikrines is asked to arbitrate, and there is much talk from Syros at least, of what is just. Is this parody? Lines 325–33 of *Epitrepontes* probably describe the plot of Sophocles' *Tyro* without parodying the tragic model.[140] Parody can be defined as the imitation with regard to the words, style, tone and more of an author in such a way as to invite mockery.[141] It has been called a branch of satire. Other definitions stress exaggeration and incongruity, either together or singly.[142] Parody can be of situation as well as of an author's style. There may not be simply mockery or contempt in the treatment of the object of the parody. There is often an ambivalence, and this 'double voice' is to be found in Aristophanes, for example.[143] It seems to be here in Menander too. Further observations on parody point out that it entails a complex process of recognition, and the different knowledges of different audience members are of critical importance. If the fourth century (Menander's century) did see a change in the position of slaves, the tone here in Menander may be serious.

Whatever any fourth-century developments may have been, a comparison of parodic 'law-court' scenes from Aristophanes shows that Menander's 'court' scene is different. Two slaves are involved, not two dogs (*Wasps*), or abstract ideas (*Clouds*); the judge is an old man, not a god (*Frogs*). Syros brings on his wife and a baby, not puppies (*Wasps*). There is a human arbiter rather than a jury of kitchen utensils, as is the case in the *Wasps*. On the other hand, although the baby situation in Menander could have arisen in real life, no real political situation is satirized, as it is in the *Wasps*, unless serious political points are being raised in relation to the institution of slavery.

The two slaves are given distinguishing characteristics, although in extant Menander they appear only in this act; one is selfish and deceitful, the other clever but honest.[144] Daos's knack of unwittingly revealing his real motives could be acted humorously;[145] there are points in Syros's speech, however, that could potentially move a listener to tears, particularly given his use of elevated, even tragic language, depending on the quality of its delivery by the actor.

But masks and costume would not allow the audience to forget that it was watching a comedy. Moreover, two slaves are accompanied on stage by their arbitrator, Smikrines, who could cut a humorous figure,[146] as he grumbles when asked to be judge and when he threatens to beat Syros with his stick. He may have made amusing gestures during the speeches, and the slaves may have done so during their own. Without stage directions it is impossible to know, although there may be clues in the text, when he himself speaks, perhaps pulling at their clothes (228–30) and waving his stick (248–9). It has been noted that Menander elsewhere tempers the seriousness of a scene by the presence of asides and the comments of another character. Compare Moschion at *Perik.* 755–826.[147]

The difference here is that Smikrines is meant to be present and has a definite right to speak: he hears not overhears. Moreover, he is silent from 293 to 353. The key difference, however, in Menander's scene, as opposed to the scenes considered above in Aristophanes, is what the audience know that the characters do not. In the, most likely, lost prologue the audience were probably told the identity of the baby. As has been observed, the long dispute would lose its dramatic effect if the audience were unaware that the child had any connection with the characters already introduced. Smikrines, who adjudicates, is unaware that on his decision depends the fate of his own grandson.[148] Also Smikrines, it seems, cannot be a really bad character, as he chooses well on behalf of the baby.

There are other ironies too: those who are battling over the infant are themselves slaves; one does not care if the baby becomes a slave too: the other, as interpreted here, wishes to help him achieve freedom. The fate of the baby therefore gives the scene weight in various ways, but very significantly in relation to the themes of slavery and power in the play, particularly as Smikrines' decision reunites the child with his property but does not secure his future as the tokens remain unrecognized.[149]

Slavery established as a theme of the play

The scene is a rhetorical *tour de force* and presumably would please some members of a fourth-century audience purely in that way. The specific imitation of established rhetorical devices would allow appreciation of the scene on another level by those with some kind of experience of public speaking, of whom there would be many.[150] As to whether it is a parody or not, this partly depends on historical evidence which is lacking, namely, the nature of real fourth-century arbitrations, the status of slaves, and whether a baby could have rights in law. Not that any changes in mid-fourth-century Athenian law are being parodied in the sense of being ridiculed, but a knowledge of the law at the time would help identify points where gentle fun is being made of it and the characters.

There is a feel of parody about the scene, however. This is not slapstick with serious political parody, like that in the *Wasps* trial by Aristophanes, nor fantastical debate like the argument in his *Clouds*. Gentle irony seems to be the flavour, given what the audience know, with some humour if Syros is seen as a little pompous, but with a serious undercurrent enhanced by tragic language and reference to tragic motifs. Irony and parody creep in, as this child is free but no great hero of myth, like Neleus and Pelias. Those who knew tragedy, the *Wasps* and other legalistic *agones* would enjoy thinking of other parallels; again, appreciation on a slightly different level. Given the length of the scene, the sympathetic portrayal of the slave characters and the possible fate of the baby at its centre, this is comedy with a serious edge and the action establishes as a central theme of the play slavery and what it really means to be a slave.

Onesimos and Syros 376–418

It is immediately following this memorable scene that Onesimos the family slave reappears. Syros has finally lost patience with Daos and told him to get lost (376). He asks his wife to take the trinkets in to his master Chairestratos. The word Syros uses to refer to his 'young master' Chairestratos (377) is *trophimos*. The use of a *persona muta* here is skilful; having a wife present adds a dimension of a certain masculinity to Syros's character and Syros has a kind of dialogue with her, in the sense that she must have made a negative gesture when asked if she had a box (381).[151]

Onesimos re-enters at 382; he is muttering to himself that the cook is late. The scene which follows shows Onesimos to be inquisitive but also observant. He refers to his master, Charisios, as *despotes* twice, which is perhaps suggestive of a formal relationship (393 and 400) and yet he seems loyal in his concern; indeed he speaks of the ring as 'ours', as in 'of our family' (395).

Though initially Syros is happy to trust Onesimos and hand him the ring, sensing a crisis, he soon loses the cool he maintained throughout the arbitration, and his comment at 396ff that it is hard work looking after an orphan's property neatly and humorously contributes to rounding off the act, so full of arguments about just that.

It is possible that with the adjective *striphnos*, 'scrawny' (Arnott) at 385 Menander deliberately puts a non-Attic word into Syros's mouth, perhaps to give the impression that he was not born in Athens.[152] Moreover, it is interesting that Syros, and perhaps Onesimos too, are able to read the inscription on the ring (390), which suggests that these slaves represent real-life ones who were, to some extent, literate. At 403, Syros shows that his motives are still good; he emphasizes that the property is 'Baby's', not his.[153] He is again shown speaking with his wife, who is still holding the child, which reminds us that he has undertaken to be a surrogate father, another, different aspect of his masculinity. It is clear that, despite his command of rhetorical skills, which could have been employed by him to deceive, his position has been a genuine one.[154]

At 406, Onesimos drops his use of *despotes* and refers to Charisios by name. He indicates that Charisios said that he lost the ring once when he was drunk: he was told this by another slave, in fact (473). This was not the whole truth from Charisios; he lost it, if he remembers, on the occasion of his rape of Pamphile. It appears that he did not tell his slave the whole story. In reply Syros reminds Onesimos that he is Chairestratos's *oiketes*,[155] the servant of Charisios's friend. Onesimos will not trust him with the ring even so (409–10).[156] By contrast, Syros trustingly lets Onesimos hang on to it, content that the matter will be sorted out soon, if rather surprised, perhaps, by Onesimos's attitude. Onesimos puts off telling his master about the ring until the following day. The language turns legal again, as Syros wonders if he must dispute ownership of the trinkets for the second time and devote his whole life to such disputes. How ironic he is being depends partly on whether a slave had the right to act in this way in real life.[157]

Act II, then, sees gradual further characterization – three slaves compared and contrasted, used both to characterize each other, and, in the case of Syros and Daos, to show Smikrines capable of fair judgement. These slaves give colour to the play; their various arguments over the baby, amusing in themselves, also provide enjoyment in terms of rhetorical and tragic allusions. Most importantly, the stage presence now of three slaves emphasises the fate that hangs over the baby. Slavery and, more generally, power will be seen to be key themes in *Epitrepontes*.

All three slaves are clearly distinguished. Daos, a loner, is deceitful, selfish and greedy, and not clever enough to hide his materialistic motives. Syros, a married man, is an accomplished orator who has the best interests of the baby at heart, and he is shrewd enough to be able to protect them, though perhaps a little too trusting of Onesimos, once the main contest for the trinkets is over. Onesimos is inquisitive and observant, but inclined to put off unpleasant duties. He has the power, despite being a mere slave, to reunite his master with his child. Much less has been seen of this slave so far than of the other two. What is he really like? The opening of Act III provides the opportunity to get to know him better, as he voices his thoughts aloud.

Onesimos's monologue opening Act III 419–29

The ring! I've set sail more than five times to show it to my master, and I've been extremely close to it already, but just when I'm about to do it, I back off.

And I regret giving the information I gave. He keeps saying 'God blast that wretched tell-tale!' I'm afraid he'll make it up with his wife and then do away with the tell-tale who knows too much. I did well to refrain from a second piece of stirring up – the soup I'm in is quite thick enough already!

419–29

Onesimos's entrance at 419 is unmotivated,[158] but his first word, 'the ring', the subject of so much debate at the end of Act II,[159] distracts our attention from this. In this way too Menander reconnects the audience with the action.[160] Onesimos is speaking to himself, or directly to the audience, and has no reason to think that any other character is listening, so it can be assumed that his speech represents his true feelings.[161] The monologue is a feature of New Comedy, and Menander makes extensive use of it as a technique to suggest inner thoughts, including those of slaves.[162]

Onesimos seems to be quite worked up: there is alliteration of 'd' and 'p' sounds in the Greek (419–20). Expectations which may have been aroused by his mention of the ring are thwarted: he has done nothing about it. He is not proud of his irresolution: *anaduomai*, 'hesitate', receives heavy emphasis at the beginning of line 422. He uses *despotes* again (420) rather than the more intimate *trophimos* of his master,[163] perhaps reinforcing the impression that he is anxious about his relationship with him.

The slave makes use of simple metaphors, that is to 'set sail' (Heap)/'embarked' (Miller) at 419 and to 'stir something else into the soup' (428),[164] the latter being perhaps a favourite one, as he uses it again at 573. He also uses direct speech, as he quotes Charisios's words of annoyance with him at 424 as a 'tell-tale' (Miller). In this way the estrangement of master and slave is underlined and Onesimos is shown expressing his emotions freely. He goes on to refer to his mistress as Charisios's *gynaika*, his 'wife' or 'the lady' (426). Such indirect references could suggest a certain distance between this slave and those for whom he works. Compare Demeas's oblique references to Chrysis in the *Samia* when estranged from her.[165]

So great is his fear, apparently, he cannot bring himself to refer to what Charisios may do to him, other than by the vague phrase at 427 to 'get rid of/ do away with'[166] (Miller/Balme). He persuades himself that inaction was the best course to avoid further trouble; he is the opposite of the stereotypical scheming slave. As Charisios himself has not yet appeared, and little has been said of him, it cannot be known whether or not Onesimos's fears are justified.

However, Onesimos's expression of his worries for his own future provides a hint that a reconciliation between Charisios and Pamphile may be possible (indeed, he thinks it possible they may make up their quarrel (425–6)). The comment could mean either that Onesimos is not a cynic after all, or that he knows them both quite well. Onesimos's report of his master's feelings has been compared unfavourably to Sosias's monologues at *Perik.*172ff and 354ff: 'while Sosias pities Polemon (358–60), Onesimos ... considers the possible reconciliation only as it affects himself.'[167] This may be too harsh, however. That his own well-being is his primary concern does not necessarily mean that he does not care about the happiness of his master and mistress.

Onesimos and Habrotonon[168] 430–42

Habrotonon enters at this point; Onesimos continues speaking to himself and she also voices her thoughts without noticing his presence – 'an unusual interlacing of two quite independent speeches'.[169] The *hetaira* is interesting in two ways for this study of Menander, since she can be looked at both as a female character and as a slave like Onesimos, Daos and Syros.[170] As has been noted, interest in the *hetaira*'s character has already been aroused. For example, her annoyance earlier at being ignored by Charisios (432ff) is intriguing.[171]

Whereas Onesimos may be concerned only about what is going to happen to himself, Habrotonon, despite her rejection by Charisios, does express sympathy for him (436–7). Both characters are given interesting monologues. Here is a contrast of gender with a comparison of status; a contrast of personality, but a similarity in the way the characters are revealed.

Onesimos and Syros with Habrotonon listening 442–63

At this point Menander reintroduces Syros. He is in a hurry, his patience has run out – he sums up Onesimos's choice for him: either he shows the ring to Charisios or he hands it back. This draws attention to Onesimos's indecision. But Syros is still polite to Onesimos: at 443, he addresses him *o agathe*, 'sir' ('a term of gentle remonstrance').[172] Onesimos decides to confide in him his failure to show the ring. Again he refers to Charisios as *despotes* not *trophimos*, though here the former term does occur in conjunction with his name. But to address Syros Onesimos uses the less courteous, indeed frequently contemptuous, *anthrope*,[173] 'man/mate/my friend' (Balme/Miller 446) in reply. It seems that Onesimos protests here against Syros's impatience.[174] Syros's[175] use of *abeltere*, 'you idiot', in reply (450) suggests that again he is losing his cool. Onesimos explains what he thinks has happened, and how he is pessimistic about the good of saying anything to his master, unless the girl who was raped can be found. He does appear to have more than just his own interests at heart when he says:

> But without her evidence we'll only produce suspicion and chaos.
>
> Miller 457

Syros tells him rather unsympathetically that that is his problem. Indeed he imputes ugly motives to Onesimos; if he is threatening to keep the ring and blackmail him into buying it back, he has another thing coming. That did not sound like what Onesimos had in mind. However, the Arbitration Scene left the impression that Syros is a good character,[176] and if he thinks Onesimos is up to no good, then perhaps he is.

The intransitive use of the Greek word for 'make trouble' at 458 (*anaseiein*) is unparalleled. It has been speculated that the unusual word is chosen to suggest Syros as in some way learned. The same effect could be intended by *merismos*, 'going shares' (461), a 'new-fangled abstract' of Hellenistic Greek.[177]

When Syros says that he does not 'go shares', we are reminded of his struggle with the materialistic Daos. Perhaps the audience is supposed to wonder if Onesimos is mercenary too. At 461 he protests he does not want to do anything of the kind Syros has suggested. Syros curtly accepts this and again trusts him, going off into town on an errand. The audience are left wondering what Onesimos will in fact do with the ring, which he has had for so long.

Onesimos and Habrotonon 464–556

Habrotonon's question about the baby at 464 shows that she has overheard the conversation and has quickly realized what has happened. She expresses sympathy for the child and talks of its rights: compare Syros's behaviour in Act II. Onesimos, on the other hand, speaks of it as the 'thing' that happened to have his master's ring (*despotes* is again the word he uses of Charisios).

Habrotonon is an *hetaira* who, contrary to probable expectation, likes babies, and whose character throws into relief Onesimos's lack of concern for the infant in the play.

Yet this baby is Onesimos's *trophimos*, the baby being a person in his own right.[178] The danger that hangs over its head, of growing up a slave, if its identity and free status are not established, is spelt out by Habrotonon at 468–70:

> Then, if he really is your master's son, can you stand by and watch him being brought up as a slave? That would be a capital crime.
>
> Miller

She uses the Greek word *doulos*, to emphasize how the baby will be treated and *trophimos*, perhaps to highlight Onesimos's duty towards the child, and his apparent lack of tenderness towards it.[179] Habrotonon's attitude, in not wishing her lot as a slave on anyone else, commends her as a character. It also adds a serious note, in what is otherwise a comedy, about the institution of slavery.

Onesimos protests at 470 that the important thing is to find out who the mother is. At 472, he defends Charisios's behaviour at the festival up to a point by mentioning that he was drinking when he lost his ring; having been drinking was a conventional excuse in comedy for rape.[180] Habrotonon, by contrast, seems in her reactions to criticize Charisios, as will be seen below.

Onesimos mentions that he was told about the drink by the *paidarion*, 'young slave', attending Charisios; it might be observed that he was not asked to go himself, but perhaps he is too old for such outings with his master. Given that many people would warm to Habrotonon, with her liveliness, compassion and sensitivity, Onesimos's ironical 'yeah, right!' at 479, expressing scepticism about her former purity, could sound cruel and cynical.[181] When she protests, he does not apologize but merely puts a question to her about the girl she saw. Moreover, he does not get distracted or moved by Habrotonon's account of the rape, but sticks to the facts – whether or not the girl had the ring.

Although Onesimos has followed the story carefully, he still has no idea what to do and asks Habrotonon for help only in an indirect way: 'I wonder what to do now.' (Miller 492–3). Habrotonon, however, is in no doubt – he should tell his master (494–5). Her decisiveness contrasts with Onesimos's irresolution. She emphasizes part of what it means to be free when she says:

> If the mother's a girl of good family, why shouldn't he know what's happened?
>
> Miller 495–6

Finally, Onesimos does ask for her help, calling Habrotonon by name (497–8); they must find the girl. His fear of getting things wrong by accosting his master has, however, been understandable.

Habrotonon's speech at 499ff deftly describes her as a woman used to the company of men. This makes her comment at 478–9 that she did not know about men when she was at the Tauropolia only the year before intriguing. Onesimos has not been shown in the company of women in the way that Syros, for example, was given a wife. His reactions to Habrotonon could be considered partly from the point of view of this gender difference. Onesimos offers no ideas to Habrotonon at all; just exclamations of encouragement; these serve the purpose of building the excitement: 'she's the best'[182] (520), 'Yes, by the Sun – splendid!'(525), 'Good!' (528), 'Herakles!'[183] (532).

Habrotonon as the scheming slave

It is Habrotonon, the female slave, who thinks up the scheme in this play. Onesimos, who prefers to dither,[184] compliments her at 535 that she is 'ready to do anything' (Sandbach) and 'wicked' (Furley), again using her name.[185] Perhaps he is sexually impressed too.

If Onesimos has been physically attracted to Habrotonon as she outlines her plans, he does not show much understanding of her as a person. He commends her cleverness rather than her compassion, and assumes a partly ulterior motive:

> One point you haven't mentioned – you'll get your freedom.
>
> Miller 538–9

Charisios, he thinks, would buy her in order to manumit her if he thought she was the mother of his child.[186] Habrotonon appears not to have considered this in depth, but admits it would be nice (541). This does not mean that it has not crossed her mind, but it need not have been her primary motive in suggesting her plan, as Onesimos insinuates it was.

Onesimos is impatient with her protest, indeed, he is sarcastic, and, instead of being pleased for her, asks what is in it all for him. He cannot see the funny side when Habrotonon says that she will say he will be 'responsible/to blame' for all she gets (543–4). Indeed, he is afraid she will betray him. Habrotonon's reply is interesting:

> Do I look like a girl who is desperate to have children? May I just get my freedom, that's all the reward I want.
>
> 547–9

This contrasts with her apparent lack of concern about her freedom at line 541.[187] There is the question anyway of how someone like her would benefit from her freedom. The expression of the wish to leave slavery behind draws from Onesimos the simple word(s) 'may you get it'. Deep down they share the same desire. There is pathos here, especially if a freed slave could never be the equal of someone who was born free.[188]

But even sharing this painful, heartfelt sentiment ('slave voices'?) does not elicit Onesimos's trust. He likes the *hetaira*'s plan, but again warns Habrotonon not to double-cross him. In fact, he threatens to fight her (551), claiming that he has the power.[189] It is not until 554 that he hands over the ring, now passing to its fourth slave. It is important that, despite the fact that it is gold-plated (387), none of these slaves has actually stolen it.[190] Only Daos, indeed, has been interested in its monetary value.

Onesimos's monologue 557–82

Habrotonon's monologues are very brief; Onesimos's thoughts are expressed at greater length. This speech is over 25 lines long, and that which opened Act III was 11 lines long. Onesimos commends Habrotonon, but the words he chooses are not wholly complimentary. She is *topastikon*, 'smart', rather than 'kind' and a *gynaion* – this could be affectionate or contemptuous.[191] His summary of her motives is unnecessarily callous and may be quite wrong: he thinks that having tried love to get her freedom (558) and failed, she is attempting another scheme. He uses the metaphor, 'Off she goes on the other track' (Miller 559–60), as he did another kind in his previous long monologue (419). Suddenly he reveals why freedom sprang to his mind as Habrotonon's motive for getting involved:

> But me, I'll stay a slave forever, drivelling (and) paralytic, quite incapable of a scheme like this.
>> Miller 560–1, brackets added to emphasize the asyndeton in the Greek

The strength of the adjectives, and the asyndeton, suggest a bitter outburst, again, a kind of 'slave voice'. Perhaps, given that women's lives were restricted at the time, there were ways in which being a slave was more humiliating and therefore harder for a man. Onesimos also resents Habrotonon's intelligence, since he recognizes that, although a man, he is unable to devise a plan.

Not only is he a slave, but a female slave has proved more resourceful than he is capable of being. In addition, he may be jealous that, being a woman, she can manipulate Charisios in ways he cannot, although he, Onesimos, has been his slave a long time and she has only recently been hired. Such tensions between slaves might well reflect real life.[192] Onesimos hopes instead for some benefit from Habrotonon's plans (562–3): that would be *dikaion*, 'just' he says; the phrase is emphatic, occurring mid-line between pauses, echoing the exchanges of the slaves in the Arbitration Scene and being an implicit comment on his and Habrotonon's lack of freedom. More bitterness is hinted at in lines 563–5; he will be a fool if he expects gratitude 'from a woman'. A pessimist, he puts away hopes of an improvement in his situation and settles instead for staying out of trouble (565–6).

Some members of the audience might nevertheless sympathize with Onesimos; he does go on to express concern for his mistress, though again he uses the formal *kektemene*, 'mistress' (literally, 'she who owns me'), when speaking of her being in danger; she may be deserted by Charisios in favour, as he thinks, of another freeborn girl, if such a girl turns out to be the actual mother of the baby (568–70).

But soon his encouragement of Habrotonon's plan is forgotten, and he is congratulating himself on having avoided getting embroiled, using the same metaphor of 'stirring up' at 573 as he did at 428. He vows to give up meddling and gossiping (574–6). This is reinforced somehow in 576. It has been suggested that Onesimos says his teeth can be pulled, if he does it again, where, perhaps, the audience expects the word for testicles.[193] The arrival of Smikrines provides Onesimos with a reason to leave: he fears there will be trouble and that someone has told Smikrines the truth.

Power as an extension of slavery as an explicit theme

The theme of slavery is taken up by Pamphile in her opening words at the beginning of Act IV: if Smikrines does not persuade her to obey him but forces her, he will not be her father but her *despotes*, 'master', as of a slave (715). Through the baby's predicament, Syros's and Daos's argument and Onesimos's conversation with Habrotonon, the kind of existence a Greek slave might expect has been explored. Now it is seen that freeborn women too have their freedom restricted, in that they are always subject to the control of men.[194]

Similar and contrasting status

The encounter between Habrotonon and Pamphile which follows is a dramatic and touching one.[195] It is given added poignancy by the new turn given to the traditional recognition scene: a slave *hetaira* and a young freeborn woman engaged in discovering the identity of a baby and thus saving the child potentially from life as a slave. The conversation ends with considerable warmth between the two women, despite the difference in their status. Habrotonon's generous nature is very prominent, as she displays no hint of jealousy at Pamphile's advantages in life, only compassion for her unhappiness.[196] For a short while, freeborn and slave are intimate, even friends.

Onesimos's monologue 878–907

The two women exit and Onesimos rushes on. He delivers a kind of messenger speech, which describes Charisios's behaviour. His alarm and excitement, together with Charisios's emotion, are conveyed at once by the repetition and alliteration, the chiasmus and the double oath:

> He's mad, I swear it[197] quite loopy, really raving, absolutely crazy!
>
> Miller 878–9

There is humour too, as he repeats himself, running out of words to say what he wants to say.[198]

Does Onesimos act here as a kind of *servus currens*?[199] It seems likely that Onesimos's speech has the flavour of comic tradition and parody. At 880 Onesimos makes it clear whom he means: 'My master I mean, Charisios.' That Charisios eavesdropped on his wife and her father suggests a certain anxiety on his part. Onesimos recounts the extent of his master's emotion, and, interestingly, how he reproaches himself for double standards. Note also how Charisios does not approach Pamphile at once, but addresses her with affection whilst he is still alone, a hint of a difficulty in showing his feelings.[200] In this way a slave is used to characterize his master, as the baby, whilst a focus for the theme of slavery, also draws out the characterization of speaking characters.

Onesimos reports all this in a characteristically lively mixture of direct and indirect speech:[201]

'Sweetheart,' he cried, 'what wonderful words!' And he punched himself hard on the head.

Miller 888–90

The Greek word for 'hard/with vehemence' here (*sphodra*) is a word common in comedy and colloquial in type: therefore its presence serves to defuse somewhat the serious nature of Onesimos's report.[202] *Meleos*, 'miserable', quoted from Charisios at 891, is by contrast a word from tragedy.[203]

But Onesimos's thoughts are mostly centred on himself; at 901 he gets back to what is really significant:

I'm terrified, my mouth dry with fear.

Miller

Moreover, he interprets remorse as anger, just as he misread Habrotonon as selfish. In the line immediately following he emphasizes his fears of the possible repercussions of recent events for himself: *auton...me* is a particularly emphatic expression for 'me'.[204] He has 'slipped out' (904) rather than face the music, and continues to be indecisive:

But where to turn? What to do?

Miller 905[205]

His last word is characteristically 'me' (907) – a prayer to Zeus to save him. This oath is emphatically placed first in the line, a less common placing for it than last in line would be; oaths, however, create warmth between the character and the audience.[206] This one also suits well a hurried exit or attempt to hide.

Monologue[207]

Monologues often create empathy with a character in some members of the audience: they may feel a special relationship with a character if they have heard his or her private thoughts. In *Epitrepontes* the significantly long monologues go to Onesimos with briefer confidences from Habrotonon (see 431ff). Perhaps the first actor[208] demanded Onesimos's role, a slave role.

Onesimos's monologue is immediately followed by one by Charisios. This is probably Charisios's first appearance in the play and Onesimos has prepared us for it. Onesimos's report only anticipates Charisios's, it whets the appetite and raises the tension, but does not tell the whole story. After Onesimos's parting words an angry exchange might have been expected, as Charisios caught him trying to flee, or a fierce soliloquy directed against his slave by his master. Instead, Charisios castigates himself and expresses at some length his affection for his wife; only hints of this affection have been given by Onesimos.[209]

The monologues delivered by the slave and then his master can be compared in that they both report Charisios's words. But Charisios's is a more introspective speech than Onesimos's. Many different kinds of monologue are possible, as are, sometimes, different interpretations of the same monologue.[210] Prologues and epilogues may be distinguished from other monologues which rely on a direct relation between performer and audience and from the semi-direct asides, which constitute audience address of a qualified nature, that is, short and explanatory speeches forming commentaries on the action; indirect monologues may be categorized as those in which, for example, the speaker predominantly addresses himself:

> 'the realization of a communal mode which is not (as in some other communal forms) opposed to subjectivity but is a deepening and then a transformation of it'.
>
> Williams

These are only guidelines for interpretation, however, as individual monologues can contain a mixture of the direct and indirect.[211] Onesimos's monologue at 878ff is largely explanatory; Charisios's could be explanatory to the audience at first, but it certainly ends in self-address and self-reproach.

Charisios's reference to the 'Power', and quotation of its words, continue the slavery theme, forming a parallel with Onesimos's fears of him as his master: that is, as someone who is in a position of power over him. The young man says:

> Well, some Power above has well and truly turned the tables on me, and quite right too. I've finally shown that I'm human.
>
> Miller 911–12

Pamphile and Habrotonon's references to the gods earlier (855 and 874) may be echoed here. There is alliteration in the Greek (*kappa, pi, delta* and *chi*), and emphasis too, in the way *daimonion*, 'power', and *anthropos*, 'human', are at opposite ends of the same line. Charisios is human; Onesimos is too in wishing for his freedom. *To daimonion* is not found elsewhere in Menander or the remains of New Comedy, and is therefore 'no banal phrase'.[212] The speeches by slave and master are juxtaposed, and Charisios's lively quotation of the Power's words[213] echoes the similar reporting of his own words by Onesimos. Everyone is in the power of someone or something.

Whether or not Onesimos exits at 907 affects the interpretation of his character. Some scholars think he does.[214] Others, however,[215] assume that he remains on stage, and is present throughout Charisios's speech. His presence, whatever he was doing, would affect audience reaction to his master's words, since his being there would provide a comic distraction from the serious sentiments of his master. Moreover, Charisios would be eavesdropped upon as he eavesdropped himself, inviting a comparison of slave and master in terms of their inability to trust. Of course to eavesdrop is also a dramatic convention of New Comedy and of comedy in general.

Onesimos's oath at 906, as noted, would suit a hurried exit or running to hide. He says that he hears the door – this is a conventional comic signal for another's entrance and an excuse for someone speaking to withdraw or leave altogether. However, Charisios does launch straight into his speech, leaving little time for Onesimos to get off stage.

Onesimos, Charisios and Habrotonon 932–78

Onesimos's words at 932–4 could equally plausibly be spoken on re-entering, or in response to having overheard Charisios again, since he was already convinced before that Charisios's mood was sure to mean trouble for him: 'Oh dear, I'm a terrible mess', he says, aside, and calls on Habrotonon for help. Yet he denounces her without hesitation at 951:

> The woman tempted me, I swear she did.
>
> Miller, based on a restoration

This shows little loyalty to her, despite her help and goodwill. A good joke would be lost at 935–6, when Onesimos denies he has been eavesdropping, if he is not lying.[216] Whether he stayed or not at 907, he certainly listened well enough on a previous occasion to report Charisios's words to us at 878ff. On the other hand, the motif might be dull if repeated in this way. If Charisios were alone on stage for his monologue the overall effect would have been a more serious one. It is interesting for their relationship that Charisios suspects him of spying (he accuses him at 934–5), though there is some hypocrisy in his words, given his own actions. Moreover, *hierosule*, 'good-for-nothing' (Furley), is hardly a term of affection.[217] One scholar at least feels there is a suggestion that the confrontation between Charisios and his slave is acrimonious'.[218] Others, however, think that Onesimos and Habrotonon enter together, or almost together, taking Onesimos's protest at 936, 'I've just come out', at face value as 'the truth'.[219]

Act V: Traditional 'slapstick' endings

Onesimos's behaviour to Smikrines in the last act of *Epitrepontes* can be compared with that of the slave Getas and the cook Sikon to Knemon in *Dyscolus*: in each case fun is made of an old man. At 1078–9 Onesimos is rude to Smikrines, calling him 'Grumpy'. He says that Smikrines has come for dowry and daughter, implying that the former is his priority. This is to someone of whom even his master, a freeborn man, whatever his character, was afraid in the previous scene: at 928ff Charisios can only rehearse what he will say to his father-in-law. Onesimos is shown in a new, carefree mood, but this is also plausible, as reconciliation with Charisios is now possible. The slave's behaviour is part of a traditional, happy, comic 'slapstick' ending. The scene also suits the way in which the story of Charisios and Pamphile is played out in the lives of other people, their reconciliation being not directly represented on stage, but the excuse that lies behind the merrymaking.[220]

Onesimos, Menander and philosophy

The repetition of a phrase at 1081 is again used as a technique of characterization, since Onesimos's ironic 'yes, indeed' to Smikrines at 1080, as he announces Smikrines' arrival, recalls his use of it at 479 to Habrotonon.[221] He then launches (1084ff) into philosophical discourse.[222]

The height of New Comedy writing coincided with very intense and productive work in the field of ethics by the Peripatetics and then by the Stoics and the Epicureans. Menander would be appealing to his audience's interests by introducing some well-known maxims and arguments and, with them, different levels of humour, depending on the extent of the individual spectator's familiarity with philosophy.[223]

The fact that Onesimos can introduce these 'scraps of various current ideas', for example, 1091ff (Epicurean)[224] shows that he, a slave, has a certain level of intelligence and education, however these ideas were acquired. Such philosophical content need not suggest any comment by Menander himself on the action. The slave's words at 1092ff are jumbled. However, the general sense, that character influences events,[225] and that behaving well brings happiness, does fit with the underlying theme of Menander's plays.

At 1102–3, the philosophy becomes more down to earth. Onesimos challenges Smikrines, as perhaps some members of the audience have done in their minds since his argument with Pamphile in Act IV. The slave asks if it is *agathon*, 'something good' (Furley), to take a daughter from her husband. There is some loyalty to Charisios implied here. Smikrines replies (his response a human one):

Who says it's good? It's just necessary.

Furley 1103–4

Onesimos's scornfully expressed repetition of this aside to Sophrone (1104ff) seems, by contrast to his direct treatment of Smikrines at 1079ff, to be really unkind. In twisting what Smikrines has said (1104–5), that wrong is necessary, however, he shows himself to be clever. At 1108, the Greek word *t'automaton*, 'chance', is a grander word than *tyche*, also 'chance' (personified in the prologue to *Aspis*).[226] There is some truth in his description at 1111 of Smikrines as 'rash': he did make false assumptions about his son-in-law.

Perhaps Onesimos means well, but his reference to Smikrines' grandson at 1112 is certainly delivered rather suddenly and tactlessly. Nor does he apologize for being so abrupt. In fact, he insults Smikrines:

You were thick[227] too, though you thought you were so clever.

Miller

He rubs Smikrines' ignorance in: 1115 is cruel, implying as it does that Smikrines is to blame for his daughter's predicament, by not taking proper care of a young girl.

Onesimos goes on to recount what happened at the festival and says that Sophrone, as Pamphile's old nurse, can confirm it. He reports that Charisios and Pamphile have recognized one another (1121). This passionate *anagnorismos*, 'recognition' (here another Greek noun ending in '–*mos*', as favoured by Onesimos)[228] must be imagined from one sentence – effective economy on Menander's part. This is the closest Onesimos comes to any expression of personal pleasure on his part, now that his master and mistress are back together.

He continues to insult Smikrines, calling him *moros*, 'stupid' (1124).[229] He threatens to quote a whole speech from Euripides's *Auge* at him.[230] The tragic allusion, like the slave's philosophizing, might appeal on different levels, depending on the extent to which it was realized how closely the plots of the two plays resembled each other.[231] Onesimos's last extant remark, after taunting Smikrines that the old woman got the allusion before he did, is finally to exclaim at the *eutychema*, 'piece of good luck/ good fortune' (1130) that has brought Charisios and Pamphile back together: this is not an 'everyday word'.[232] Onesimos is glad, after all, for his master.[233]

Further reading

The introduction to this chapter draws on work done on the ancient Greek slave trade commissioned by the website 'Civilisations in Contact': see www.cic.ames.cam.ac.uk accessed on 25 June 2018.

Images

Slaves seem to be portrayed in art as smaller than other adults: see further Wrenhaven (2011): at 105ff she comments on the difficulty of distinguishing slaves in art from children. For slaves in the theatre, see further Green and Handley (1995), 66 and 80ff on figurines of slaves taking refuge at an altar, as one does in Menander's *Perinthia*.

Slaves in literature

Wrenhaven (2012) and Alston, Hall and Proffitt (eds) (2011) investigate ancient literature and art as sources for ancient slavery. See especially Proffitt's own essay in the latter, an important study of the slaves in Menander's *Epitrepontes*. The difference between Aristophanes' treatment of slaves and Menander's is explored to some extent in Akrigg and Tordoff's (2013) collection of essays.

Slavery: an introduction

Fisher (2001) is a good, clear introduction to the subject. See Cartledge (2002) for an overview of the scholarship. There is a more general survey of Greek slavery in Cartledge (1993) ch. 6. See also DuBois (2008) on the difficulties for scholars when writing about slavery in the ancient world, given the previous 'idealization' of antiquity in the scholarship (30). For a comprehensive set of essays on all aspects of ancient slavery, see Bradley and Cartledge (2011). See Braund (2011) on the ancient slave trade. For real pirates in certain areas trading in slaves, see Braund (2011), 118.

Slavery as an institution and modern slavery

See further on Equiano: https://www.standrews-chesterton.org/church-history/olaudah-equiano/ (accessed 16 July 2018). Orlando Patterson (1982) conducts a thorough overview of slavery in a variety of places and periods. At 93–4 he discusses paternalism (pointing out that slaves still wanted to run away) and at 339 how élite Romans were realistic about the reality behind their society's ideology. Garnsey (1996), 8, however, discusses the importance of care in comparative observations. Hall, Alston and McConnell (2011) provide an interesting collection of essays on ancient slavery and abolition.

Slave voices

For actual slave voices, but sometimes doctored to suit best the abolitionist cause, see the memoirs of Olaudah Equiano, rev. edn. (2003), originally published in 1789. He features as one of the main characters in the film *Amazing Grace* (2006), directed by Michael Apted. Another example of such a first-hand account as Equiano's is that by Frederick Douglass, originally published in America in 1845 (1986). *Unheard Voices* collected by Malorie Blackman (2007) provides more accounts: Blackman's powerful *Noughts and Crosses* series (2006–) imagines a world in which blacks and whites have their roles reversed, a serious version of comedy's frequent reversal of the roles of masters and slaves.

Barbarians and tragedy

Slaves in tragedy are usually found in minor roles, as confidants, pedagogues and nurses: Garlan (1988), 18. Tragedy is no more a straightforward reflection of society than comedy: Hall (1997), 94. The term 'barbarian' is Greek in origin: Hall investigates this and distinguishes (a fine distinction) the attitude of the Greeks from that of racists, since the idea of biologically determined ethnic inequality was not central to their view. They did, however, believe that their culture was superior and that this legitimized its oppression of others. The barbarian is often portrayed in tragedy as the opposite of the ideal Greek with strange language and negative characteristics, such as being emotional, stupid, cruel, subservient or cowardly: Hall (1991), 1, 17.

Stereotypes and other representations (see also Slave names and stereotypes)

See Weiler (2002), 11ff on *kalokagathia*, 'beauty-goodness', which was a concept associated with the Greek male aristocrats and citizens. In it, the aesthetic and the moral were combined. For example, in the Aristotelian *On Physiognomics* a person's character would be as indicated by his appearance. The ideal served to exclude non-citizens and foreigners and contributed to perceptions and the stereotyping of slaves, as in their portrayal in art as smaller than the freeborn. However, in Ps.Xen. *Ath. Pol.* 1.10 the complaint is made (against the freeborn, says Wrenhaven (2012), 146 with n. 52) that, as regards how they dress, slaves and freeborn, poor citizen men cannot be told apart. For their appearance in comedy, with grotesque masks that may contradict their behaviour, see the Further Reading to chapter 1.

See the introduction to this chapter on the stereotyping of slaves in war as cowardly. They came to be viewed in Rome as the opposite of the 'moral' citizen: McKeown (2007), 119. In tragedy, barbarian slaves could be noisy and talkative. In Aristophanes, slaves can make mistakes in their speech (linked with views of barbarians). Wrenhaven (2012), 25ff gives examples of slaves shouting and mourning excessively, and, more specifically, discusses the Phrygian slave in Euripides' *Orestes*. Slaves' manner of speech can demonstrate their inferiority (29). The Archers in *Lysistrata* are over-eager and incompetent (28). See further Hall (2006), 227ff on the extensively caricatured language of Aristophanes' female Scythian archer-politician in *Lysistrata* and 234–5 on lines 184ff, where the male Assembly is parodied. On literary stereotyping, see Wrenhaven (2012),117ff on gossiping and derogatory images of slaves with 121 on confidants and bold, assertive slaves. However, no wholly disloyal slave is depicted, and slaves in comedy are critical but rarely openly in revolt.

Slave names and stereotypes

MacCary (1969) investigated whether names are related to type; for example, whether Daos in Menander is always clever and Parmenon always faithful (277). He found some common ground for Daos in relation to scheming, but comparisons between *Aspis* and *Epitrepontes*, for instance (282ff), show that a name does not tell the whole story. If 'Daos' signifies 'Phrygian' (Gomme and Sandbach (1973), 290–1), neither Daos in *Epitrepontes* nor his counterpart in *Aspis* is cowardly or effeminate, which Phrygians were apparently expected to be (Gomme and Sandbach (1973), 79 on *Aspis* 206). However, giving a slave a new name related to his or her origin would in real life remind everyone that the slave in question was not Greek.

See also on names Wiles (1991), 169–70, particularly the Syrians as the epitome of greed, a characteristic which is given to Daos rather than Syros in *Epitrepontes* (a reversal of expectation, unless Iversen's negative interpretation of Syros's character (2001) is correct). Perhaps the name directs the audience to expect another dishonest slave, whereas Daos reveals his selfish motives without meaning to do so. Syros's good character would then be a surprise, and the contrast with Daos make the scene more effective drama. 'Parmenon', a slave in *Samia*, possibly denotes a manumitted slave, derived from the Greek *paramone*, 'obligation to continue in service', because still required to continue living with his master until the latter's death.

See further Goldberg (1980), 66 on the importance of the careful characterization in *Epitrepontes*. Ireland (2010), 219 comments on how the more impressive speech brings the scene to a climax, with Daos's preceding speech disguising the need to describe what has happened in chronological order, as a messenger scene would do. Wilamowitz-Moellendorff (1961) on *Epitrepontes* 138 notes that the three slaves (he includes Onesimos but not Habrotonon) are wonderfully different types from one another. He observes that Daos is slow in thought and speech, selfish but not mean, whereas Syros is shrewd and puts the little knowledge he has smugly on display, leaning slightly towards Iversen's more negative interpretation referred to above.

The silver mines at Laurium

The silver mines produced considerable wealth both for Athens and for individual citizens, such as Callias and Nicias. The latter had at one time in the fifth century 1,000 slaves rented out there (Fisher (2001), 47–50). See Xenophon's *Poroi*, 'Ways and Means', 4.15ff. At 4.21 branding is proposed, the custom with other slaves. The mines relied mostly on slave labour. Excavations have revealed many mineshafts and tunnels, together with slave accommodation. Conditions were dangerous and unhealthy. See Fisher's figs. 4 and 5. In modern times, people trying to explore the labyrinths of the mines have been unable to find their way back and have died there.

The Arbitration Scene

A Daos and Syros are also paired in *Georgos*. For a comparison between this scene in Menander and the arbitration in Plautus's *Rudens*, Act IV, 3 and 4, see Scafuro (1997), 154ff, and on the treatment of the baby here see Heap (2002–3), 99ff.

Hurst (1990), 112 notes that Syros implies that he finds himself before an arbitrator who is 'un homme cultivé'. On the *Alope* connection, see Green (1994), 51, who notes how Menander's comedies make frequent reference to tragedy, most often to Euripides, but as part of a discussion which shows that the themes and memorable moments of the tragedies seem to have become 'points of reference' in (people's) lives (56). See further Furley (2009), 152 and Heap (2002–3), 93ff with pl. 5 there, on Euripides' *Telephos* and Aristophanes' parody of it in the *Acharnians*.

Carey & Reid (eds) (1985) refer to arbitration in private cases (4), from which the evidence of slaves was excluded except that extracted under torture (95), but the passage in question there describes a public arbitration (94). The decision of a private arbitrator was final (4 n. 9 and 93–4). According to Todd (1993), 124, successful arbitration may have been common, particularly in small disputes: for private arbitrators see his notes 1–2, with Harrison (1998), v.2, 64–6, MacDowell (1978), 203–6 and Isager and Hansen (1975) 107–8, 127–8.

But, says Todd (1993), 124, 'the most illuminating and best attested example is fictitious': he refers to Menander's Arbitration Scene. Like MacDowell (1978), he avoids the question of whether slaves could really be involved. Harrison (1998), v.1, 167 n. 6 speculates that Syros could take part, because of his special status as a *choris oikon*, 'living apart' (see further the introduction to this chapter), but he is unsure if the audience would be accepting or amused. Furley (2009), 146, on lines 237–38 notes Scafuro's observation (1997), 125 that rulings in private arbitrations in fourth-century Athens were not legally binding. In any case, the fate of a baby is being decided in an informal way. Why, however, does a character like Smikrines agree to help, if a case with slaves is ridiculous in real life? Furley (2009), 147 draws attention to the irony of how Smikrines tries strenuously throughout the play to dissolve his daughter's marriage, but, by his involvement in the arbitration, he causes ultimately the recognitions which save it, by proving as they do the legitimacy of his grandson.

Forms of address

The address 'Father' at *Samia* 520 is rather neutral in tone, as used by Moschion to Demeas. Syros, of course, addressing Smikrines (231, 296, 301), is not using it to a parent: Dickey (1996), 79 identifies it as one of general politeness (perhaps flattery, especially from a slave) to older men, and as used otherwise in Menander only to complete strangers. There may be irony here, as Smikrines is no stranger to the baby, but its grandfather, though there are no addressees who are grandfathers in extant Menander (222). The extension of such addresses to people other than parents has parallels in other languages (81). Sandbach (Gomme and Sandbach (1973), 306) identifies it as an 'ingratiating' address by a slave to an elderly man (although not confined to slaves) and gives supporting references from Menander, but its use at *Epitr.* lines 301–2 seems rather to emphasize the baby's rights as a person. Ireland (2010), 218 and 222 on 296 observes that Syros's attitude is deferential.

Monologue: Onesimos's use of *andres*, 'gentlemen'

There are no stage directions in Menander, which makes the interpretation of monologues difficult. A person can speak thinking he is alone, but be overheard, whether by another character or by the audience, or both, or he can address the audience, whether implicitly or explicitly. Does the use of *andres*, 'gentlemen', contribute anything to how the audience feel about a character?

Sostratos uses *andres* frequently in the *Dyscolus*, at 194 and 666, for instance, and so does Demeas in the *Samia*, though this form of address is not confined to them, as Moschion uses it at *Samia* 683 and Sikon, the cook, at *Dysc.* 659. It is probable that spectators feel close to a character when he addresses them directly, though that does not necessarily mean that they approve of his actions. For example, Iago, the villain in *Othello*, lies (very in character) to the audience. Indirect addresses, or overheard thoughts, are more intimate. The explicit address reminds the audience that it is sitting in a theatre, relating to a stage character; thus the dramatic illusion is suspended, though the break may not always be as clear-cut as Dover (1972), 56 defines it, in relation to Aristophanes, and, by its absence, tragedy; that is, as a 'rupture' of the concentration of the characters in the play on their situation, everything being fictional.

The *Servus Currens*

It is possible that parody of messenger speeches in tragedy gave rise to this comic convention. The *servus currens* is certainly in some respects the counterpart of the messenger of tragedy (Green (1994), 59, with the references in his note). Both the *servus currens* and the more dignified messenger have important plot functions, for example, in conveying information about events offstage to the audience (see further Easterling in an unpublished paper, 'Messages and messengers in Greek tragedy'). If so, the *servus currens* was invoking a different kind of parody from that at *Sikyonios* 176ff, where there is a specific allusion to the speech of the messenger in Euripides *Orestes* and a similar situation: both speeches give an account of a debate before a popular assembly that decides the fate of a man and a woman: Gomme and Sandbach (1973), 650–1.

Anderson finds a *servus currens*, that is a standardized routine of an excited slave running in to bring good or bad news, in Daos at *Aspis* 399ff, for instance: at 410 it is stated that he is actually running: Anderson (1970), 233. Daos in *Aspis* is reporting (falsely) that Chairestratos has fallen ill, and he, the slave, quotes from tragedy, perhaps lending weight to speculations about the possible origins of this comic slave stereotype. At *Dyscolus* 81ff, there is another example of this character, when Pyrrhias reports Knemon's 'madness'. See further on the *servus currens*, Handley's commentary on this play (1992), 143 on line 81, Webster (1970b), 92–3, notes 3 and 4 and Duckworth (1994), 106–7. Sophocles reverses the motif of breathless haste when the guard is unwilling to hurry to bear bad news at *Antigone* 223ff, an example of a comic element in tragedy.

Conclusion

What has this analysis of *Epitrepontes* revealed first about the characterization of women in Menander? Habrotonon has several substantial appearances on stage;[1] she helps to characterize other people in the play by what she says, whilst remaining rather enigmatic herself. Pamphile appears late in the action, having been kept remote by frequent but impersonal references to her by other characters. When she does appear, she speaks at length, showing in the process both her own character and that of her father. Opinions differ, and may change again as more papyrus finds emerge, as to whether she is insolent or merely surprisingly assertive. The text may allow for different interpretations by the actor playing her part, and this may also be true for Habrotonon. Pamphile's character continues to emerge as more fragments of papyri are discovered, as does that of her father, which contributes to revealing hers, demonstrating how indispensable papyrology has been to the study of Menander. The extent to which Smikrines is 'disagreeable, money-grubbing', or just anxious, will affect how justified Pamphile is in her attitude towards him. Smikrines' character, for example, leads him to assume that Habrotonon is 'a gold-digger'.[2]

The comparison and contrast of Pamphile's character and status with Habrotonon's are brought to a climax with their meeting, probably an unusual one, as has been observed, for a freeborn woman and a slave *hetaira*, two women worlds apart. But Habrotonon is about the same age as Pamphile and also at a transitional period of her life,[3] since she has only just become an *hetaira* and Pamphile has only recently become a bride and a mother. When compared with the male characters, Pamphile shows herself more courageous than her husband, Charisios, in facing her father, Smikrines, and more ready to forgive Charisios than he is to forgive her. Habrotonon is also more resourceful than Charisios's slave, Onesimos. The *hetaira* in this story is, despite her greedy stereotype, like a family slave rather than what she is, less concerned with money than the freeborn Smikrines[4] and more compassionate than the freeborn Charisios is towards a victim of rape, his own victim, in fact.[5]

Habrotonon and Pamphile in *Epitrepontes* have major roles to play, in terms of how much they are seen and how much they show of others, and help to advance the plot.[6] Most important to emphasize here is the sense in which they switch roles: at the festival, the freeborn woman, who has a name that means 'loved by all' or 'loving to all',[7] has a rough sexual encounter, while the *hetaira* remains safe with the other women.[8] This constitutes an audacious playing with roles, embellished by Habrotonon's softness towards the baby (maternal instincts?)[9] and suggested affection for her client, Charisios, and by Pamphile's separation from the same man, her husband and the baby, which is hers, early on, followed by her assertiveness towards her father, which contradicts any ideal of the submissive Athenian daughter. What the spectators find behind Menander's masks for these two women is not what they might have expected.

There is subtlety in their portrayal. Habrotonon's character remains, as has been noted, ultimately an enigma. The ambiguity is in the portrayal of an *hetaira* as formerly innocent of men and uninterested in money, and in her affection for the baby.[10] This complicated presentation makes it difficult to agree completely that she gives the audience the main feminine perspective in the play,[11] although some aspects of her portrayal might have appealed particularly to women.[12] Details of her characterization might initially suggest to some a tendency to be rather concerned with money, and it might be assumed that her being a sex slave of some kind would make it unnatural for her to be completely altruistic.[13] Unnatural or unexpected?

Habrotonon's character is interesting, and, though revealed relatively little through what either she or other people say, intriguing – reserved, but warm. Habrotonon is an unusual *hetaira*, given her wistful references to her lost virginity, and no apparent jealousy of Pamphile's wealth and free status. She is used to explore issues such as rape in a comedy that is prepared to disturb.[14] This is another important point. The term 'comedy' can cover several different kinds of play, and it appears that, as Aristophanes can explore various serious political issues under the cover of fantasy or farce, so apparently trivial plays such as Menander's turn out to be anything but.

The setting of *Epitrepontes* prior to the main action, the festival of the Tauropolia, appears to have been very carefully chosen as the background to Pamphile's rape, and a knowledge of it and other questions of historical context turn out to be crucial for an understanding of the play. An important festival of that name did take place at the deme Halai Araphenides, and must be the one mentioned in Eur. *IT* 1450ff.[15] Artemis was a goddess of childbirth, a goddess whose evocation in *Epitrepontes* is appropriate, since a child has been born because of a rape.

The passage in Euripides refers to clothes dedicated to this goddess, ones which belonged to wives who had died in the pangs of childbirth, a reminder of part of what Pamphile has been through. The relationship of the Tauropolia to the Brauronia Artemis and the worship of Artemis Mounychia has been noted;[16] the *chthonic*[17] character of these cults is what one would anticipate in encountering rituals where girls' initiation into the marriageable estate and parturition aspects feature prominently. Virginity for the Greeks can be seen as, rather than a lack of sexuality, a precondition of fertility.[18] This association would suit the themes in *Epitrepontes* of virginity and motherhood, explored through two women with apparently very different positions in life. However, Menander's *Epitrepontes* is also one of the main sources of information about the festival, a key instance of the problems which have been examined in studying the social background to the plays.

Nevertheless, to pursue an investigation of the relevance of this particular festival, the bull was in every sense a symbol of male potency, and the Greek word *tauros* was used to designate a part of the male organs, behind the testicles. Moreover, Tauropolos could be the goddess who controls erections.[19] Charisios's passions and the fact that he was capable of raping a young woman are thus underlined, as well as power as a theme to be explored in the play: the extreme power of Charisios over Pamphile may be added to that possessed by her father Smikrines in what was ultimately a patriarchal society.

The playwright uses a considerable amount of irony in his treatment of Habrotonon and Pamphile, but not 'bemused detachment'.[20] *Epitrepontes* is, on the contrary, thought-provoking in its portrayal of the women characters, and the audience are, as has been noted, invited to reconsider preconceived ideas about roles and status.[21] For example, Pamphile's emotional power over her husband and her father is explored. And must Menander only be innovating when he shows that an *hetaira* can be nicer than she seems?[22] Would that not be very tame for what has been judged by some to be amongst the best of ancient drama, drama influenced by Euripides?[23] The established stereotypes of Middle Comedy, such as the greedy *hetaira*, or of Menander's own society, such as the innocent young wife, do not restrict Menander but are exploited and overturned.

This questioning of society's norms may be taken further. Konstan asserts that *Epitrepontes* 'centers on the conditions for relations between the genders … on the unequal expectations that constitute the social differences between the sexes'. However, in Charisios's lament at 908ff, attributed by Konstan to his discovering that he has fathered a *nothos*, he finds that the 'perception of the identity between male and female responsibility in the bearing of a *nothos* poses a utopian challenge to both the status and gender codes of the city-state'.[24]

Heap notes that the 'apparent feminism (in Charisios's speech) creates a problem'. Omitowoju, like Konstan, cannot easily account for Charisios's shame. Moreover, she argues away Habrotonon's sympathy for Pamphile in the description of the rape by the *hetaira*, since it does not fit the tendency to be rather unconcerned about female consent which she asserts exists in Menander as well as the orators. James instead calls Menander's treatment of rape 'impossibly sentimental … but remarkably realistic … a partial recognition of the female experience'.[25] Lape also believes that, by calling what happened to Pamphile an *atychema* or 'misfortune', Charisios is 'tacitly acknowledging his own mistake in condemning her'.[26] Furley concludes that it is 'interesting' that the argument 'assumes equal rights for wife and husband'.[27]

Slaves can play major roles in Menander in terms of time on stage. The memorable Arbitration Scene, featuring the dispute between the two slaves Daos and Syros, a shepherd and a charcoal-burner, in which the baby is in danger of being condemned to a life of slavery, dominates the play. However, other slaves, Onesimos and, as has been seen, Habrotonon, speak at some length throughout (Onesimos is given extensive monologues), whereas Daos and Syros disappear from the action. Habrotonon is a woman, but also a slave. This makes her perhaps the most interesting character and, in terms of her scheme, which reunites Charisios and Pamphile, the heroine of the play and, as suggested in the introduction, also of this book.

The two slaves involved in the arbitration are sharply distinguished from each other, Daos being selfish, but Syros being concerned on behalf of the baby.[28] The scene illuminates another character: it shows that Smikrines has a good side to him, as he makes the rather mercenary Daos give up the baby and its posessions. In addition, the audience is prepared for the more extensive characterization of Onesimos and Habrotonon, and the more difficult assessment of his personality and her motives.

Onesimos, a male family slave, and Habrotonon, a girl apparently for hire from a pimp (according to Smikrines at 136), deliver monologues about their situation which generate special audience interest. Much is made in the play of the fact that Onesimos, despite the meaning of his name, 'useful'/'helpful', does not participate much in the action, after his initial 'tale-telling', or scheme to gain advantage from recognizing his master's lost ring. A contrast can be made with the female slave Habrotonon and her plan to sort things out, though this does not seem to be in order to gain anything except, perhaps, her freedom. Expectations of the stereotypical scheming slave and of women too are overturned. However, Menander introduces all these slaves for their own sakes too, that is, as engaging characters. Thus they are not just the 'other'.[29]

It is striking that Daos and Syros are not shown, in what is extant, on stage with their masters. Daos's work as a shepherd would have taken him onto the hills on his own, and Syros, whilst he has a master, Chairestratos, who does appear in the action, is a slave 'living apart' with a different kind of independence from Daos's. Habrotonon has a pimp, but he does not, again in what is extant, appear on stage, although he could have done.[30] Onesimos eavesdrops on his master, Charisios, rather than being shown in friendly dialogue with him.

These master–slave relationships, or lack of them, contrast with the various portrayals of slave and master in other plays, such as *Aspis*, with Daos's heartfelt address to the absent Kleostratos, and *Misoumenos* with its opening dialogue between Getas and Thrasonides. For a different, initially at least more ambiguous, 'partnership', see the soldier's slave, Sosias, and his emotional master, Polemon, in Menander's *Perikeiromene*, together with the feckless Moschion's uneasy intimacy with his slave Daos. As an example of mistress and slave, there is Glykera's reliance on her maid in the same play. Demeas and Moschion interact with Parmenon in *Samia* as desperate older, and clueless younger, master respectively.

Often a slave, by scheming on his master's behalf will show himself to be more clever than the person that owns him. By being cheeky, he shows himself to be insubordinate, thereby threatening the *status quo*. There is a reversal of roles here that is allowed for the duration of the comedy. However, in *Epitrepontes*, a temporary sense of some autonomy is also achieved for the slaves by the absence of their masters from the stage and a distancing of them from those in power over them that opens up the opportunity for their 'voice' about their situations to be heard.[31]

Aristophanes' and Plautus's plays often elicit a laugh, Menander and Terence sometimes more of a wry smile. How is their work to be interpreted when there are slaves involved?[32] For some the voices of slaves on the comic stage can never be more than the 'hollow ventriloquism' of their owners. *Epitrepontes* is in one sense the product of a slave society and written by a member of the élite,[33] but a sympathetic attitude is encouraged towards slaves as fellow human-beings, so that they are given a kind of voice, one more sophisticated than that given to Xanthias in Aristophanes' *Frogs*.[34] Some have found a similar interest in slaves in Euripides to that argued for here in Menander.[35]

Scholars have been puzzled, however, by the difference in the portrayal of slaves between Aristophanes and Menander.[36] Menander's plays, whilst reflecting his society's ideology, present a glimpse of 'real' slave feelings, albeit a literary one, and so may indeed, in Fitzgerald's words,[37] expose the gaps in the surviving evidence because they preserve a kind of slave 'voice', to join the other 'voices' in the plays belonging to Menander's free citizen men, women and soldiers.

But is such a sympathetic portrayal compatible with support for slavery as an institution? Although Konstan concerns himself mainly with Pamphile and Charisios rather than the slaves, he is interested in how aspirations may be projected and transcend the ideological constraints of a given society. Konstan goes on to find in the plays a suggestion that people divided by status share a common nature.[38]

In Lape too the focus is mainly on gender, but in her conclusion she notes that the distinction between free persons and slaves can be 'upset' (she mentions Habrotonon in this context). She sees Pamphile as granted a 'kind of backhanded decisional autonomy' when she defends her marriage and recognizes 'inclusionary and egalitarian' elements which she seems willing to extend to the slave characters. She refers to historical examples. In 403/2, after the expulsion of the Thirty and restoration of the democracy, it was proposed that slaves who had fought in the democratic cause be enfranchised. After the battle of Chaeronea in 338 BCE the orator Hyperides proposed that the slaves be freed and the metics enfranchised (freed slaves had the status of metics): 'an extremely radical and innovative measure'. Neither proposal was successful, however.[39]

Proffitt goes further and draws comparisons with interpretations of, for example, Shakespeare, where Shakespeare seems to use subtle irony to allow for another point of view, whilst clear that a different world may be unattainable.[40] But others believe that social norms are affirmed by Menander's plays in the narrative outcome.[41]

Perhaps what the spectator or reader of Menander's plays (who may have been a woman or a slave) was really left with was just a deliberate question mark, like that left over Habrotonon's character, a question mark which hangs this time over the spectator's/reader's assumptions and those of his or her society.[42] What can safely be said is that Menander's slaves are interesting in their own right. The surviving texts portray slave characters who are bold or fearful, loyal, indifferent to, or estranged from, their masters. More than one slave is found in a play. Some have major parts, but this may be more in terms of monologues and participation in lively dialogue than because they actively shape the plot. Such parts would, however, despite their low status as characters, offer considerable opportunities to accomplished actors. Slaves are prominent in other ancient comedy, in Aristophanes, Plautus and Terence, and Menander's slaves should take their place with these.[43] The surviving evidence from Menander definitely suggests, however, that Plautus, whilst also following models in Aristophanes, developed and exaggerated the role of the slave.[44]

The freeborn Smikrines, who unwittingly has had the power, as arbitrator for the slaves Daos and Syros in Act II, to consign his own grandson to slavery, later has to argue with his own freeborn daughter, who does not wish him to be her 'master'. The young master, Charisios, has his life sorted out by slaves, and feels towards the end of the play as if he has to defer to some *daimonion* or superhuman 'power'. Everyone in *Epitrepontes* is in the power of someone or something, some emotion, for example, even the supposedly free. Slavery and power over others are major themes in the play.

The power of freeborn men over slaves, male and female, but also a slaves's power to influence or manipulate, part of the comic reversal of master and slave, is presented, through Pamphile and Habrotonon, alongside an alternative view of the conventional one of women as submissive. Menander's women in *Epitrepontes* may be based on stereotypes, comic or real, but they are not typical. This survey has shown that, as with those of the slaves, some knowledge of women's positions in the real society of the period in addition to an awareness of the characters' literary history can illuminate the texts and lead to surprising conclusions about their representation. Subtle characterization, in which two stock types, the greedy *hetaira* and the innocent freeborn girl, are actually gently reversed in a mirror effect, leaves a lasting impression that there may be more to people than prejudice or preconceived attitudes might suppose.

Behind the mask, or rather masks, of the characters are, in some sense, the people of Menander's period as well as the stereotypes of the comedy which inspired him. But with the help of what is independently known about Menander's society and its norms, it is possible to see where these characters deviate from those norms, contrary to preconceived expectation and prejudice, an answer to Bain's problem of contradiction between appearance and character.[45] This is achieved without the comfort, for those who prefer the *status quo* to be justified, as far as is known, of a conventional, unquestioned happy ending,[46] and despite the only apparently repetitive themes of love and status, as each of Menander's plays has its own story to tell.

Society may not change, but the audience has been invited to see a little deeper into the lives of those who are, for instance, oppressed by the power of other people, or by their emotions or their consciences. All this is done in a largely humorous context, in contrast with the ultimately tragic treatment of similar themes in Euripides. Spectators are left thoughtful rather than ultimately disturbed by what is, in effect, a kind of 'comitragedy',[47] so that at the end of the play or day, they are still, in this 'serious' comedy, and despite the intrusion of darker elements, entertained by characters who are memorably larger than life.

Glossary

agonothetes official who, from the fourth century BCE, was appointed to organize the festivals.

archon religious and judicial magistrate at Athens.

chiton tunic worn by men and women.

chlamys cloak worn by soldiers and messengers.

chthonic of the earth, the underworld.

codex ancient precursor of the modern bookform.

ephebe young man of 18–20 years undergoing military training in ancient Greece.

gynaion 'little woman', expressing endearment or, more often, contempt.

hetaira from the Greek for 'female companion': a kind of courtesan (no translation is exact) who could be independent, cultured and educated but might receive gifts or money and might or might not have sex with her clients. Should be distinguished from *porne*. A professional girlfriend.

hybris insulting and dishonouring behaviour on purpose. The Athenian law against it protected male citizens, women and children, but also slaves.

koine the 'common' form of Greek dialect spoken in Hellenistic or Roman times.

mechane crane used to simulate a character flying.

metic a foreigner in Athens.

Middle Comedy refers to the period *c.* 404–321 BCE (around the time of Alexander's death).

mina a Greek coin worth 70, later 100, drachmas.

New Comedy has been used to describe plays written from the last quarter of the fourth century BCE to the middle of the third century BCE, which includes those by Menander.

Old Comedy has been applied to the comedies of the fifth century BCE.

orchestra literally, 'dancing place', from *orcheisthai*, 'to dance'. The *orchestra* was the main space used for performing in a Greek theatre. It could be in the shape of part of an open circle, rectangular or trapezoidal.

palimpsest manuscript or piece of writing material on which later writing has been superimposed on effaced earlier writing ('again' and 'rubbed out').

pallake difficult to define: (female) partner, rather than wife, who may formerly have been a *hetaira*.

papyrus a writing material made from crushing together fibres of the papyrus plant.

paraskenion projecting wing of theatre building.

parodos or *eisodos* side-entrance to the theatre through which the audience and later the chorus entered.

phallus representation of a penis.

phlyax, a kind of farce that probably developed from phallic songs, was thought to command the stage still in South Italy and Sicily at the same period as Menander's plays, but most of the vase-paintings interpreted as depicting these plays in fact show Old Comedy still being performed outside Athens: see Taplin (1993), 38ff, 89ff and ch. 9.

porne common prostitute.

proskenion colonnaded porch, in front of the *skene*, from whose roof the actors performed.

skene the wooden structure at the back of the *orchestra* that provided a backdrop for the action and a central doorway and later two side-doorways through which actors could appear.

skenographia scene-painting.

theatron theatre building or audience.

theologeion literally 'the talking place for the gods', most probably the flat roof of the *proskenion*.

Notes

Introduction

1 Easterling (1995).
2 See the frontispiece to this book for a photograph of the third-century CE papyrus that preserves it.
3 See ch. 3 on Aristophanes and Middle Comedy, which explains problems with the use of this term for comedy from the period just before Menander was writing. It is hoped that the *Misoumenos* speech referred to here will receive a fuller treatment in a future study of the soldier character, partly as a variation on the serenade motif. For recent relevant papyri which carry verses from the monologue, see Bathrellou (2014b), 809.
4 The ancient precursor of the modern book form. See below.
5 Gallo (1986), 54. For more on the discovery of Menander, see Handley (2002 and 2011), Arnott's account in his Loeb introduction to Menander v.1 (1997 with corr.), xxviff, and Sandbach's in Gomme and Sandbach (1973), 2ff. On von Tischendorf, see further Soskice (2010), chs. 11 and 13. Von Tischendorf also discovered the fourth-century CE Codex Sinaiticus of the Christian Bible with Old and New Testaments.
6 A Greek book (*biblion* or *biblos*) took the form of a roll or (later) *codex* of *papyrus*.
7 On Egypt and the Greeks, see Bowman (2002), 197.
8 See further Parsons (2007 with plates), 11 and 14ff, Gallo (1986) and Turner (1980), chs. 2 and 3.
9 Literary papyri, including Menander, have also been discovered at Antinoopolis, founded by the emperor Hadrian and named after his beloved: Bowman (2002), 198ff with his n. 18.
10 See Handley (1990) on the contribution of these finds to scholarship on Menander.
11 For negative reactions to the literary merit of the new find on the part of some scholars, such as P. W. Harsh, see Scafuro's account in her Introduction to Fontaine and Scafuro (eds) (2014), 15.
12 See Plautus (1986) lines 494ff; Handley (1968); and below.
13 For continuing finds, see the journal *Zeitschrift für Papyrologie und Epigraphik (ZPE)*.
14 See Lowe (2008), preface. This Menander (there is also some *Dyscolus*) had been reused for a ninth-century text in Syriac. Compare the fragment found on Sinai: Wilson (2014a), 428. The discovery of the Archimedes palimpsest, for which see below, proved that there was a Byzantine manuscript tradition for Hyperides: Edwards (2015), 82. Some hitherto lost speeches emerged by this orator, a contemporary of Alexander the Great and ranked second only to Demosthenes. On the "music" in P Oxy. 3705, see Bathrellou (2014b), 807–8 (no. 76 in her table) with references and Huys (1993), together with Sandbach's comments (Gomme and Sandbach, 1973, 519ff). On the Vatican fragment, Vat. Sir. 623, see also Arnott (2004a), 53, n. 23 and Blanchard (2014), 248. For relevant websites and databases, see Bathrellou (2014b), 804.
15 Segal (1987).

16 Green (1990), 67: 'precise ancient equivalents of modern situation comedies or soap operas'. Parsons (2015), 27 refers to Menander as 'the father of sitcom'.
17 See, for example, Rosivach (1998), 1ff.
18 Konstan (1995).

1 The Treasure on the Rock: Menander and the Masks and Figurines from Lipari

1 See Heubeck and Hoekstra (1990), 43. Hraesvelg, the Scandinavian storm-giant, shook the winds out of his bag. (See Dawe in Homer (1993), 392.)
2 The earliest offerings in the pit have been dated to the sixth century BCE. On its cover was a small bronze lion: Cavalier (1991), 34. Aiolos was worshipped on Lipari in Hellenistic times too: Diod. Sic. 20.101.2–3.
3 Diod. Sic. 5.7.1 and Strabo 6.2.10; Thuc. 3.88.1–4.
4 Wilson (1996), 18.
5 The squint is 'credible', according to Arnott, *Menander* v.1 (1997 with corr.), xix: *Suda* biography (Test. 1). For the portraits of Menander, see Richter (1984), 159ff with plate 121. For the Mytilene mosaics, see Charitonidis and others (eds) (1970). For the bronze, see the Getty Museum handbook (2010), 177 with Walton & Arnott (1996), pl. 2, and for the statue see ch. 2 here.
6 Zanker (1995), 78. Fig. 45 shows a reconstruction 'imaginatively realized' from various copies by K. Fittschen with the help of plaster casts (Göttingen University, Archäeologisches Institut). Zanker cites Fittschen (1991) for the relevant evidence and a complete list of copies used. Zanker warns that it does not give 'the complete picture', as it cannot take account of every existing copy at once.
7 See Richter (1965), v.2, 225, citing Pausanias's *Description of Greece* 1.21.1.
8 Richter (1965), v.2, 225: it was embedded in a wall behind the stage. A marble base was discovered near the theatre of Eretria on Euboea, inscribed with Menander's name, of the kind which indicates that there was a second statue erected around this time.
9 Richter (1984), 17–18 and (1965), v.2, 235.
10 See Green and Seeberg MNC³, 56.
11 See further Heap (1994).
12 The following account is derived from Geddes-Brown (1988). For more on Stevenson, see her husband's book, Stevenson (2009).
13 Trendall (1969), 1.
14 Two years later, the Cairo codex of Menander was found (see the Introduction here). For the dramatic terracottas in the Stevenson collection, see Webster (1969), 6–7 and 28.
15 *ANT* (1999), 255–6 carries an obituary by Sebastian Tusa: he calls Brea 'a sort of sacred icon of world archaeology', relating how he refused a comfortable university chair to remain on his digs.
16 The literary period to which they belong has been termed by scholars 'New Comedy'. See ch. 3. The Lipari figurines show action and movement in a way figurines from the period immediately before, 'Middle Comedy', do not. See MNC³, 55 and *passim* for other similar artefacts with Bain's review in CR N.S. 48 (1998), 547–8.
17 See further Green and Seeberg MNC³, 56.
18 Webster (1969), 6–7. They are very similar. The important Athenian series of figurines called the Loeb Group were exported to and copied in many different places (see

MNC³, 55 and further Green (1994), 34ff: plate 2.13 there depicts the New York Group, a Middle Comedy set, more static in appearance and manufactured solid (my thanks to Richard Green for pointing this out). See the Glossary and Introduction.

19 A small number of New Comedy masks have been found in a necropolis on Stromboli, another of the Aeolian islands. See Brea (2001), 274.

20 See the index to Trendall and Webster (1971). Given the date of the terracottas, any seating and stage structure that existed belonging to a theatre may have been constructed out of wood. The Spanish fortifications of the sixteenth century would have destroyed any stone remains, if the theatre was built up against the slopes of the acropolis, as it was at Athens. See Brea (2001), 277.

21 Webster (1969), 7. See also Green (1994), 34–8 and Harvey and Wilkins (eds) (2000), ix–x under List of Illustrations.

22 *MNC³*, 53; Green (1994), 69, 107.

23 *MNC³*, 54. For a pie chart giving geographical distribution, see *MNC³*, 55; see also Green (1994), 109 for a bar chart, with 34ff on the introduction of the figurines in the later fifth century.

24 *MNC³*, 53–8, 85–6.

25 Green (1994), 109–11, 115, 137, 139 and 141. See also *MNC³*, 53–8.

26 Green (1994), 38. See above on the New York and Loeb Groups.

27 Brea (2001), 274: they are found associated there with the polychrome pottery of the Lipari painter and his successors and with small portrait masks of famous men, many of Menander himself.

28 By contrast, Dionysus appears on stage in Aristophanes's *Frogs*. Gods do deliver prologues in Menander, however. See ch. 2 with Further Reading there for the continuation of fifth-century rituals in the Theatre of Dionysus in Menander's time. See Green (1994), 117, with reference to fourth-century vase-painting, on Eros and Dionysus appearing together with a mask, masks becoming symbolic of parties and good times. 'Romantic' love is a key theme of Menander's plays.

29 See Brown (1984), 110 citing Holloway (1967), 403 for suggested tombs of actors.

30 *MNC³*, 3. For attempts to recover the masks of the actual performances, see Williams (2004), 417 and Wiles (1991).

31 Green and Seeberg in *MNC³*, 7. See also Calame (1986), 128.

32 Green (1994), 120, *MNC³*, 56 and Brea (2001), 275: the hair is sculpted, but would have been a wig. Nearly all have a little hole at the top, as would their originals, to hang the mask up and store it.

33 The 'Hellenistic Age' is a term conventionally used of the period between the death of Alexander the Great in 323 BCE and the Battle of Actium in 31 BCE, when the Roman Empire of Augustus and his successors was beginning to emerge.

34 See further Pickard-Cambridge (1988), 177–9. See also on the sources Csapo & Slater (1994), Appendix A, 393–402, which provides a translation. For comparing Pollux with the archaeological evidence, see Green and Seeberg *MNC³*, 6ff. Green (1994), 153–4 believes Pollux's work derives from a source which knew and described the masks and costume of the transition from Middle to New Comedy.

35 Wiles (1991), 69.

36 Brea (1981), 15.

37 Masks for comic actors during the fifth century were not very stereotyped and there was a strong tradition of special masks caricaturing individuals, Socrates in the *Clouds* being one example (Green (1994), 80). Standardized masks and costumes then start to appear, the artificial appearance more marked as time went on (Green (1994), 132).

38 See further Heap (1998b), 32–3.
39 Wiles (1991), 80 and Brown (1984), 112.
40 See Williams (2004), 422: he argues that the plays are written with an awareness of the perceptual issues involved. The prologue speakers, a special case, are represented in the Lipari finds only by Pan. Pollux mentions only tragic personifications, not comic, such as Tyche in Menander's *Aspis*. The Baby probably did not have a mask (see Heap (2002–3), 113.
41 See, for their importance, Further Reading on the "Masks for Menander" project carried out by the University of Glasgow and Brown (1984), 109 with *MNC*³ (1995), 56. Bain (1998), 547–8 sadly found the archaeology a distraction from literary criticism, but was forced to point out that 'the verbal subtlety and visual grotesqueness in New Comedy need explanation'. This book aims, in part, to answer his question.
42 As observed by Brown (1984), 109.
43 Wiles (1991) *passim*.
44 The Greek word for 'mask', *prosopon*, also came to mean 'character' in later Greek; the Latin *persona* is a borrowing from it via Etruscan. This draws attention to the link between the theatrical prop and the personality portrayed.

2 All the World's a Stage: Menander in Performance

1 For Menander's and Philemon's victories, see Pickard-Cambridge (1988), 119 and 278 with n. 2 respectively; he cites Quintilian x.i.72. Philemon was not, allegedly, above cheating: *ambitus*, *gratia* and *factiones* ('intrigue', 'favour' and 'partisanship'), according to Aulus Gellius *N.A.* 17.4.
2 For a survey of all the material, see *MNC*³, usefully reviewed by Csapo (1997). The individual plays are *Achaioi* (Bulgaria, at Ulpia Oescus), *Perikeiromene* and *Sikyonioi* (Ephesus) and *Theophoroumene* and *Synaristosai* (Pompeii).
3 See Charitonidis et al. (1970), especially 12 and 90, Berczelly (1988), 122 n. 25, 123 with notes 25 and 34, 124 and Ling (1998), 29 and 31 with Ling (1991), 219. See also Goldberg (2007), 130–1.
4 Green & Handley (1995), 72.
5 See, for example, Taplin's arguments (1999), 44ff on non-Athenian elements in tragedy and below on theatres in the Greek world.
6 See Winnington-Ingram (1989), 29 and Webster (1970a), 97.
7 Handley (1989), 115.
8 Pickard-Cambridge (1988), 99 and Wilson (2000), 23.
9 Handley (1992), 5.
10 See Cole (1993), 28 with n. 18, 25, 29 with n. 30: 'traditional elements survived and did not lose their own particular meaning' (34).
11 Goldhill (1990),105–6, Chaniotis (2007), 55–6, 65 and Cole (1993), n. 24.
12 See Graf (2007) for a discussion of ritual and drama; he notes (64), that comedy's gods are not randomly chosen; for example, Pan is the god of Knemon's countryside in the *Dyscolus*.
13 Csapo & Slater (1994), 103 warn against overestimating the religious context of drama. Frederiksen (2002), 81ff notes that Athens was unusual in having separate buildings for political meetings. Theatres elsewhere could be multi-functional.
14 This was the funding of a chorus by a rich citizen, a *leitourgia* or 'public service', one of about a hundred each year.

15 See Wilson (2000), Appendix 4: 'The date of the reform of the *choregia*'. See also Pickard-Cambridge (1988), 91ff and Rehm (2007), 189ff. On the theoric fund, another important change, see below.

16 Goette (2007b), 149.

17 See Wilson (2000), 273 with Pickard-Cambridge (1988), 86ff and Rehm (2007), 191. The role of the chorus in comedy had changed by this time, but Wilson finds that the *agonothetes* continued to spend lavishly, though less competitively (270), with evidence for plenty of choral activity (4–5). On the *choregia*, see further Wilson (2000).

18 Arnott (1997 with corr.), xv-xvi.

19 Meritt's view (1938), 116ff, no. 22, fragment A, 251/50 BCE line 10, based on a single inscription from the Athenian agora; Test. 29–31. Pickard-Cambridge (1988) 41 n. 11 (revised by Gould and Lewis) points out that the evidence is uncertain for 255/54 BCE at the Lenaea, however.

20 See Arnott (1997 with corr.), xx.

21 See Camp (2001), 145 with Pickard-Cambridge (1946).

22 See Glossary with Dugdale (2008), 47 and Simon (1988), 2. On the *skene*, see below. Compare and contrast, for example, Shakespeare's Globe Theatre in London, a polygonal structure with a three-tiered gallery surrounding an open yard, or some of today's modern Western theatres.

23 Pausanias' *Description of Greece*, II.27.5. See fig. 2.2.

24 Dugdale (2008), 54: the theatre is based on the cubit derived from the human lower arm and the precise mathematical proportions of the human body carried religious significance.

25 Dugdale (2008), 54–5. Compare the Theatre of Dionysus at Athens: Pickard-Cambridge (1988), 263.

26 For example, Argos, Corinth, Cyrene, Miletos, Syracuse and all the larger and well-known *poleis* (cities). See Frederiksen (2002), 65ff, however, on how a nuanced view is needed and a study of all localities. Some which were visible and are described in travellers' accounts have now disappeared (66). Many continue to be uncovered (69). See further the tables in the Appendices and Levi (1984) 148–9 for a map with descriptions.

27 Frederiksen (2002), 69 and Green & Handley (1995), 58. 'Every Greek city with any cultural pretensions had one by the mid third century' (Taplin (1993), 3). The demes, for example Thorikos, and cities outside Attica had before this imitated the City Dionysia, building their own modest theatres: Csapo (2007), 100 and Frederiksen (2002), 79–80.

28 Linked by Camp (2001), 145 to the chorus in comedy becoming diminished in size and role, but see Rothwell (1995) and Wilson (2000), 4–5 for evidence on how the chorus continued to flourish, albeit in a different form. Round orchestras may be a late development: Thorikosis is earlier than Athens and rectilinear (146). Csapo (2007), 106 suggests that it would be difficult to shape wooden seating to fit a circular plan, a case of 'simple, practical economics'.

29 On ancient theatre design, see Vitruvius *De Architectura* 5.3, although he is vague about what he means by 'a Greek theatre' (McDonald & Walton (2007), 6). See Green & Handley (1995), 58 for the theory that acoustics are improved for large audiences by a circular orchestra backed by high-reaching stone seating.

30 Simon (1988), 4. Dugdale (2008), 52: a low stage may have been used by the actors in Menander's time. See also Camp (2001), 146.

31 Webster (1970a), 1. See Csapo & Slater (1994), 105 and Cole (1993), 27.

32 On how various practices were the same at festivals in honour of Dionysus around the Greek world, see Cole (1993), especially 31.

33 Dugdale (2008), 51–2, 140 and Simon (1988), 5.
34 See Pickard-Cambridge (1988), 52 and 189. Construction began before Lycurgus, in fact: Csapo (2007), 112, 114. The theatre was possibly completed in about 340 BCE (Goette (2007: 116) prefers 329 BCE).
35 Pickard-Cambridge (1946), 141ff.
36 Pickard-Cambridge (1988), 263. Film acting requires the opposite, as described by Michael Caine in a televised workshop on acting in movies in which close-ups of the actors' face influence their methods of acting.
37 Pickard-Cambridge (1988), 263 and Green & Handley (1995), 35.
38 Frederiksen (2002), 88 n. 119.
39 Csapo & Slater (1994), 287. The fund was instituted by Perikles, according to Plutarch *Per.* 9.2–3, to help the poor pay their entrance-fee and obtain seats, for which there was fierce competition. Most historians doubt, in fact, that there was a *theorikon* before the latter half of the fourth century: Csapo (2007), 103 finds that it is directly attested only after 343 BCE. Roselli (2011), 96 and 17 thinks that later developments may have generated revenue for the state from ticket sales and made the audience 'more ideologically homogenous'. Theatres and opera houses today struggle to fund performances as well as making tickets affordable for everyone.
40 See Gerö and Johnsson (2001) on Old Comedy and for a review of the debate. If they saw tragedy, they also saw satyr-play (87). See also O'Higgins (2003), who concludes that, although there were most likely women present, the evidence is ambiguous, suggesting 'an ambiguous situation' (137). Women were present in Shakespeare's audience, but female parts were also all acted by men: Bate (2007), 31.
41 Sourvinou-Inwood (2003), 184 finds the passage 'meaningless' if there were no women there and Csapo and Slater (1995), 291 agree.
42 See Pickard-Cambridge (1988), 265ff.
43 See ch. 4.
44 See Gerö and Johnsson (2001), 87 with n. 1.
45 Goldhill (1994), 347. See further Goldhill (1997).
46 See Henderson (1991), especially 133–4, 144, 146–7, Csapo & Slater (1994), 286ff and Podlecki (1990).
47 Goldhill (1994), 362 on fragment 1 of the Greek play. See the opening scene of Plautus's *Cistellaria*, which is based on Menander's *Synaristosai*: Arnott (2000), 327–8.
48 See further on audience address, Csapo & Slater (1994), 287ff, who argue that such formulae are only evidence that women are conceptually invisible. Handley in his commentary (1992), 304 suggests that it was not the done thing to appeal to the women for applause, and Pickard-Cambridge (1988), 264 wonders if 'no lady' would clap.
49 Taplin (1993), 112. Pickard-Cambridge (1988), 269 lists references that may show women seated separately from men, courtesans seated separately from other women and foreign women seated in particular places.
50 See again Plato *Gorgias* 502b–d on rhetoric used in theatres and Theophrastus *Characters* 9.5; see Pickard-Cambridge (1988), 265, where the Gorgias reference is noted as explicitly about theatrical performance, not reading. The Theophrastus character who takes his paedagogue to the theatre with someone else's money is the 'Shameless Man'. See also Csapo & Slater (1994), 286. It is known from the prologue to Plautus's *Poenulus* that they were certainly present at Roman festivals:

'Let no slaves crowd in, but leave room here for free men
or else pay cash for manumission' (lines 23–4)

(The prologue also tells us the play was adapted from the Greek *Karchedonios*; plays of this name by both Menander and Alexis are known: see Gomme and Sandbach (1973), 7, which argues for Alexis.) Only citizens and metics were present at the Lenaea. For more on audiences, see Roselli (2011), 3 on how they were, and are, neither a 'mass' nor individuals, but groups, that is, social and cultural categories, such as metics, foreigners with special privileges.

51 The role of the chorus changed over time, but it is not certain how. See ch. 3.
52 Facilitated by the use of masks. See Sommerstein (2002), 12–14, Gomme and Sandbach (1973), 14ff and below.
53 Pickard-Cambridge (1946), 54–5 and Simon (1982), 5ff. For the later *paraskenion* (side wing) see Glossary and below. For the *mechane* in drama and in Aristotle, see Dugdale (2008), 70ff.
54 See Csapo & Slater (1994), IV 77A (268ff).
55 Gomme and Sandbach (1973), 20ff with n. 3 for references.
56 Pickard-Cambridge (1946), 54–5. See further Wiles (2000), 119–20. Pickard-Cambridge's comments in this context in his Appendix (172ff) and his discussion of Menander and Philemon's 'allegorical personages' predate the discovery of the *Dyscolus* and Pan's appearance, but at 54–5 with n. 1 he gives analogies for Euripides' divine prologues being performed on the same level as the human characters, as opposed to the divine appearances at the end of a play. The latter are not found in extant Menander. On whether Pan's presence was retained as a statue on stage, see Gomme and Sandbach (1973), 134: statues were often used as 'stage furniture'.
57 See Miles (2014), 75 for the scholiast on Plato to whom this quotation is owed.
58 Miles (2014), 79 and 86.
59 Webster (1970a), 9 argues for the wheeled platform. Padel (1990), 360 n. 92, thinks with Taplin that one was used to reveal interior scenes in tragedy and that this is parodied in the passages in Aristophanes, but admits that the evidence is inconclusive.
60 See Csapo & Slater (1994), IV 78A (270ff).
61 As was done respectively in a student production in 2016 at University College London and several years ago in a production directed by Russell Shone. For the *ekkyklema*, see Dugdale (2008), 67ff with Handley in his commentary on *Dyscolus* (1992), 263 for Aristophanes's parody involving Euripides's appearance in this context at *Ach.* 407ff and *Thesmo.* 95ff (Agathon's, with his exit at 265). Pickard-Cambridge (1988), 100–3 with the index) favoured either finding a simpler way to stage scenes in which its use has been suggested, or a simple wheelchair or couch.
62 See fig. 2.2.
63 The nature of the stage in the 'Theatre of Lycurgus' at the end of the fourth century has been 'hotly disputed'. See Gomme and Sandbach (1973), 10, with n. 3. For a longer discussion, see Pickard-Cambridge (1946), 156ff, Dugdale (2008), 52 and Simon (1982), 7.
64 Although the natural alignment with the sun at a particular time might be exploited.
65 Dugdale (2008), 65 warns that not every feature in a play will have been represented in some way in the set. Aeschylus's *Suppliants* 710–23, for example, describes in detail the view out to sea of an approaching armada. Webster (1970a), xiv urges extreme care in using ancient plays as a source for scenery and costumes, as the playwrights increasingly had a reading public in mind. He believes, however, that it is often difficult to know where words are relied on alone for effect and where they are reinforced by visual or other aids (3). As for the natural setting of the theatre building, there are many possibilities since Menander's plays were performed all over the Greek world (see above).

66 Similarly, the financial difficulties of the BBC in the 1980s may have made the economy of form of Alan Bennett's single actor *Talking Heads* monologues an attractive project to decision makers and presented a challenge to the author with nevertheless excellent results: Dick (1996), 9.

67 Phyle is appropriately remote, being about thirteen miles from Athens, near the border wih Boeotia: Ireland (Menander, 1995) on line 2. Knemon is remote 'spiritually': Gomme and Sandbach (1973), 137. See also Handley's commentary (1992), 23–5.

68 Aristotle (*Poetics* 1449a) says that scene painting in perspective was introduced by Sophocles. A date of towards 460 BCE would be suggested if it had already been used by Aeschylus: Simon (1982), 22ff with this conjecture in n. 84.

69 See Simon (1988), 22–4, with figs. 3 and 4 for suggested reconstructions, and pl. 10; see also Csapo and Slater (1994), I 129, 62–3 and Pickard-Cambridge (1946), 124–5. See Dugdale (2008), 64 with pl. 3.5. It predates any archaeological evidence for the *paraskenion*, which could be shown (a projecting wing of the theatre building): this was part of the theatre of Lycurgus in Menander's time (52–3 with plate showing the elevation of a typical Hellenistic theatre). Any wooden structures representing a palace façade would have perished. On scene-specific vase-paintings, see Taplin (1993) *passim*. Hughes (2012), plate 12 shows Hellenistic grooves at Aphrodisias in Turkey which may have been for scenic units, but the theatre dates from the third century BCE (see 221 for an explanation).

70 See Simon (1982), pl. 11.2 with discussion at 25–7 and 230. Webster (1970a), 26–7 thinks it 'probable' that the paintings copy actual scenery; Pickard-Cambridge (1946), 226 is doubtful, wanting independent evidence. See also Ling (1991), 112.

71 On the importance of such scenes in Menander, see Brown (1995). The production at University College London had no doors and the Chloë production used curtains; the lack of banging doors diminished the comic effect.

72 Handley in Menander (1992), 21, n. 1. See Pan's prologue for the description of Knemon's house, the shrine and Gorgias's house.

73 Pickard-Cambridge is doubtful, however, based on modern experiments, that the mask was a kind of megaphone: (188), 196. People probably came to recognize a particular actor's voice. See Wiles (2007) for his experiments with masks.

74 See on this Handley (2002).

75 See Csapo & Slater (1994), 222, where actors' competitions are said to begin in 449 and 432 for the Dionysia and Lenaea respectively. See also Pickard-Cambridge (1988), 94.

76 Csapo (2010), 109, n. 49.

77 See Green (1994), 34. Comic actors are shown on vases wearing masks, but the actors in the vase painting referred to above (Simon (1982), pl. 10), a backdrop to a tragedy, do not wear masks. Vase painters often omitted the masks from such tragic scenes. This phenomenon needs more explanation.

78 For example, see Chairestratos at *Epitrepontes* 169ff (Menander (2009), 135) and Lape's comments in Further Reading.

79 The choral element may only appear to have been 'atrophied' in these plays: Sommerstein's word in his edition of *Wealth* (Aristophanes 2001), 23. Hunter (1979) assesses the internal evidence and concludes that there were choral performances at *Eccl.* 729–30 and 876–7, *Wealth* 321–2 and 626–7 and perhaps elsewhere in the latter play (33). More choral interludes are indicated in these two plays than separated the five acts in Menander: Arnott (2010), 293–4. Hunter (1979), 23–4 argues that it may be assumed from *CHOPOU* in the manuscripts of Menander, as well as variations of the formula in the plays to introduce this break in the action, that there was a choral performance of some kind.

80 See some of the ideas in Wiles (2000), such as (117), that the chorus helps (the other characters and the audience?) with the interpretation of a character by their comments and (125–6) that they are an extension of the audience (perhaps meaning that they act as a kind of 'buffer' for emotional involvement).

81 Easterling (2002), 332 and Csapo (2010), 103ff.

82 See Csapo (2010), 177 and ch. 3. Easterling (1999), 165 observes that actors became like athletes and musicians in their networks of patronage, organization and life style. The replica masks and figurines of actors on Lipari have in the past been connected with the worship of Dionysus. Actors did dedicate their masks in sanctuaries of Dionysus: see below and ch. 1 Further Reading.

83 See Wilson (2007), 5ff, Ghiron-Bistagne (1976), Le Guen (2007) and Taplin (1993), 92 with Frederiksen (2002), 87 and Csapo (2010), 85ff with Pickard-Cambridge (1988), 281.

84 Known already from the plays of the Sicilian Epicharmus: Green and Handley (1995), 50 and 16. Vases have a use-value and an aesthetic appeal that can go beyond a dramatic decoration, but the imported figurines must surely be representions of comedy: Csapo (2010), 101.

85 Earlier than the Loeb Group: see ch. 1.

86 But see ch. 1. See also Green (1994), 34ff, with pl. 2.13 for the New York Group and 38 on the lack of context. Many figurines were found in graves, which could be only because graves, being smaller, are easily and therefore more readily explored by comparison with housing areas, depending on what is being sought. See also 64–5, 69, 107, 110, 72.

87 These have been compared with those on monuments commemorating comic victories. See Pickard-Cambridge (1988), 214 and 231 with Webster (1970a), 56 on the Aixone relief (pl. 19, B31 with pl. 16, B10,), two examples from the fourth century BCE. See further on the standardization, Green (1994), 37.

88 Green & Handley (1995), 58ff.

89 See Pickard-Cambridge (1988), 231 and on costume in the service of character, Compton-Engle (2015), 147–8: the *Dyscolus* and Sostratos's 'fancy cloak'. See also Further Reading.

90 Wyles (2011), 43–4 contrasts tragedy only with Aristophanes for drama without a hint of the actor beneath the costume.

91 See ch. 3.

92 Green *MNC*³, 1, Green (1994), 36–7, 104. See also Simon (1982), 28 and Webster (1970a), 74 for the gradual disappearance of padding and the wearing of long chitons by free men except soldiers. The Lipari finds, from Menander's time or before show padding and a *phallus* for slaves. For Menander's plays as 'realistic', see the introductions to chapters 4 and 5 on social background.

93 Osborne (1987), has a fourth-century Pan figurine as his frontispiece. For various different representations of Pan (some like goats and some more human in form, and one wrapped in a cloak), see Boardman (1997). For Tyche see, for example, Tyche of Antioch (Roman copy of a colossal Greek bronze original by Eutychides, *c.* 300 BCE) with LIMC for both gods (suppl. 8.2 for Pan).

94 *MNC*³, 4. See Pickard-Cambridge (1988), 230–1 on women's costume, but based on Pollux (see comments below on young men), and Green & Handley (1995) for some illustrations, for example, *hetairai*, 65, plates 39–40, with 61, plate 36 for the nurse (see ch. 1, fig. 3 for another version) and a young woman, plate 37.

95 Wiles (1991), 177.

96 *MNC*³, 4. On women's costume, see further Bieber (1961), 95–9, figs. 347–68 and Brea (1981), 208–34.
97 Pollux IV, 118–20. See Csapo & Slater (1994), 393–402, Appendix A for *Onomasticon* 4.99–154.
98 *MNC*³, 4. Pollux is called 'oddly precise' by Green and Seeberg, who point out the discrepancy.
99 Wiles (1991), 188, 191. At 188 he quotes from Donatus, who says they wear less because they are poor, or so they can move more freely.
100 *MNC*³, 4–5.
101 See fig. 5.2 with *Epitr.* 302–3. For the baby in Menander see Heap (2003) and chapters 4 and 5.
102 See Menander's *Perinthia* for the plot motif and Bieber (1961), 102–5, figs. 388–413, with Green and Handley (1995), plates 41, 53–55 and 66.
103 Wiles (1991), 188, 190. At 191, Wiles does not distinguish, as he should, between a *chlamys* and a *chlanis*: it is the former which was a military cloak. A soldier renouncing violence might show this by wearing civilian clothes (see Polemon in Menander's *Perikeiromene* (179 and 354) for this possibility: Furley (2015), 124).
104 On the *pilos* or *kausia*, see *MNC*³, 4, with n. 16 (it may be Eastern or Macedonian in origin). See also ch. 3 and Green (1994), 100–1 on how the masks and figurines of young men might imitate Alexander the Great.
105 Bieber (1961), 99 and figs. 368, 369a-b, 370, 371.
106 *MNC*³, 4.
107 See above on the colour of the costume of young men.
108 See Green (1994), 24.
109 See Green (1994) at 24ff for discussion of a particular vase which highlights several possible interpretations of a theatrical scene.
110 See Trendall (1991), 151ff and (1989), 239ff on the Lipari Group; Green (1994), 90–1. See also above on actors and the 'Artists of Dionysus' with Further Reading.
111 See Pickard-Cambridge (1988), 60 for his statue being escorted to the theatre from Eleutherai. His priest had a front seat: see above.
112 Green & Handley (1995), 99.
113 The Pronomos Vase, the Cleveland Vase and all those with comic scenes were made for the *symposium* (drinking-party): masks came to be one of a series of motifs evoking this: Green (1994), 95, 116. On the 'equivalences' in the iconography between the stage world, Dionysus's world and the actors who attend him and the world of wishes or expectations in love, see Green (1994), 118ff and Further Reading.
114 See, for instance, a marble relief in Princeton, perhaps after an early Hellenistic original, of Menander with masks of a young man, an old man and the so-called false maiden (Green (1994), 83, pl. 3.21), the image on the cover of this book.
115 Green & Handley (1995), 99.
116 See ch. 1 with Heap (1994), Brown (1984), 110, with his references, and Brea (2001), 276–7.
117 See Green (1994), 107 on Apulian vases and 116ff for the growing cult of Eros and his link with Dionysus, and the vase discussed by Trendall (1991), 157 with pl. 64, which shows Dionysus with Ariadne under a flying Eros. See Further Reading and Hunter (2002), 200 on a sexy performance at dinner about Dionysus and Ariadne: Xenophon. *Symp.* 9.2ff.
118 Wiles (2007), 9.

119 Green (1994), 80–1. Wyles (2011) suggests that costumes may have been dedicated as well (44).
120 Williams (2002), 125. Wiles (2000), 160 suggests that having the same actor playing different roles, which was facilitated by the use of masks, may have added subtle nuances to the drama. High-born actors may have played low status roles (in Greece but not Rome).
121 As has been assumed by traditional scholarship on, for example, Middle Comedy. See further ch. 3 on stereotypes, such as the courtesan and cook and the introductions to chapters 4 and 5.
122 Wiles (2000), 208.

3 Alexander, Aristophanes and Beyond: Menander in Context

1 On Theophrastus and history, see Lane Fox (1996), 127ff, 143ff on the Women's Agora, 154 on the values and 157.
2 For the masks from Lipari, see ch. 1.
3 Menander's plays throw light 'on a lost way of life': Walton & Arnott (1996), 134.
4 The people of Aristophanes' time are examined by Ehrenberg (1962).
5 For the period after the death of Alexander, see Scott (2009), ch. 17.
6 Walton & Arnott (1996), 28 and Shipley (2000), 113. Mikalson (1998), 298 and 312, claims that initially the Macedonian occupation isolated Athens from foreign contact, by cutting it off from trade with the rest of the Greek world and in particular from religious influence. Cartledge (2004), 89 has Athens as the exception for Philip at least: free at that point from a garrison, and retaining democracy: he dealt with Athens in this way to ensure his use of its navy. Alexander deliberately did not use it, but at some strategic cost: Cartledge (2004), 94.
7 Cartledge (2004), 53, Shipley (2000), 108 and Walton & Arnott (1996), 26.
8 Shipley (2000), 128. On the *theorikon*, see Pickard-Cambridge (1988), 266ff, Scafuro (2014), 199 with n. 1 and Csapo and Slater (1994), 293. Scafuro thinks poorer Athenians may have denied themselves other things in order to continue to attend the theatre (200).
9 It is likely, of course, that they were read as well as performed. But poorer people were less likely to be able to read or get access to papyrus copies.
10 The kings had their own civic traditions, and those were much older than is implied by Arrian 7.9, for which see Austin (1981), source 15 with Shipley (2000), 108–9. There was a highly cultured aristocracy, if the Dervéni papyrus of 340–320 BCE, found in Thessaloníki (a philosophical text composed around 400 BCE) is in any way typical (111). Alexander arranged dithyrambic and tragic competitions in Tyre, for example: Plutarch *Alexander* 29 as quoted by Csapo & Slater (1994), 236–7, with comments by Green (1994), 106–7.
11 Shipley (2000), 2, with 1ff on the problems associated with the term. See further Cartledge's introduction to Cartledge, Garnsey and Gruen (eds) (1997), 1–19, especially 2 and Ogden's introduction to Ogden (ed.) (2002), ix-xxv, 1.
12 The anecdote is recounted by Alciphron 4.18–19 and the elder Pliny (*HN* 7.111 = Test.10). For a television programme on Greek theatres of the period see Scott (2017), episode 2. For companies of actors, the festival circuit and patronage, see Easterling (2002), 331ff, citing Csapo & Slater 231–55, and ch. 2 here. Some actors became diplomats. See also Wilson (2007), 6.

13 The ancient records are confused and contradictory about precisely when Menander
    was born and died.
14 Walton & Arnott (1996), 25 stress the expanded geography and talk of 'a new vision of
    humanity'. Shipley (2000), 2ff emphasizes continuities with the fifth century, because of
    colonization across Greece's cultural boundaries.
15 See ch. 2 here. On Philemon see also below. One story tells that Philemon died
    laughing at one of his own jokes (Valerius Maximus, who lived *c*. 30 CE, ix. 12. ext.6).
16 See Kraus's entries in *Kl. Pauly* (1970) with Pickard-Cambridge (1988), 119–20.
17 For example, the Cambridge Greek Play in 2013 was Aristophanes's *Frogs*; University
    College London's Classical Play was the *Dyscolus* in translation in 2016. The University
    of Sydney produced the *Dyscolus* in 2009 (available on DVD). Menander's *Samia* has
    now been set for undergraduates to study at Cambridge.
18 See above and Diog. L. 5.79 = *Test*. 8. Demetrius's nephew, Telesphorus, is said to have
    intervened on Menander's behalf.
19 When Demetrius fell from favour, some of the many statues of him were made into
    chamber-pots: Diog. L. 5.77.
20 Demetrius would have been familiar with Aristotle's collection of books: Casson
    (2002), 29. On Demetrius of Phalerum, see Further Reading and Habicht (1997),
    chs.1–4; 2.3 on Demetrius. On Antipater, see above. Demetrius went to Egypt after
    Cassander's death in 297. Ptolemy Soter was, like Alexander, taught by Aristotle.
21 Diog. L. 5.36 = Test. 7 and 5.75. Diggle (Theophrastus (2004)) 8 calls Diogenes 'a late,
    dubious source', however. According to Alciphron 4.19.14 (writing in the second or
    third century CE, however, and so also late) Menander was a friend of Theophrastus.
    Demetrius of Phalerum was a philosopher himself as well as a political leader. On
    Menander's life, see further Lefkowitz (1981b), 114.
22 Cartledge (2004), 37, 51–2 and 203–4. Later they fell out.
23 Sharples (2006) , 225–26 and 223–4 on scepticism and hedonism, Shipley (2000), 177ff
    and Konstan (2014), 286 on Demetrius of Phalerum and Poliorcetes.
24 See further, on the dating of these individual *Characters*, Theophrastus (2004), 27ff.
25 A better translation of the title *Characters* would be 'traits': Rusten in Theophrastus
    (1993), 11. '*Behavioural Types*' or '*Distinctive Marks of Character*' are suggested by
    Diggle (Theophrastus (2004)), 5. 'A wide range of purposes' have been proposed (Lane
    Fox (1996), 139) who doubts a coherent didactic reason for their composition. They
    were 'meant to amuse, not teach' (141). Diggle (Theophrastus (2004)), 15ff suggests
    that they accompanied lectures on ethics.
26 Diggle (Theophrastus (2004)), 8 observes that 'comedy furnishes much the same cast
    of players': see his n. 26 for references. On their relevance to Menander's
    characterization, together with Middle Comedy, see further Traill (2008), 82ff: the
    assumption is shared by Theophrastus's characters and Menander's that someone's
    tropos, 'character', does not change.
27 However, none of the Characters is 'a caricature of youth' (Lane Fox (1996), 132).
    Menander, on the other hand, depicts the young man in love more than once: see
    further Lane Fox (1996), 139–40.
28 Webster (1974), 44ff and Diggle (Theophrastus (2004), 6ff. But, as Diggle says,
    Theophrastus, unlike Aristotle, gives us 'a real individual'.
29 Ussher (1993), 5 with n. 13 and Rusten in Theophrastus (1993), 21. See further Hunter
    (1985), 148–9. Again, it has been suggested that the *Characters* have connections with
    ethics (Ussher (1993), 7–8). See further Fortenbaugh and others (eds) (1992), 2. On the

Characters as social history, see Millett (2007) with Lane Fox (1996). On influences from Aristotle, see Lord (1977) and Fortenbaugh (1974).

30 Strabo 14.638 = Test.6 (Arnott (1997 with corr.), xvi) with Alciphron 19.14. See O'Sullivan (2009), 236ff, partly on Cicero's comments about Demetrius and his own debt to philosophy.

31 See further Hofmeister (1997), 316ff.

32 See Fortenbaugh and Schütrumpf (2000), 31 and Shipley (2000), 182–3.

33 Sharples (2006), 230: there were statues of Epicurus in such communities and his birthday was celebrated as a festival. See also Hutchinson's Introduction in Epicurus (1994), xi: 'on equal terms with the men ... completely out of line with the social norms of the time' and Konstan (2003), 251.

34 Theophrastus had a slave, Pompylus, who was a philosopher, according to tradition: Diog. Laert. 5.36.

35 For replicas of these masks, see ch. 1. See further Sharples (2006), 227ff also for how Epicureanism relates to ideas of free will and responsibility.

36 Friendship in the plays is another theme which would bear further research. On Menander and religion, see also Further Reading.

37 This section owes a debt to the author's entries on comedy in Shipley et al. (eds) (2006).

38 See Glossary.

39 See Walton & Arnott (1996), 7.

40 The title of Hunter (1985) is one instance, although it is obvious from his wide-ranging approach that he regards the differences between Greek and Roman Comedy as important (vii).

41 Ruffell (2014), 164, citing Green (1994), 37.

42 Rosenbloom (2014), 300: Isoc. 8.14 *On the Peace* and *Laws* 935d-936a.

43 See ch. 2. Only three of Menander's plays are known to have been set outside Athens: *Perikeiromene* (Corinth), *Leukadia* (Leucas) and *Imbrians* (Imbros).

44 See Athenaeus 8.336d.

45 Athenaeus was a scholar who had had access to the great Library of Alexandria, founded by Alexander the Great. Menander and other ancient Greek authors owe a great debt to this institution for the transmission of their works.

46 See Hunter in Eubulus (1983), 21 and Arnott (2010), 280–1, citing Handley.

47 Some subject matter would derive from real life of course: another such plot motif would be capture by pirates. See further for the influence of tragedy on Menander, Hurst (1990) in French, Walton & Arnott (1996), 7ff and Omitowoju (2010).

48 See ch. 2 on the chorus.

49 Alexis allegedly taught Menander: Test. 2: Arnott (1997 with corr.), xiv.

50 Theophrastus, Menander's teacher, was also a non-Athenian, from Eresus in Lesbos. For theatre iconography from Southern Italy, and performances beyond Athens generally, see ch. 2, and above here for Euripides receiving patronage from the kings of Macedon.

51 Richter (1984), 187–9 with plate for Poseidippus and (1965), 236 for Philemon. For Menander's statue, see ch. 1. Poseidippus is clean-shaven too and sitting on a similar chair.

52 Ireland (2010), 335–6 with n. 11.

53 Aulus Gellius 17.4.1.

54 Plutarch *Moralia 6: On Restraining Anger* 458A, K.-A.Test.9: Scafuro (2014), 204–5.

55 Webster (1970b), 126–7, 151.

56 Athenaeus VII 288cff = K.-A. fr. 82.

57 Ireland (2010), 340ff.

58 See further on the *Amphitruo* the essays by Dupont (2001) and Slater (2001) and the edition by Christenson (Plautus (2000)), 45ff on other possible influences.

59 Hunter (1985), 4 and Ireland (2010), 341.

60 On Menander and the Roman adaptations, see the useful analysis in Gomme and Sandbach (1973), 4ff and Duckworth (1994). Only one significant parallel passage for a Greek model and its adaptation is extant so far, namely *Dis Exapaton* and Plautus's *Bacchides*. Nevertheless, the flavour of the Roman plays would bear reassessment in the light of the growth of the rest of extant Menander. According to one tradition Terence drowned at sea after hunting for more Menander: Goldberg (1986), 95 n. 2, citing Suetonius's *Life of Terence* 5. He allegedly brought back 108 plays.

61 See further Nesselrath (1997) on politics in Middle Comedy. For Neaira, see ch. 4.

62 On Demetrius, see above.

63 See further Hofmeister (1997), 303ff.

64 Lape (2004) argues well, for example, at 13ff and in her conclusion. See also, for a similar approach, Omitowoju (2002).

65 Nesselrath (1997), 285.

66 See Gomme and Sandbach (1973), 555–6, Arnott (2000), 12 and Sommerstein (2013), 135.

67 For example, in relation to the popularity of Theocritus's *Idylls*, the assumption made by some that the expansion of the Greek world through Alexander's conquests led to a yearning for escape to the country has been questioned by Hutchinson (1988), 3.

68 There are echoes in the arbitration of *Epitrepontes* of Euripides' *Alope*, for example, and of tragedy in general in the opening of *Aspis*. See also the recognition scene in Menander's *Perikeiromene*, Act IV (See Furley (2014), Menander (2015), 155ff and Furley (2015)). There is not room here to explore Menander's extensive debt to tragedy and Euripides in particular. For brief references to mythology in Menander, see *Samia* 499ff and 589ff, the stories of Phoenix and Danae respectively. For Menander's treatment of the gods, see above and ch. 2 for their appearance on stage.

69 See further Rosenbloom (2014), 310–11, 301, 309, 313 on later comedy and politics in Menander.

70 On the opening of *Aspis*, see further ch. 5.

71 Arnott's edition of Menander's *Alexis* (1996), 21.

72 On a possibly continuing role for the chorus, see ch. 2. See further Hunter (1979), 24 and especially 37–8 on act-breaks in Greek and Roman comedy, and Handley (1987), 300, on the marking of acts in Menander (but perhaps not by his contemporaries) with the interlinear note CHOROU ('by the chorus') in the earliest papyri. Act division in Roman comedy was introduced originally by scholars in the first century BCE. No music or record of any choreography survives as yet from Old or Middle Comedy but there is musical notation for a line of Menander's *Perkeiromene* (796): see the Introduction to this book. Some passages in ancient comedy, especially monologues, seem to have been written as a gift to particular actors: Arnott (2010), 310. The number of monologues in Menander may reflect the growth in the status of the actor: see, again, ch. 2.

73 See further Lape (2006) and ch. 2. The chorus is not necessarily supportive of the central character in earlier drama, of course.

74 Lane Fox (1996), 140 on other debts than to Theophrastus.

75 Csapo (2000) and the important essay by Sidwell (2014), arguing against Arnott (2010). Certainly any "development" may mean only a different kind of comedy, for which see Merchant (1972) and Hokenson (2006). See further the Conclusion to this book.

76 Sidwell (2014), 75 and Olson (2007), 22–6.

77 See Ruffell (2014), 149, 152, 154–5 and 163. As for names, Moschion will suggest a young man in love (as in *Samia* and *Perikeiromene*, for instance), Polemon a soldier, from the Greek word for 'war'. The study of stereotypes crosses disciplines, such as literature, history and sociology, as was demonstrated at a conference at Cambridge (CRASSH 2005), 'Stereotypes and Binary Divides'.

78 *Pace* Ireland (2010), 350, who warns that too much is uncertain for too detailed a sociological approach. Ruffell (2014), 166 refers interestingly to 'shorthands' in assessing characters in New Comedy on which social and fictional interactions depend.

4 Women in *Epitrepontes*: Habrotonon and Pamphile

1 No woman is known to have performed on stage in ancient Greece: see Lightfoot (2002), 212 but also Webb in the same volume for later female performers.

2 There has not been room here for a study of the male characters as such in Menander, but a further study is in progress on Menander's *Samia*.

3 See Hubbard (ed.) (2014) and Skinner (2005), xii for its popularity with scholars.

4 Fantham and others (1994), 7.

5 See further Fantham et al. (1994), ch. 2 for how the experiences of Spartan women, for instance, may have differed from those of Athenian women; they were contrasted by Athenians with their own experiences or ideals, as being free to go outside the house and speak to men. This 'Other' may have been embellished. Menander does sometimes set his plays outside Athens.

6 See, for example, Schaps (1981), 9, n. 55 on a woman's retaining her personal attendants throughout her life, based on Demeas's actions towards Chrysis in the *Samia* when he throws her out.

7 Where women's speech is reported, for example, what survive are men's impressions of how women spoke, which may not be accurate (Dickey (1996), 242).

8 Lefkowitz (1981a), 48. Discussions of Menander and history are relevant to his use or otherwise of politics, for which see ch. 3 here.

9 Brown (1990), 249.

10 See further the important study by Christodoulou (1997). The role of the *pallake* will be explored in more depth in relation to Menander's *Samia* in a sequel to this study here.

11 See Glossary and ch. 3 with Athenaeus Book 13, 567d and 568a and Olson (2007), 339ff and Appendix IV for translations of the passages discussed. Tragedy has no *hetairai* to provide literary precedents for Menander's characters.

12 See Carey in Apollodorus (1992), 16. Rhodopis, for instance, is described by Herodotus at 2.134 as *hetaira gyne*. See Gomme and Sandbach (1973), 30, Brown (1990), 248–9 and Henry (1985), 3.

13 Pomeroy (1975), 89.

14 Neaira, for instance, for whom see below.

15 Compare the modern English euphemism 'escort'.

16 Thus Aspasia was called an *hetaira* by her critics, although she was Pericles' partner. See Further Reading.
17 Davidson (1997), 109ff, especially 112.
18 Carey in Apollodorus (1992), 16.
19 Wiles (1989), 42.
20 See below on line 646.
21 Brown (1990) feels that 'prostitute', working 'in the trade', is not an adequate translation for *hetaira*: see 249, for instance.
22 *Epitr.* 136. On all these distinctions, see further Halperin (1990), 111–12.
23 Gomme and Sandbach (1973), 30 n. 4, Brown (1990), 249. For the *pallake*, see further Chrysis in Menander's *Samia*.
24 Or possibly 'forced into prostitution'.
25 Carey in Apollodorus (1992), 3–4.
26 These Greek terms are not translated because of the difficulties of finding English equivalents, as discussed above on the *Hetaira*.
27 This quotation uses 'a restricted sense' of the word *hetaira* according to Carey in Apollodorus (1992), 148. See also Foucault, v.2 (1985), 149.
28 Just (1989), 7.
29 Harding (2008), 157–58.
30 Sissa (1990a), 2 and 105–6, with Sissa (1990b), 349.
31 Lefkowitz (1995).
32 Scholium to Theocritus II. 66: see Sissa (1990a), 77 n. 15. See also below on *Epitr.* 438–40.
33 On Artemis in this context, see Sissa (1990a), 77, 86–88, with Sissa (1990b).
34 Xenophon, *Oec.* 7.5. On the existence or otherwise of women's quarters, see further Nevett (1992), 136–7 and Nevett (1995): 'it is possible that there was no such area in the literal sense that men never entered' (373). The movement of male visitors may have been as restricted as the movement of female occupants. Nevett (1999), 163 suggests male female contact on a daily basis, with some rooms used more habitually by one gender than another. But in the Introduction to Ault & Nevett (2005), 5 she notes that although a *gynaikon*, 'women's area', is 'frequently mentioned' in literary sources (for references, see Morgan (2010), 118ff), very few Greek houses that have been excavated seem to be divided spatially in this way.
35 Omitowoju (2002), 230–1. See further Taylor (2011), *passim* and in particular 704.
36 In particular here, see Foxhall (2003).
37 Just (1989), 113.
38 See Further Reading for an example from Menander's *Dyscolus*.
39 Cohen (1989), 8. The *oikos* would have had to have been rich enough to employ enough slaves to do the work (9). See the introduction to ch. 5 for the many jobs slaves were expected to do by those who could afford them.
40 See above on the *Hetaira*.
41 For a full discussion of rape and rape in Menander, see James (2014).
42 See further Deacy and Pierce (eds) (1997).
43 See Harrison (1998) v.1, 19 with n. 2 on men being forced to marry.
44 See further Just (1989), 68–70. The extent of adulterine bastardy in an historical society is unknowable, however: see Ogden (1996), 7ff.
45 Harrison (1998), v.1, 35. The influence of alcohol was another mitigating factor regarding young men's behaviour: but see further below on the *Epitrepontes*.
46 See Todd's commentary (2007) on Lysias 1.32–3. He suggests (130) that what is being read out is not a rape law but a law that could be used against rapists. Harrison (1998)

v.1, 35 accepts that seduction was more severely dealt with than rape, but says that the details cannot be certain.

47 Todd (1993), 276ff.

48 Cantarella (2005), 242.

49 Harris (1990), v.1, 371. Ogden (1996), 147ff agrees with Harris (1990), 375 that death was not excluded as a penalty for rape: Lysias's statement reflects real anxieties in society about adultery. See further Carey (1993), 53–5, who argues from Aristophanes that sexual humiliation of adulterers was one option as a punishment (55). See also Sommerstein (1998).

50 See above on Virginity.

51 Cantarella (2005), 243.

52 Harrison (1998), v.1, 36, 38: he refers to the classical period, however.

53 Ogden (1996), 143.

54 Harrison (1998), v.1, 37.

55 For sympathy for the rape victim as the historically silent female perspective, see James (2014). For the view that female consent was not regarded as important, see Omitowoju (2002), 122 and 131 and Further Reading here.

56 Ogden (1996),145.

57 Cohen (1990),148, n. 3.

58 Harrison (1998), v.1, 37; he refers to Aeschin. *Timarch.* 1.14 and the procuring of a freeborn boy or woman for immoral purposes. This was probably not an explicit doctrine, however, or there would have been different rules about attacks on women past childbearing. On adultery as worse than rape, see further Ogden (1996), 146ff with Patterson (1998), 172ff.

59 See Humphreys (1993), 46, 49 on the problems in assessing the evidence for social structure and experience from one period and area to another. Modrzejewski (2005), 344 argues for the influence of Athenian law on the law in Hellenistic Egypt. See also Pomeroy (1997).

60 Foucault, v.2 (1985), 147 comments on the lack of a category of 'mutual fidelity' in Greek marriage (before Musonius Rufus, a first century CE stoic: Paul Cartledge pers.comm.).

61 Cox (2011), 231 draws attention in the context of marriage to the fact that ancient Athens was a shame culture.

62 See further Cox (2011), 232 on *engye* as a rite essentially concerned with legitimacy and citizenship and Patterson (1998), 107–109 with 258 and her n. 2 to ch. 4.

63 Just (1989), 151, Fantham and others (1994), 101.

64 Isaeus 8.8; 2.3–4, 3.37; 6.14. See Isager (1981–82), 86.

65 See Ps.Dem. 59.122 and MacDowell (1978), 87 with references there: an alien who joined the *oikos* of a citizen as husband or wife (*synoikein* implies marriage, not mere concubinage) could be prosecuted by *graphe* and, if found guilty, was sold as a slave. A citizen (the man) in such circumstances was fined 1,000 drachmas. See also Harrison v.1 (1998), 26–8.

66 See further Harrison (1998), 1–2. He also points out that it is difficult to determine what constituted a valid marriage.

67 Harrison (1998), v.1, 18, 50, MacDowell (1978), 81, 203–4, 97–8.

68 For a useful summary of the problems, see Cox (2011) and Cohn-Haft (1995): for instance (9), there is no evidence that there was any legal concept of adequate grounds for divorce.

69 See further Pomeroy (1997).

70 Cox (2011), 232.

71 Harrison v.1 (1998), 40.
72 Cox (2011), 233.
73 An expression from the Roman period for the official at Athens who gave his name to the year.
74 Just (1989), 70 (on Dem. 59 (Neaira), 87), Todd (1993), 212 n. 13 and 276ff, especially 278–9.
75 Lacey (1980), 108 (on Dem. 41, 4). Todd (1993), 214 cites Harrison v.1 (1998), 31 on Menander's *Epitrepontes* 657–9 and 714–15 as suggesting a father retained some power over a married daughter. See also Petrides (2014), 28.
76 Cox (2011), 234–5. She points out that the potential loss of the wealth represented by a dowry was a favourite theme in drama, citing Euripides's *Andromache* 864–79.
77 See Harrison v.1 (1998), 12 for next of kin unable to force a divorce if there was a son, with MacDowell (1978), 88. Petrides (2014), 272 n. 49 summarizes the debate. See further Rosivach (1984) who discusses *Epitrepontes* but also draws heavily on Roman comedy.
78 For the arguments between scholars, see Kapparis (2002) 154ff with Golden (2011a), 272–4 on Ariès's original questioning of parents' emotional investment in their children in high mortality populations. G. thinks ancient parents would still be devoted. See also Laes (2011), 315.
79 Gomme and Sandbach (1973), 34–5. Todd (1993), 184–5, n. 32 comments that exposure may have been 'a form of social infanticide', it being thought better for an infant daughter to end up in a brothel than to starve, but unacceptable to sell her openly. Boswell (1988), 41 warns, however, that, whatever the period and culture, exposure should not be conflated with infanticide.
80 Kapparis (1992), 155.
81 See Further Reading.
82 See Garland (1990), 91–3.
83 Eva Lassen (pers. comm.): Aristophanes *Thesmo.* 502ff assumes that infants could be supplied to childless women, implying a willingness to dispose of unwanted children. The *Thesmo.* passage is discussed by Gardner (1989), 55–7. (See also *Peace* 675–7, Dem. 21.149.)
84 Prof E. W. Handley (pers. comm.): evidence exists for more modern times which does not for ancient Greece; for instance, hospital records and newspapers, but the fictional, such as Shakespeare or *The Importance of being Earnest* cannot be ignored, since it must relate in some way to reality. (But see Witzke (2014) on Menander as an influence on Wilde.)
85 Lacey (1980), 166 n. 83; 167 and 167 n. 88.
86 The same verb, *apoballein*, is used (*LSJ*) of exposure in the Gortyn Laws (Crete) at least (4.9).
87 See Kapparis (2002), 154–5. For a study by Menander of an adoptive relationship, see his *Samia*.
88 Boswell (1988), 84 with n. 112. If so, a shift in opinion could have a parallel in the possible changing attitudes to slavery at that period (see further ch. 5 on slaves).
89 Donatus's commentary on the play, which might have answered this question, has not survived.
90 Samos was notorious for its prostitutes (Bain (1985 with corr.), 113). See above on The *Hetaira*.
91 See further Heap (2002–3), 81ff.
92 A further study on the male characters in Menander will look at characterization in the *Samia*, and therefore at Chrysis, and at Polemon in *Perikeiromene* as a variation on the young man in love.

93 Gomme and Sandbach (1973), 514.

94 See ch. 1. Green and Seeberg in fact suggest Pollux's Mask 42, the Little Torch, a description of the particular hairstyle, for Habrotonon in *Epitrepontes*, based partly on her youth: *MNC*³, 49–50.

95 See fragment 1. Now confirmed by P. Oxy. 4020: see *Oxy. Pap.* 60 (1994), 27–9 and Parsons' comment on lines 3–5. For the development of the dialogue with Chairestratos present too, possibly forming a plan, see Handley *Oxy. Pap.* 73 (2009), 26 on P. Oxy. 4936.

96 The definite article is used in the Greek, conveying the idea 'our friend': Gomme and Sandbach (1973), 292.

97 Gomme and Sandbach (1973), 292. Fr. 264, line 4 from *Methe*, however, translated by Balme (2001), 267–8 associates *psaltriai*, 'harp-girls' and *auletrides*, 'flute-girls' and the legal maximum charge was the same for both (Arist. *Ath. Pol.*50.2). See Davidson (1997), 81–2 and McClure (2003), 21–2 on female entertainers and their associations with sex.

98 As noted above, it seems from the speech *Against Neaira* (for which see the relevant section above) that to have a relationship with an *hetaira* was not in itself something that would occasion moral condemnation, unless one pretended that she had the rights of a married woman.

99 A drachma was worth six obols and an obol was a relatively small amount of money, a sixth of which would buy a cheap bottle of wine. See further Ireland in *Menander* (2010b), 213. Talents were worth a great deal more and used to measure dowries (see below on line 134). Charisios is spending the equivalent of, perhaps, a good bottle of wine on a daily basis for Habrotonon's services: see Arnott's comments (1997 with corr.), 397 n. 1 and Menander (2010b), 212 on how Smikrines's complaint reflects partly on his own interest in money when he is not poor (see below on the dowry he has been able to afford). As a slave, and as a woman, Habrotonon would not have seen much if anything of her earnings. (See ch. 5 on slaves, for sex workers and freeborn but poor women).

100 The comment is preceded by the information that Charisios does not consider himself 'to be sharing (his wife's) house', but sleeps out. Gomme and Sandbach (1973), 296–7 note that it is a stock idea that a rich wife makes her husband her servant, sometimes the meaning of the word *oiketes* in the Greek, but that the word may just mean 'sharer of the household'. Whichever is the case, the word may have some bearing on the themes of slavery and power over others in Epitrepontes, which will be explored in ch. 5 on slaves. There is a picture of a figurine of a pimp in Green and Handley (1995): see plate 52. The pimp is mentioned but does not appear, as far as is known, in the *Epitrepontes*, but this might have been the image conjured up for the audience, although the statuette is dated to the second century BCE, as these figurines were part of a continuing tradition.

101 On the other hand, the wine was not ridiculously cheap either (Gomme and Sandbach (1973), 295).

102 Admittedly, four talents (line 135) was a great deal of money as a dowry.

103 Menander could have brought such a character on stage; indeed, a speech by a pimp survives at *Kolax* E225ff, Arnott (1996b), 153, being one of the excerpts from the main papyrus source for that play. The prominence given to the pimp would affect perception of the *hetaira*'s character, as an *hetaira* in a semi-permanent relationship would have no need of a pimp. Ireland (1992), 65 would like the detail to explain the degree of self-interest that is apparent in her later behaviour; perhaps it mitigates

Smikrines' condemnation of her, since certain characteristics, such as greed, might
have been associated by many people with women owned by pimps (see above on the
Hetaira).

104 Sandbach discusses how extravagant or otherwise the sums involved were, at Gomme
and Sandbach (1973), 298. Halperin (1990), 107–12 studies in detail the prices
charged for sex, and in the process distinguishes the different kinds of arrangements
involved: he refers to this passage at 109, but is unsure whether it shows that
Charisios is extravagant or Smikrines tight-fisted. The general tone of the passage
suggests the latter.

105 Something that might be more expected of an *hetaira* and that has resulted from
Charisios's actions.

106 Gomme and Sandbach (1973), 299.

107 See above for a discussion of *nymphe*, a probable reading.

108 The division of speakers is uncertain. Sandbach tentatively gives 160 to Smikrines,
but against this see Kassel (1973), 6. Furley (2009) gives the information that
Smikrines is the father of the bride and the observation on his appearance to
Chairestratos.

109 It is not clear whether there are any premises involved, as would be the case with a
'brothel-keeper': Smikrines refers to a *matryleion*, 'a brothel' at 692, but he
exaggerates. At 136 he has been more vague, saying Charisios 'sleeps out': in fact,
Charisios is at his friend Chairestratos's house. See Marshall (2013), 175 for the
pornoboskos as a specialized slave dealer, with 177 on Habrotonon.

110 Gomme and Sandbach (1973), 327, where he notes the 'you' singular in the Greek
between plural imperatives. The distinction has to be made explicit in English.

111 Xen. *Cyr.* 5.1.10, Herod. 9.108, Eur. *Hipp.* 32, Plato *Symp.* 181b.

112 Goldberg (1980), 133 n. 7 notes this unusual Greek word *theion*, among others, as
contributing to Habrotonon's colourful language.

113 For Habrotonon's perjorative use of *anthropos*, compare Lysias 1.15 (there of an old
woman). Interestingly, for what follows about power games in terms of the theme of
the *Epitrepontes*, it can also be used in this way of a slave.

114 See Gomme and Sandbach (1973), 569 on line 269 of the *Samia* for references.
Sandbach's examples of the use of this address include Demeas and Moschion, an
older and a younger man respectively, Onesimos, a slave, in this play, and Sostratos, a
young man and Sikon, the cook in the *Dyscolus*. Women do not appear to use it. See
Dickey (1996), 26–7, who finds that it is commonly used by a man to address a group
of men. She does not appear to discuss its use in drama, however.

115 The picture is of a man drowning his sorrows, in contrast to the assumptions made
by Smikrines earlier (Ireland (1992), 72).

116 See further Davidson (1997), 99 on such disapproval. Lacey (1980), 172 cites Plutarch
Alcibiades 8, Andocides 4.14 and Dem. 59.22; the latter is also quoted by Just (1989),
141–2.

117 It does, as has been seen, make him the subject of Karion's gossip at the beginning of
the play, however.

118 Arnott (1997 with corr.), 440 n. 1 on line 440.

119 Gomme and Sandbach (1973), 329.

120 Gomme and Sandbach (1973), 329 says that the word is 'as usual' sympathetic. But
see also Dickey (1996), 161–2, who notes its double function, that is half the time in
expressions of genuine or ironic sympathy, and half the time in scornful rebukes. See
also Bain (1984), 33–5.

121 Gomme and Sandbach (1970), 131, comparing Glykera in *Perikeiromene*. For more on Habrotonon's language, see Further Reading.

122 Gomme and Sandbach (1973), 328–9.

123 Dickey (1996), 162–3, with 246, remarks that *talas*, 'poor thing', conveys genuine sympathy here, and notes that in Aristophanes, Menander and some other poetry it is used by women rather than men. See Heap (2002–3), 102ff. Dickey (1996), 211 observes that there are in Menander a number of addresses to babies by women who are not their mothers; the babies' names are never used, but terms of pity or endearment, sometimes combined with *teknon*, 'child', with tragic connotations.

124 See Heap (2002–3), 99ff.

125 Compare Chrysis's behaviour in *Samia*, also variously interpreted: see Heap (2002–3), 81ff and the enigmatic references by Habrotonon to her virginity above. Traill (2008), 232 and 238 is sceptical, however, about any maternal feelings on Habrotonon's part. She notes simply (228) that Habrotonon's sympathy is given 'a plausible basis' in that she herself is a slave and sees the baby in danger of becoming one too. See against this Heap (2002–3), 105.

126 Babies are used elsewhere in Menander as a measure of people's characters: compare Moschion's baby in the *Samia*, where the *pallake* Chrysis shows more concern for it than its father and grandfather. See Heap (2002–3).

127 See Todd (1993), 184 with n. 32: slavery in Athens was chattel slavery: 'the most dehumanized form of dependant labour'; to treat a Greek in this way would have been unacceptable behaviour. For penalties, Todd refers (187) to Dem.1.23, where Menon is executed for keeping a citizen boy as a slave.

128 Traill, 229 regards Habrotonon as serving as an intermediary (she is still in touch with Pamphile's friends: 481, 500–1) 'between the female world of the Tauropolia and the male world of the symposium'. Bathrellou (2012), 183, (2009), 267 thinks, however, that the main emphasis of the Tauropolia was on young men and their transition to adulthood. The festival is referred to three times in the space of about 70 lines (451, 472, 517) and it therefore seems likely that the particular festival is significant for the events described and for themes in the plays: Bathrellou (2012), 152 has come independently to this same conclusion. Bathrellou (2012), 185, (2009), 267–8 regards the inclusion of references generally to festivals in Menander as enriching the audience's understanding of the characters, giving the plays social and political importance.

129 Gomme and Sandbach (1973) on 482 (333) says it is the girls' mothers who are meant there; see, however, also Arnott (1997 with corr.), n. 1 on 477, who thinks it was Habrotonon's virginity that made her, a slave, able to share in freeborn girls' amusements; could it also be meant that Habrotonon was at that point in her life more accepted in the company of freeborn girls? See further ch. 5 on slaves for other possible forms of familiarity with masters and mistresses. Compare, as Traill does (2008), 235, how the *pallake* Chrysis is accepted by her freeborn neighbours at *Samia* 37–8. But perhaps being a freeborn *pallake* made a difference to the degree of acceptance. Demeas refers to Chrysis as a free woman at *Samia* 577.

130 At *Epitr.* 517, discussed below, Habrotonon uses *parthenos* as part of her description of her supposed rape and the audience is (again) invited to think of her as a virgin (Traill (2008), 229).

131 The exclamation is one used only by female characters. It begins the line at 480, unusually for an oath, and so is potentially emphatic. However, this particular oath, due to its length, can only occupy a position like this.

132 Gomme and Sandbach (1973), 333 reads empathy here with Pamphile's loss of
     virginity, which would support Traill's (2008) observation that the audience is invited
     generally to compare as well as contrast the two women (228ff). The punctuation is
     disputed (see Sandbach's discussion). There may be the nature of men as well as or
     rather than actual virginity involved in Habrotonon's remark, as is reflected in Balme
     (also Arnott) and Miller's different attempts at translation given above.
133 See Ireland's (1992) interpretation (73): neither would have lost their virginity by
     choice, Habrotonon being a slave in the power of a pimp.
134 *O theoi*, 'Gods!' (Habrotonon at 489) is used only by women in Menander:
     Sommerstein (1995), 65 n. 13. Indeed, most of the instances are spoken by
     Habrotonon: Bain (1984), 41. Gomme and Sandbach (1973), 525 think its
     commonest use is to give emphasis, and that it is also characteristic of Habrotonon's
     talk (Sandbach (1970), 131). The fact that it is a woman-only oath, stresses one
     woman's pity, or rather sympathy, for another woman in an often particularly female
     kind of suffering, that is, rape.
135 Gomme and Sandbach (1973), 334, where they think the German scholar
     Wilamowitz 'had a weak spot for the girl' (they are paraphrasing W.'s commentary on
     the play (1961), 78ff. As has been noted, Traill comments (228) that Menander makes
     Habrotonon's sympathy 'plausible', being here partly about damaged clothes, but not
     how the fact that they are damaged again emphasizes that the rapist has been rough.
136 See Further Reading on seduction and rape elsewhere in Menander.
137 Traill (2008), 226 observes that at this point Habrotonon emphasizes Charisios's
     virility whilst carefully avoiding provoking anxiety or guilt.
138 Gomme and Sandbach (1973), 336. The Greek word is related etymologically to the
     English word 'theatre'.
139 Hurt professional pride is another possible interpretation of her words there.
140 Traill (2008), 227 remarks on her 'chatty, informal style', appropriate for one of the less
     educated *hetairai*.
141 The use of this particular word is not just the sympathy of another young woman for
     Pamphile: compare Parmenon's criticism to his face of Moschion's actions (that is, a
     male slave of his young master) at *Samia* 67, and *Georgos* 30 (an old woman of a
     young man). See Further Reading.
142 Contrast, however, Polemon's protests at *Perik.* 471–2, that he has had only 'one cup':
     Menander, Miller (1987).
143 Ireland (1992), 74 cleverly notes how the slave's interjections break up the details of
     Habrotonon's plan, 'enlivening the various phases of its revelation'.
144 See Gomme and Sandbach (1973): various comments referred to above, Henry
     (1985), 53–4, Wilamowitz-Moellendorff (1961), 78ff.
145 See ch. 5 Further Reading on his use of the audience address *andres*, 'gentlemen',
     although this address was possibly not open to Habrotonon as a female character, as
     explored above on 430ff.
146 *Kompsos* (466) seems less casual than just 'nice', in the light of this.
147 It is part of the *hetaira*'s world to understand things from different viewpoints (Prof.
     E. W. Handley, pers.comm.); compare Habrotonon's feeling at 436ff that Charisios is
     wasting his money on her, her sympathy for Pamphile's plight at the festival (486ff),
     and Chrysis's implied experience of men when she says at *Samia* 80ff that Demeas,
     like Moschion, is in love.
148 It would be poignant (Prof. E.W. Handley, pers. comm.) if an *hetaira* like Habrotonon
     had not much hope of manumission in real life, or if freedom would in practice make

no difference. On manumission and how a stigma and obligations remained attached to the freed Greek slave, see ch. 5. For a contrast with the rewards some Roman slaves could expect, see Garnsey (1996), 97ff. An older woman was able, however, to gain her freedom from her master elsewhere in Menander: Demeas complains about the ingratitude of Moschion's nurse at *Samia* 238.

149 See Further Reading.

150 There are no specific moral overtones in the Greek here, although the verb used can carry them: see Creon's opening speech at *Antigone* 162ff for one example (Eva Lassen, pers. comm.). But Habrotonon has argued for justice previously, at 468–70, on behalf of the baby.

151 Gomme and Sandbach (1973), 339.

152 See further Voigt (1937) and Buxton (1982), (31ff), where he discusses inscriptions which testify to Peitho's connexion with *hetairai*, and with Aphrodite, and (37) for a prostitute named Peitho and sacred prostitutes alluded to by Pindar as 'servants of Peitho'.

153 Lacey (1980), 173 and note 129: Isaeus 2.1, Dem. 46, 14, etc. See further Just (1989), 209ff.

154 Voigt (1937), 194 and Buxton (1982), 35 find a tradition that links Peitho with marriage; this adds an extra dimension to Habrotonon's prayer for the young couple. Ambiguity, or rather ambivalence, is also one of Peitho's fundamental qualities (Buxton (1982), 66), which would suit Habrotonon's enigmatic presentation (see Character of Habrotonon: summary below).

155 Buxton (1982), 44. (He dismisses (n. 53) Wilamowitz's argument (85 of his commentary), that, to 'dignify' the invocation, the Athenian Peitho was more exalted and unerotic than her counterparts elsewhere in Greece.)

156 See Furley (2013), Römer (2012a and b). As has already been noted in the introduction to this chapter, if an *hetaira* is indistinguishable from a *porne*, how can Smikrines insult Habrotonon in this way? The text there actually invalidates the translation of *hetaira* as 'prostitute'.

157 Gomme and Sandbach (1973), 353: 'a rare word (in the Greek), perhaps of non-Greek origin' (and therefore emphatic).

158 See further Henry (1985) 32–48.

159 Henry (1985), 58 observes that Habrotonon's language often refers to money, however, which serves as a reminder of her profession.

160 See, for example, Traill (2008), 7.

161 Compare how Polemon is deceptively portrayed as the violent soldier at the beginning of *Perikeiromene*.

162 Traill (2008), 224 agrees in the sense that 'her motives are unclear', but observes too, strongly, that 'Menander leaves plenty of room for doubt'. Note in particular how Habrotonon is made a chaste *hetaira* by having her reminisce about when she was a virgin (Henry (1985), 60 and Omitowoju (2002), 219). Traill (2008), 229 observes that 'despite her expertise, she is not strongly associated with the sexual side of her trade'; this reassures the audience that she is not a rival for Pamphile (230).

163 A name historically borne by *hetairai* as well as respectable women: Gomme and Sandbach (1973), 291, meaning 'beloved of/to all' or 'loving to all'. It perhaps invites comparison or contrast with Habrotonon, whose name could suggest a bitter taste or a cause of bitterness (it comes from the herb 'wormwood': but see Gomme and Sandbach (1973), 291 and 466 on its qualities as an aphrodisiac). On the two women taken together, see Traill (2008), 229. For the possibilities concerning her mask, see

Brea (1981), 138 fig. 226, Mask 32 *IBT* 5 at *MNC*³, 40 and Green (1994) (a suggestion here, not his), 113, fig. 5.6: a small terracotta plaque from Kavalla, early Hellenistic with a selection of masks, bottom centre. See Furley (2009),18 for a more tentative comment that the young bride might be represented by the False Maiden.

164 Furley (2009), 198–204. See above on The *Hetaira* for the exact nature of the insult at 646.

165 Gomme and Sandbach (1973), 353, where they quote Andokides 4.14 (*Against Alcibiades).* See Harrison, 40–1 on marriage dissolution due to a husband's behaviour with courtesans.

166 See Bathrellou (2009), xix and *passim* for an extensive treatment of this part of the play. There have been several notable discoveries relating to other plays by Menander too. See Arnott (2004a) with (2004b) on finds relating to *Epitrepontes* in particular and Furley (2013). For more updated material from the same papyrus roll as Gronewald (1986), see Furley (2013) and Römer (2012a and 2012b): the end of Smikrines's speech and the beginning of Pamphile's are now nearly complete (114).

167 See originally Gronewald (1986). In the final scene of Act III, Chairestratos and Smikrines were on the stage: see Arnott (2004a), 39. Arnott suggests that Chairestratos was eavesdropping on Smikrines (41) and draws attention to possible hints that the former was in love with Habrotonon (42).

168 See further Cohn-Haft (1995), 3. The text is fragmentary, but it seems that the father here would prefer his daughter to initiate the divorce (5), although he does not use the Greek verb *apoleipein*, 'to leave' a husband, but rather *apienai*, a general word for going away. Perhaps, if she did not, it might affect her reputation (7 n. 27). He assumes a responsibility to protect, rather than just referring to the law (6), an interpretation which would leave open the possibility that he is motivated by affection for his daughter and not just a determination to recover her dowry. These questions are discussed by Petrides (2014), 28 with reference to Harrison in n. 30, Furley (2009), 28 and 147 and Rosivach (1984).

169 See Petrides (2014), 28ff on a tragic parallel for her words in Sophocles's *Electra* 597–8, but not her more conciliatory tone, and Traill (2008), 222 on Euripides's heroines.

170 Arnott (2004a), 43 notes the debt to such *agones*, 'competitive exchanges', in Greek tragedy: see ch. 5 on the Arbitration Scene which gives *Epitrepontes* its name.

171 Sandbach rightly claimed that the situation is different, since there the husband's only fault is losing his money. In *Epitrepontes*, Smikrines cares about the dowry, but also that his daughter has been rejected. Diction and metre in the Didot speech did suggest comedy rather than tragedy, but Sandbach found the style stiff and formal for Menander, although he considered the sentiments worthy of him. For Sandbach's views in full, see Gomme and Sandbach (1973), 723–4.

172 See Traill (2008), 213ff on such a scene as a stock motif of New Comedy.

173 See Schaps (1977) and Sommerstein (1980) *passim* on the conventions for avoiding the naming in public contexts of freeborn Athenian women by Athenian freeborn men. But a high proportion of these impersonal references to Pamphile are by a slave or a slave *hetaira*, Onesimos and Habrotonon, both of whom could have used her name (Sommerstein (1980), 393). In any case, the way in which Menander presents the characters could have led to her not being named, with the result that she seems distant. Compare Plangon in *Samia*, where it is not clear, because of the naming convention, whether Moschion's late use of her name (630) has indicated a certain distance in his attitude towards her up until Act V.

174 See above on Rape and Seduction with Further Reading on the Tauropolia.
175 The term *parthenos* can have a strong nuance: see Virginity above for Greek myth in this context.
176 Prof. E. W. Handley (pers. comm.). Compare the gradual technique to prepare for Knemon's entrance in *Dyscolus*, and the opposite technique (whether derived from Menander as he thinks, or not) for Euclio in Plautus's *Aulularia*. More importantly, no other young, wealthy, raped citizen woman ever has a speaking part in extant New Comedy: Bathrellou (2012), 178.
177 See above on Divorce, where the evidence is not conclusive.
178 See the conclusion to ch. 5 on slaves and power as a theme in *Epitrepontes*. Persuasion gives *hetairai* like Habrotonon and other women power over men.
179 See above on Rape and Seduction, discussions of the historical issues by Ogden (1996, 1997), Omitowoju (2002), Lape (2004) and Harrison (1998) with Further Reading and the Conclusion to this book.
180 It is hoped that illegitimacy, the *oikos* and a full discussion of Charisios's motives will be dealt with in future in a study of the male characters in Menander.
181 It was Pamphile who exposed it with Sophrone's help in order to conceal it from Charisios: Arnott (1997 with corr.), 387, probably based on line 1118, where Onesimos says that the nurse knows what he is talking about.
182 See Omitowoju (2002), 232, for example, and Petrides (2014), 42ff and 48.
183 Traill (2008) finds her lacking in deference, down to Smikrines' character and their 'underdeveloped emotional bond' (219–20), but observes some different ways in which an actor could portray her, such as 'hopelessly impractical' or 'coy, slyly calculating' (222). Bathrellou (2009), 107 finds her tone 'neither imploring nor dismissive'. Römer (2012a), 117 finds her 'a self-assured young woman'.
184 Römer (2012a), 118ff thinks she alludes to wronging him as he realizes he has wronged her but Furley (2013), 88ff. disputes some of her interpretations.
185 On the boards of Gynaikonomoi to oversee women's activities see Gagarin (2000), 352. See further Gagarin (2001) on how women are portrayed in the orators for the ideal versus reality.
186 Line reference as in Arnott (1996b): Gomme and Sandbach (1973), 303ff. Getas says 'Pig on the mountain . . .' of Demeas just before this, which Arnott (323n. c) takes to mean 'unreasonable stubbornness'.
187 That use of her name has been delayed (see above) draws attention to it.
188 See the new text in Römer (2012a and b) and Furley (2013).
189 Prof. E. W. Handley (pers. comm.): his point is, perhaps, that they do not know what is going on. One might suggest 'the family' as a translation.
190 Gomme and Sandbach (1973), 350 comments on the pleasant irony.
191 See Arnott (1997 with corr.), 471 and Harrison (1998), v.1, 43 with n. 1, using evidence from Demosthenes, Isaeus 3 and Ps. Andocides 4.
192 She reminds her father that she owes her ability to reason to the education he gave her, according to Römer (2012a), 117 on lines 801–3, but see also Furley (2013), 87, who disagrees.
193 Following Austin (2008). Furley (2009), 211 on line 705, however, taking note of Arnott (2004b), still has this as a disputed reading. Another suggestion is that Pamphile utters an exclamation of distress.
194 Note the slightly different emphasis from Traill (2009), 188 on Smikrines as mercenary.

195 Gomme and Sandbach (1973), 357. Bathrellou (2009), 160 thinks the sense is more
    that Pamphile speaks of her eyes as blurred with tears. This returns her to a more
    traditionally feminine state than standing up to her father has been.

196 See Gronewald's (1986) notes (11) on v. 35 of the new frag. 2, with Römer (2012a)
    and Furley (2013).

197 Blundell (1980), 34 n. 17.

198 Bain (1977), 111–12, 125 thinks, surprisingly, that she has already recognized
    Pamphile. He does not discuss the absence of a third 'asides' character. For
    Bathrellou, however (2009), 161, it is 'simpler to assume' that Habrotonon comes out
    of Chairestratos's house to soothe the baby and first addresses Pamphile at 858.

199 Traill (2008), 233 comments on the contrast between her appearance and the fact that
    she is nursing a baby.

200 On the other hand, Chrysis in *Samia* is reported by the young man Moschion to be
    well accepted by her freeborn neighbours (36–38); this in spite of the fact that her
    background was presumably known, although she would not have dressed as an
    hetaira as such.

201 When she enters is disputed. See Bathrellou (2009), 161.

202 Habrotonon may seek to avoid 'the hostile response' that she might expect due to her
    profession (Ireland (1992), 77). See further below.

203 The verb used by Pamphile to ask if Habroton knows her, *gignosko*, is from the same
    root in Greek as the word for the recognition motif, *anagnorisis*. Pamphile would be
    remembered easily by Habrotonon, but not Habrotonon by Pamphile, because of her
    distress after the rape, and perhaps too because of Habrotonon's slave status.

204 Habrotonon is 'sweet' not bitter, as her name has implied. See above. Taking *gynai* to
    be a term of respect or affection, she could be 'maintaining the social divide' here, as
    Ireland (1992), 77 suggests. Sandbach points out that this is the only place in
    Menander where the vocative *gynai* begins a sentence (Gomme and Sandbach
    (1973), 359): emphatic, therefore. Dickey (1996), 86ff finds a range of tones, noting
    how in this passage the term is used reciprocally by two women.

205 See Furley (2014) on *anagnorisis*, 'recognition' as a theme in Menander, the superficial
    motif concealing the exploration of character.

206 Gomme and Sandbach (1973), 359.

207 This address, *philtate*, already used to Pamphile by Habrotonon, expresses genuine
    affection (it is more frequent in tragedy): see Dickey (1996), 120, where she compares
    its use at *Misoumenos* 614 and 709 of Arnott (1996b), (213 and 308 of Sandbach's
    text), used by a daughter to her long-lost father and a man (quoted) pleading with his
    beloved respectively. Gomme (1957), 255 comments that respect turns to affection
    between free woman and slave.

208 Traill (2008), 233–4 notes the growing rapport between the two women, also giving a
    detailed analysis of their language here.

209 Although Bathrellou (2009), 167–8 notes that the phrase conveys emotion and has
    religious connotations, marking Pamphile's renewed status as a married woman.

210 She is a slave, after all, and some kind of sex slave too, probably: see the introduction
    to ch. 5 for a reminder of what this could mean.

211 Gomme and Sandbach (1973), 358.

212 On one reading, even *teknon*, the tragic word for child. On the baby, see further Heap
    (2002–3). What is the norm for talking to/about babies? See further Golden (1995),
    29 on *paidion* ('child') as a pet name. Compare the nurse at *Samia* 242, who definitely
    uses *teknon*, and see further Dickey (1996) 65ff, with references, and 211, 246.

213 See Traill (2008), 234 on the wife ironically receiving the *hetaira* into the family home.

214 See Gomme and Sandbach (1973), 294 on how, again, the audience cannot have only learnt the truth with the characters if the arbitration scene is to have dramatic effect.

215 Onesimos's direct quotation of Charisios's emotional words prepare for the impact of his actual entrance on stage finally at 908.

216 Gomme and Sandbach (1973), 370–3.

217 If Habrotonon did gain her freedom, her rise in status would parallel Pamphile's becoming a *gyne*: so Traill (2008), 240 on Pamphile's 'happy ending'. See further Gomme and Sandbach (1973), 374–5 on 1018ff: perhaps Onesimos and Habrotonon were freed.

5 Slaves in *Epitrepontes*: Habrotonon, Onesimos, Syros and Daos

1 There will be some overlap in the characters chosen for analysis, because several characters may be categorized in different ways.

2 It is hoped to explore elsewhere the power of women over men, and the stereotypical comic soldier as, in one way at least, another 'young man in love'.

3 Garnsey (1996), 6. On slaves in literature, see further Fitzgerald (2000), 8ff.

4 Richard Re (2002), as cited by http://www.bbc.co.uk/ethics/slavery/modern/modern_1.shtml (accessed 16 July 2018). For definitions of slavery, including being forced to work and being treated as property, see antislavery.org.

5 For examples, see www.antislavery.org and http://www.troniefoundation.org/about-us/rani-hong (accessed 16 July 2018). Rani Hong has spoken about her experiences as a child trafficking survivor. Mauretania retains a slave population in spite of the UN Universal Declaration of Human Rights: https://www.theguardian.com/global-development/2018/jun/08/the-unspeakable-truth-about-slavery-in-mauritania (accessed 16 July 2018).

6 The plaque is outside St Andrew's church in Chesterton. The slave was Olaudah Equiano (also called Gustavus Vassa).

7 Richard Re (2002), as cited by http://www.bbc.co.uk/ethics/slavery/modern/modern_1.shtml (accessed 16 July 2018).

8 Cartledge (2002), 261–2.

9 See Cartledge (2002), 255–6 on whether natal alienation together with social 'living death' (Orlando Patterson's description of slavery) gives the essence of the slave or whether it lies in being property or an outsider. See Patterson (1982), 5–7, 13 and 113 with 105ff on the various means of enslavement. See also Braund (2011), 131–2 for an epitaph dated *c*. 350–300 BCE (IG II 2.10051) about the displaced Paphlagonian Atotas, though it is not clear whether Atotas was literate in Greek (his master may have written the inscription down for him).

10 A notable exception to this observation is the helots who were Spartan slaves, for which see Cartledge (2011): they were treated symbolically as conquered, however (89). See further Garlan rev.ed. (1988), 93–8 and 155–6.

11 Braund (2011), 120–3.

12 See Cartledge (2004) 57–8, 80ff and Lane Fox (1973), 88 with references at 513.

13 Wrenhaven (2012), 14 points out that the same word could be used for 'kidnapper' as 'slave-trader'. Despite the Greeks' reliance on slaves, as she notes, this word *andrapodistes* could be used as an insult. See Casson (1991), 102–3 (with 75 and 177) for pirates as an ever-present danger to shipping and the consequences for personal losses on the part of the merchants. For state cooperation with piracy, see, for instance, Demosthenes' First Philippic 34, where Philip, Alexander the Great's father, finances his wars by preying on sea-borne commerce.

14 Casson (1991), 177.

15 Barbarians would trade slaves for Greek goods: Braund (2011), 123, 126ff.

16 See Herodotus v.6 describing the Thracians as selling their own children. Sometimes the slaves' families hoped for a better life for them thereby.

17 The evidence is, unfortunately, largely literary: see Garland (1990), 89. If drama may be believed, infants were left out in the open or in large *pithoi*, 'jars', with 'recognition tokens', items which it seems their parents hoped might one day lead to their being reunited with their children. The same sort of trinkets were, however, buried with dead babies. See ch. 4.

18 Demosthenes' speech *Against Nicostratos*, 53 (probably by Apollodorus, son of the slave Pasion), composed in the fourth century BCE, tells a complicated story in the course of which Nikeratos's brother receives Nikeratos's letters after he has been sold as a slave from Athens to Aegina, but he fails to ransom him. The events are in fact part of a scam (Dem.53.6–7). The initial 26 minae being allegedly demanded before the balance had to be paid was roughly ten times the average price of a slave: Braund (2011), 118 on 53.10.

19 See Marshall (2013), 185ff (with 187 n. 51) for a reference in the prologue of Plautus's *Mercator* to buying a girl or 'sex slave' on a trading trip to Rhodes and bringing her back by ship. Plautus's play is adapted from the Greek by Philemon, but this may reflect the Greek original.

20 Casson (1991), 128, 158, 162.

21 By the time they reached the sea, slaves might have been sold several times already and then be sold on in any direction: Braund (2011), 129. See Casson (1991), 99ff for a description of what happened when ships arrived at Athens' port the Piraeus and all the different goods that were unloaded there, including, presumably, slaves.

22 Slaves were often exchanged for wine: Braund (2011), 121. See Casson (1991), 107 for slaves carrying sacks of coins, for maritime loans, to the ships; traders might also entrust the cash and the voyage to a slave agent with authority to act in their name.

23 De Souza (1995), 188 emphasizes the distances and how these would lessen the likelihood of rescue, escape or survival.

24 See Marshall (2013), 175ff who discusses the evidence for sex slaves from ancient comedy and compares modern examples from South East Asia. For the *hetaira* as a kind of sex-worker, see ch. 4.

25 See Trümper (2010) on possible structures for the sale of slaves (it is difficult for archaeologists to identify such buildings) but covering the Graeco-Roman period only, reviewed by Hitchner (2011). Crete was popular as a market in the Hellenistic period: De Souza (1995), 188. See further generally Braund (2011), 122 and 129 and Casson (1991), 70 on the Black Sea, with 71 on Byzantium or Byzantion as Megara's colony. At Delos, in the second century BCE (see above on piracy), the pirates, who often sold their goods themselves, had a market which could allegedly take in and send away thousands of slaves in one day: Casson (1991), 165–7.

26 See Wiedemann (1987), 10 on slaves being deprived of basic rights. See also Xen. *Oec*.9.5 (Ischomachos's slaves are not allowed to breed without permission) and Braund (2011), 124. See further on the mines, Fisher (2001), 47–9 with plates.

27 Aeschines *Against Timarchos* 1.97, cited by Braund (2011), 130. See further Scheidel (1995, 1996).

28 See above on traders' slaves. Braund (2011), 131.

29 Patterson (1982), 8, 52; 50, 62ff. See further Golden (2011b), 136ff and Xenophon's *Oeconomicus*. No dedicated Greek slave quarters have been found: Cohen (2011), 482, citing Cahill on Olynthus.

30 Braund (2011), 127.

31 Urbainczyk (2008), 30–1 mentions the Spartan helots and a revolt on Chios (led by one Drimakos) a century after Menander. See further Vogt (1974), 79ff.

32 On stereotyping by society and in literature, see Further Reading: Slave names and stereotypes.

33 Gomme and Sandbach (1973), 290.

34 Marshall (2013), 182ff.

35 See the cover of DuBois (2008). The photograph (1863) is of Gordon, a former slave (escaped) from Louisiana. Whip marks can be seen on his back.

36 See further McKeown (2007) on the difficulties of interpreting the evidence.

37 Braund (2011), 113.

38 DuBois (2008), 29, 152ff and 162.

39 Hall (1997), 93 observes that only fictional representations of excluded groups like slaves could address the public, in the theatre, through the 'multivocal form of tragedy'. At 111 she discusses the slave voice in tragedy as almost completely that of those who were once free. See, for example, *Troades,* 'Trojan Women', with Rabinowitz (1998), and Further Reading: Barbarians and Tragedy. See also, on Euripides, Synodinou (1975).

40 Hall (2006), 200.

41 *Politics* (1255b). Gill (1996), investigates Greek thinking about the self but does not appear to address the paradox at the heart of Aristotle's views that slaves are humans as well as like animals.

42 *Politics* 1253b20–23, 1255a3–12: they argue that slaves are not different by nature and are enslaved by force.

43 The slave trade itself is 'couched in discourse of property and exchange': Braund (2011), 119.

44 Hunt (1998), 2–3 and 12–13: instances are treated in isolation or misleadingly described as emergencies. See Further Reading: Stereotypes and representations.

45 Harrison (1998) v.1 164ff, Todd (1993), 184 with n. 32.

46 Hall (1989), 2–3. 'Barbarian' was a term coined by Greeks to describe non-Greeks. Todd (1993), 189 notes that comparative evidence from other slave societies suggests that paternalism is one way in which owners come to terms with their position. See further Patterson (1982).

47 See further Wrenhaven (2012), ch. 1 on 'The Language of Slavery', especially 17.

48 Finley (1981), 98, 133.

49 See further Wrenhaven (2012), 14–15: it appears most often in a military context. There it covers the newly enslaved, those, technically, still free (14). In time, however, it became a general word for 'slave', perhaps connecting slaves and animals by its derivation from the Greek for 'footed', as in 'four-footed' for wild and domesticated beasts (15). Such removal of personhood helped to justify the enslavement.

50 Garlan (1988), 22.

51 See Gomme and Sandbach (1973), 320 on 377ff.
52 Harrison (1998), 170.
53 Todd (1993), 96, 187, 172.
54 Harrison (1998), 167.
55 See the word play by Habrotonon at *Epitr.* 468–9. The latter word for 'young master' is rare in both tragedy (three times in Euripides) and other Greek authors, including what survives of Diphilus and Philemon, where it might be expected because of the subject matter. Dickey (1996), 95ff discusses *despotes* in the vocative case including metaphorical uses, concluding that it denotes the direct power of the addressee over the speaker.
56 On freedom see further Patterson (1992).
57 Cartledge (1985a), 38 and Garnsey (1996), 7 and 97.
58 See further Fisher (2001), 68.
59 His activities are described in Isocrates 17. See above on Transport and trade and A slave voice? and Pomeroy (1997), 183ff.
60 Todd (1993), 190 with n. 39.
61 Gomme and Sandbach (1973), 567 on *Samia* 237.
62 Pomeroy (1994), (Xen. *Oec.* 65–6). This work predates Menander, however: see Further Reading.
63 Todd (1993), 187–8. On such slaves, see above with ch. 2 on the audience. It is possible that slaves were not allowed in the gymnasium in the fourth century BCE (Wrenhaven (2012), 63ff, citing Aeschines 1.138).
64 Harrison (1998), 182 and 171.
65 See Glossary and Fisher (2001), 68ff, Todd (1993), 174 and Harrison v.1 (1998), 236–7.
66 Todd (1993), 193.
67 Wiedemann (1981), 3.
68 Austin and Vidal-Naquet (1977), 147, citing Gernet. For more on attitudes to slavery at this period, see Vidal-Naquet (1986), 168–83, although the discussion there is inconclusive. See also Todd (1993), 192ff, who gives details of the cases on which the argument depends, that is, Aeschines 1, Demosthenes 34 and one mentioned in some inscriptions from *c.* 320 BCE, the *phialai exeleutherikai*, which record some manumissions, but ones which had to be paid for by the ex-slaves.
69 Arnott (1997 with corr.), 383–4: 'firm evidence' for the date of the play, such as some reference to a dated external event, is, however, lacking.
70 Compare Hall (2006), 200 with n. 57 on the substantial role of Xanthias in *Frogs* (405 BCE) being perhaps a reaction to a recent emancipation of slaves who had been rowers at the battle of Arginusae the previous year.
71 Bradley in Hornblower, Spawforth and Eidenow (2012), 434.
72 Wiedemann (1987), 12. See above on the reluctance to enslave other Greeks and below Further Reading: Barbarians and tragedy, Slave names and stereotypes, Stereotypes and representations and Ruffell in Revermann (ed.) (2014), 161ff on slaves in Aristophanes.
73 Garnsey (1996), 9.
74 Compare Getas, Thrasonides's slave, at *Misoumenos* 34–5, if the lines are given to him rather than to his master. Bathrellou (2014a), 43 points out the contrast between a loyal slave and Smikrines, a greedy and therefore bad citizen.
75 See above on Terminology. Note the probably derogatory diminutive and the neuter plural which gives an impersonal tone, as the people are already becoming 'things'. The word and its derivatives are, interestingly, not common in either tragedy or Aristophanes (Wrenhaven (2012), 15). See above.

76 This is noted by Konstan (2013), 145ff, who wonders whether there is irony or sympathy here. See above on deportation and colonization.

77 Literary evidence against the negative effects of natal alienation.

78 Bathrellou (2014a), 44 n. 22 feels that the hope here is 'not necessarily' for freedom, but it does seem to be implied. For the possibilities of escaping slavery in real life, see above on Greek manumission. Ireland in Menander (2010), 74 compares the self-interest, disputed by other scholars, of the *hetaira* or slave courtesan, Habrotonon, in Menander's *Epitrepontes* in seeking the mother of the baby in that play. For Habrotonon, see below and ch. 4.

79 On the waiter see Bathrellou (2014a), 43ff. He refers to the mills, a place for slave punishment.

80 Marshall (2013), 182, n. 36.

81 The prologue is probably spoken by 'some divine personage': Gomme and Sandbach (1973), 636.

82 The large, inland old capital of Caria, about half-way between Miletus and Halicarnassus. The capital had moved to Halicarnassus by 355 BCE: Hornblower (1982), 68. Several Macedonian colonies were established there in Hellenistic times. The modern town of Milas covers the site, and the whereabouts of the ancient market is not known (Arnott (2000), 211, n. 3.).

83 Another impersonal neuter plural.

84 See above on kidnapping and piracy, poverty and ransoms.

85 Gomme and Sandbach (1973), 665 on line 355 and Arnott (2000), 275 n. 5.

86 Interestingly, the man who is also for sale addresses his fellow-slave at line 13 as *beltiste*, 'sir', not a word the man could expect to be used to him normally, since being born into slavery or losing his liberty. See Gomme and Sandbach (1973), 638. See further Bathrellou (2014a), 51 on the slaves' preserved self-respect, with her notes.

87 Gomme and Sandbach (1973), 637.

88 Literary evidence for a slave appearing to care for a mistress, as the girl is found to be freeborn (Arnott (2000), 205). In *Hero* (see 15ff) a slave falls in love with his mistress, even representing himself as the father of her child (see Gomme and Sandbach (1973), 385).

89 Underlined by Getas's reference to being put in charge of the *parapompe* or 'spoils' (literally 'escort', 'transport') at line 35: he is a soldier's slave like Sosias in *Perikeiromene*. (Miller gives the lines to Thrasonides.) Krateia may have been sold as a slave in Cyprus (Arnott (1996b), 253 with n. 1 and 263 with note *a*).

90 A popular literary motif, as it is hoped to explore elsewhere. See the frontispiece to this book for this speech on papyrus.

91 The word used is derived from *hybris*: see Glossary. Getas is surprised that this is at the hands of a woman.

92 The suggested reading is *despoina*, the female equivalent of *despotes*, 'master'.

93 Gomme and Sandbach (1973), 290. There is word play on the name in the New Testament in Paul's letter to Philemon.

94 Quoted by Sandbach (Gomme and Sandbach, (1973), 291). The cook's status as a character may be slave or free. See Cox (2013), 168 with n. 44. Karion is also a slave name in Aristophanes.

95 Gomme and Sandbach (1973), 302.

96 See Further Reading on Slave names and stereotypes. The interpretation of Daos's character here depends partly on the positive view taken below of Syros's motives.

97 'A word which cannot readily be translated': see further Todd (1993), 92–4. See also Harvey (1990), 107ff.

98 Gomme and Sandbach (1973), 306.
99 Cohoon (1914), 157: it may be intended to be overheard by the judge, in order to prejudice him.
100 A charcoal burner was a common occupation (Furley (2009), 149, citing Aristophanes *Ach.*, for example, 664ff). Sticks from the woods were treated in special ovens and converted into fuel for the city. The Mytilene mosaic of this scene labels the slaves incorrectly: see ch. 2, fig. 2.1.
101 Compare how Daos in *Georgos* has, as one of his functions, being someone with a great deal to say, thus giving a vivid account of events off-stage. That play also pairs as two slaves a Daos with a Syros (see line 40).
102 On the baby in Menander, see Heap (2002–3).
103 For example, Cohoon (1914). 173. Ireland in Menander (2010), 219 lists Daos's negative qualities.
104 Gomme and Sandbach (1973), 305 calls the garment in question a 'poor man's cloak', but it is a garment for work, and a poor man's because workers in the countryside are generally not rich; one could not easily operate a *dikella*, 'fork', with a cloak in a wind. It is Sostratos who wears a cloak in *Dyscolus* and it marks him out as rich. The translation 'jerkin' is better.
105 See Miller's direction *ad.loc.* (1987), 86; see also Gomme and Sandbach (1973), 311: if this other slave is elsewhere called Syros, although his naming as such in the (late) Mytilene mosaic of the play is not reliable evidence in this context, the diminutive, which is extant only here in *Epitrepontes*, must carry some significance; it would be being used deliberately by the speaker (that is, Daos).
106 'Breathless', says Sandbach (Gomme and Sandbach (1973)), 311.
107 See further Dover (1974), on Daos's feeling here (238 n. 12). Ireland (1992), 70 compares the comic effect of Daos's comments here with Gripus's reaction to his loss of the trunk in Plautus's *Rudens*, 1184ff.
108 These characteristics, despite slave stereotypes, for which see Social Background, are not confined to slaves in Menander: compare Smikrines's avarice in *Aspis*.
109 See above on Terminology.
110 On the Greek word *beltiste*, 'sir', as a form of address, see Gomme and Sandbach (1973), 185–6 on *Dysk.* 319 and Handley's edition of the play (1992), 155 on line 144, where Handley's examples suggest 'formal politeness' with 'a hint of self-righteous reproach', with Dickey (1996), 61, 110. See Ireland in Menander (2010), 218 as well (line 224) on the fitting politeness of the optative form of the Greek verb for 'sparing time' which is used. Dickey (111) finds that Socrates uses *beltiste* at times of triumph, when refuting an opponent, or taking pleasure in being about to do so; in Plato it is one of a number of familiar addresses 'largely restricted to the one character who plays the dominant role in a given dialogue' (113). See also 120 for other uses in Menander, and 139 for how *agathe*, 'my good friend', by contrast, always occurs in Menander in contexts where the speaker is dominant.
111 See Further Reading: Forms of address.
112 See above and Cohoon (1914), 157 for this interpretation.
113 Compare how Smikrines interrupts Daos in the opening scene of *Aspis* above, relieving the serious mood and showing his mercenary nature.
114 Compare Pamphile later to her father, the same Smikrines. Did Peitho, 'Persuasion', perhaps speak the prologue?
115 Furley (2009), 152 cites Dem.21.187, where the orator complains he has no babies like Meidias to give him an advantage with the jury.
116 Gomme and Sandbach (1973), 312–13 and Ireland in Menander (2010), 222–3.

117 Arist. *Ath. Pol.* 52.1 is cited by Gomme and Sandbach (1973), 313: calling Daos this kind of robber in the Greek is 'unfair' here, they say, but Ireland in Menander (2010), 223 thinks the word aptly describes his underhand behavior.

118 Gomme and Sandbach (1973), 313.

119 Cohoon (1914), 211: 'a mocking repetition of Daos's phrase' and 212.

120 Gomme and Sandbach (1973), 314.

121 See above on Manumission and freedom.

122 Gomme and Sandbach (1973), 315. The three matching phrases, 'hunting lions, bearing arms, Olympic running' (lines 324–5) add to the elevation.

123 This may refer to the *stadion* or 'sprint'.

124 Furley (2009) comments (5) on tragedy as a kind of 'meta-language' for Athenians for emphasis or to add subtle meaning to their arguments. On metatheatricality (theatre within theatre, or attention drawn to the unreality of the drama) and the tragic references here see further Slater (2002); it is not just parody: 3–4; the degree of comedy may vary: 6. See also 239 on its presence in Menander, with Hunter (1985), 135, below on the Effect and purpose of the Arbitration Scene and Further Reading: The Arbitration Scene. On acquaintance with tragedy in Menander's time, see further chapter 2 here with Xanthakis-Karamanos (1980).

125 For the paucity of evidence bearing on the presence of slaves at the theatre (Plato *Gorgias* 502b–d and Theophrastus *Char.* 9), see Pickard-Cambridge (1988), 265 and Csapo (1995), IVBi, 290–1. Daos might also have seen these stories performed, therefore. It is certain that slaves were present at Roman festivals: see Plautus's *Poenulus*, the prologue, at 23ff.

126 And authority: compare how Daos at *Aspis* 399ff resembles a tragic messenger, lending credibility to his story (Hurst (1990), 97). But some have found Syros 'pretentious': see MacCary, although he does not (1969), 291 n. 25. Against the argument for dignity, his undignified comic slave mask would contrast with his tragic hero voice, but the effect might be to overturn expectations of a slave character.

127 Exposure of babies was probably common in Menander's time, but for a child to be reunited with its family was uncommon except in fiction. See ch. 4. Of course, in discussing its context, it should be remembered that the plot of *Epitrepontes* is thought to be based on a tragic plot which was centred around the exposure of a child, that is, Euripides' *Alope*; see Gomme and Sandbach (1973), 303.

128 Gomme and Sandbach (1973), 316. See Sandbach further on how Syros's style 'keeps rising towards that of tragedy'.

129 One of these being an attraction betweeen brother and sister, as in Menander's own *Perikeiromene*: Ireland in Menander (2010), 224.

130 See Further Reading: Slave names and stereotypes.

131 See Furley (2009), 143ff: there are differences, but the audience would appreciate the tragic precedent. Smikrines may, as a result, have been expected to recognize the baby's tokens.

132 See above on Manumission and freedom for a possible change in attitudes to Greek slaves in the fourth century BCE.

133 See Further Reading: The Arbitration Scene.

134 See, however, Ireland's (2010) and Furley's (2009) commentaries on the *Epitrepontes*, Porter (2000) and Profitt (2011), an excellent analysis, in Further Reading: The Arbitration Scene.

135 Cohoon (1914), 229.

136 Ireland in Menander (2010), 224.

137 The size of the jury varied according to the seriousness of the issue: in the fourth century there is evidence of a range from 200 to 2,500 (Carey and Reid (eds) (1985), 2, and Harrison v.2 'Procedure' (1998), 47). On audience sizes and the evidence for the possible presence of slaves in the theatre, see ch. 2.

138 See Omitowoju (2002), 161–2 and Proffitt (2011), 161ff, 164; Furley (2009), 155 points out that reference to myths as paradigms would have frequently found their way into court cases.

139 Furley (2009), 143–4. See further Heap (2002–3).

140 Hunter (1985), 134–5.

141 Cuddon (1991), 483.

142 Dover (2012).

143 Goldhill (1991), 207–10.

144 *Pace* Iversen (2001) on Syros.

145 Compare how Smikrines stupidly reveals his mercenary motives at the beginning of *Aspis*.

146 Smikrines being freeborn but perhaps a less attractive character than the slave, Syros, an interesting contrast, again recalling Daos and Smikrines in the *Aspis*.

147 Katsouris (1983), 31.

148 Gomme and Sandbach (1973), 294.

149 Babies are used in Menander to characterize; see ch. 4 with the comments below here on Habrotonon and Onesimos at lines 464ff. This is one of their main functions, rather than to demonstrate the affection of couples (Post (1939)). See further Heap (2002–3) with its critique in Proffitt (2011). See also Ireland in Menander (2010), 225. Proffitt (2011) expands on the baby's important contribution to the theme of slavery already noted by Heap (1998) and (2002–3).

150 Cohoon (1914) *passim*. The effect of a pair of adversarial speeches in a play would be a compound of experience from real life and from other plays. Real life here would include education as well as jury service.

151 The Mytilene mosaic of this scene includes Syros's wife and the child: see fig. 2.1.

152 See Gomme and Sandbach (1973), 321: the exact nuance is not clear. The slaves are not, in general, distinguished by their language.

153 Kinship terms are among the class of familiar appellations which are used without the article. There may be irony that a kinship term is used by Syros, not Onesimos, to whose master the baby belongs. Dickey (1996), 71 finds the Greek word *paidion* indicates affection rather than age. Compare Syros's comments about wrong to a person at 318, using *soma*, a Greek word meaning 'body' which in other contexts can mean 'slave'; this similarly draws attention to the baby's predicament over its identity. See above on neuter words for 'slave' and the acquiring of foreign (non-Greek) slaves.

154 *Pace* Iversen (2001) and his negative interpretation of his character.

155 For this word, see above on terminology.

156 Compare the humorous but crucial disputes over a ring on an epic scale in J. R. R. Tolkien's *Lord of the Rings*. One could add the Rings of Gyges and Polycrates and Wagner's Ring Cycle.

157 See above on the Arbitration Scene.

158 Frost (1988), 69.

159 Repeated references to this simple object have gradually intensified the sense of crisis: Onesimos has the one crucial identifying factor in his hand.

160 On verbal echoes between the end of an act and the opening of the next, see Handley (1968), 20, n. 8.

161 On monologues generally, see further below. If his monologues represent Onesimos's true feelings, such speeches and monologues by other slaves such as Habrotonon come close to a kind of slave 'voice', but see further above on this concept. The one word, *andres*, is the extent of his audience address at line 887. There is no pretend conversation with, or even vilification of, the audience, as occurs in Aristophanes. Nevertheless, the effect would be to defuse slightly the serious nature of Onesimos's report.

162 Blundell (1980), 5. Blundell discusses Onesimos's monologue here at 28–9. See also Bain (1977), 135ff.

163 For the terminology, see above.

164 Compare Getas in *Misoumenos*, who compares Krateia to the 'Magnetic Stone' (A43) (Menander, Miller (1987)). The sailing metaphor is not developed by allusion to tragedy as it is by Demeas at the beginning of *Samia* Act III; tragedy is also used by Syros in the Arbitration Scene above when talking about the baby's experiences. Simple metaphors are part of Onesimos's characterization. Later in the play he quotes philosophy (1087ff), though 'comically distorted': Arnott (1997 with corr.), 513, n. 1.

165 See on *Samia* lines 336–7, for example, where he calls her his 'Helen' of Troy.

166 Gomme and Sandbach (1973), 327 observe that the 'imprecise' word in the Greek 'does not imply killing'. Rather, Onesimos fears that he may be sold into a less pleasant form of slavery, such as, perhaps, working in a flour mill, a fate threatened by the young man Moschion to his slave, Daos at *Perik*. 277–8. See Arnott (1996b), *Hero* line 3 and his note b, and above on punishments.

167 Blundell (1980), 28.

168 For more on Habrotonon the *hetaira*, see ch. 4.

169 Blundell (1980), 28–9.

170 Slavery and femaleness intersect in her: Joshel and Murnaghan (1998), 3 of a female slave.

171 She may have feelings for her master: contrast what is possibly merely implied there with Daos's words at *Hero* 15: he is explicit about his love for a girl whom he knows may not really be a slave.

172 Plato's *Protagoras* 311a, for example (*LSJ*). See Dickey (1996), 113 on the use of this form of address by the person dominating the argument (Plato), with 119–20, 139 on how it is neutral as to friendliness but often indicates superiority (Aristophanes also) and is close to these usages in Menander, including here.

173 Gomme and Sandbach (1973), 329–30, Dickey (1996), 150–4. Contemptuous, as to slaves (*LSJ*); frequently in Plato, but only once in tragedy. Or 'brother', as in P. Oxy 215.1.

174 Gomme and Sandbach (1973), 329–30.

175 The speaker is disputed here, however. Onesimos more characteristically speaks in the Loeb by Arnott: see the note by Ireland in his commentary (2010), 232 and his reference to Arnott (1977), 20. Furley (2009), 174 disagrees with both, giving the address to Syros and translating it 'rogue' (104).

176 *Pace* Iversen (2001).

177 Gomme and Sandbach (1973), 331 under notes on line 458.

178 Onesimos's use of *despotes* for Charisios is possibly neutral in tone and appropriate, because, although he did not know it, he already has a *trophimos*.

179 There is word play here in the Greek with *trophimos . . . trephomenon* from the verb 'to bring up': see Gomme and Sandbach (1973), 292 on the etymology.

180 The Greek word is *paroinon*, which may be a little negative in nuance. On drunkenness and rape, see ch. 4. See also Gomme and Sandbach (1973), 338 on line 522 where

Habrotonon is imagining Charisios's confession: Sandbach thinks that for *methuon* there the translation 'drunk' is too strong, but that describes how he will be when she tricks him. Compare Gomme and Sandbach's note on *Perik.*142 and the use of *methuon* again there by Agnoia to describe Moschion's habitual behaviour in that play; the verb is also found at 471 used by Pataikos to Polemon. They do not feel, however, that any great degree of intoxication is implied: 'tipsy' might be the best translation.

181 Habrotonon may have had no choice about the loss of her virginity, as a victim of rape has none (Ireland in Menander (2010), 234): but see ch. 4 for differences between *hetairai* and *bordello* prostitutes or streetwalkers, that is, *pornai*.

182 Gomme and Sandbach note that Wilamowitz saw a 'scurrilous meaning' in Onesimos's words which goes unnoticed by Habrotonon because she is too modest. Gomme and Sandbach dismiss this interpretation, however (Gomme and Sandbach (1973), 337). Does she perhaps ignore his tone?

183 He expresses astonishment at her 'resourcefulness': Gomme and Sandbach (1973), 338.

184 Contrast Daos in *Aspis*, who takes charge of the situation and is close to his master. Onesimos is hardly networking with his fellow slaves either, in the way that Bathrellou (2014a), 47 wishes to see everywhere in Menander.

185 The sense of the adverbs is not necessarily negative here.

186 Slaves were sometimes rewarded with freedom: see Gomme and Sandbach (1973), 567 on *Samia* 237 (we may remember that Demeas frees Moschion's nurse), although it seems this was less common in Greece than Rome (see above). Furley (2009), 191 comments on how it is not clear if this was the outcome for Habrotonon, but that Onesimos fears that she will then have no motive to look for the real mother. See further on Habrotonon's hopes ch. 4.

187 On how altruistic Habrotonon is, see Ireland in Menander (2010), 236 on 541. He rightly defends her against other scholars' accusations that freedom is her prime concern, but notes that she is 'someone whose role in society would make total altruism unnatural'. For her prayer on exiting to *Peitho*, Persuasion, see ch. 4 with Furley (2009), 192. Gomme and Sandbach (1973), 339 observe that the elevated style wins her sympathy.

188 Being freed from slavery carried a stigma and fewer opportunities in Greece (see above).

189 The verb in the Greek can have this sense, though his claim may be ironic and poignant, since he is only a slave.

190 Contrast, for example, a black maid in the film of Kathryn Stockett's novel *The Help* (2011), directed by Tate Taylor, who finds a ring belonging to her mistress and takes it to put her children through college, having been refused a loan for this purpose by her employer.

191 For this word as expressing endearment, see *Wasps* 610 and *Thesmo.* 792. It is, however, more frequently contemptuous: And. 1.130, Dem. 25.57, Ar. *EN* 1171b10.

192 See above on how the slave trade for women often, but not always, meant being traded for sex. See also ch. 4 on the *Hetaira*. There were probably possibilities for female sex or domestic slaves to exploit the affectionate feelings of good masters as well as the risks of sexual maltreatment by bad ones. Such opportunities may also have existed for male slaves, however.

193 'A notorious puzzle' (see Gomme and Sandbach (1973), 344–5). Obscenity is rare in Menander, and where it does occur, it has an explanation; for instance, Sosias at *Perik.*

483–4 is drunk and a soldier's slave, whereas here it may be part of Onesimos's characterization. See Kassel (1996), 58.

194 On this dialogue between Pamphile and her father, extended by continuing papyrus finds, see ch. 4.

195 See the discussion of this scene in ch. 4.

196 Of course, she may stand to gain from this approach: see the discussion of her motives above.

197 Oaths by Apollo are almost exclusively male in Menander: see Sommerstein (1995), 65–6, especially 66. It may serve to draw attention to unmanly hysteria in Charisios. At 951, for another example of such an attitude, Onesimos seems to be stressing that a woman led him, a man, astray (that line is not complete, however).

198 Gomme and Sandbach (1973), 360.

199 See Further Reading. Furley (2009), 226 notes that slaves generally, 'being in close attendance on their owners', make good messengers to the audience, presumably as they are often privy to family secrets.

200 Though, as noted elsewhere, it was probably conventional not to stage such meetings between husbands and wives or lovers.

201 At 887 he uses explicit audience address *(andres,* 'gentlemen'). See below on Monologue. Furley (2009), 228 sees scorn also at 'the capers of the free' in his choice of *lalein* for Smikrines speaking (emotionally) to his daughter at 886, translating the Greek verb as 'went on about' (compare Demeas's description of the nurse's babblings while he is trapped in the pantry at *Samia* 241).

202 See Heap (1992), 57, although Arnott (1995), 151, n. 5 requires more evidence that *sphodra* is colloquial. Dover (1987), 57 does remark on the fact that there is no *sphodra* in Aeschylus or Euripides, so to that extent it is a comic rather than a tragic word. 'Prosaic' may be a more precise description.

203 See further Furley (2009), 226ff with reference to Porter (2000) on the tragic language elsewhere in Charisios's reported speech. (Porter also discusses the effect of the Arbitration Scene.) He notes with references that it is a tragic motif to prepare the ground for 'the appearance of a character suffering from emotional distress'.

204 Gomme and Sandbach (1973), 362.

205 There is something secretive about the Greek verb for 'to slip out' (904), and Onesimos speaks like a distressed hero in tragedy: Furley (2009), 231.

206 Dover (1987), 64 and 48 of writer and reader.

207 Menander's *Samia* employs extensive use of monologue.

208 For the increasing role of the actor in the fourth century BCE, see ch. 2. Greek actors enjoyed a higher status than Roman ones, yet a slave role might be coveted.

209 For more on Charisios's monologue, see the conclusion to this book.

210 Williams (1983), 40–50. For Ireland in Menander (2010), 249, for example, Onesimos's address to the audience at 887 is merely one of the examples he gives of similar 'mild ruptures of the dramatic illusion ... at moments of high emotion ... hardly felt and readily ... understandable' in a theatre without stage lighting. He goes on to refer to how monologues are at one level artificial, as their purpose is to impart information.

211 The quotation is from Williams (1983), 49. He discusses *Hamlet* and *Macbeth*. Blundell (1980), 75 on Menander notes that variation between different forms of address in a speech is to be found where feelings are strongly aroused. See further Bain (1977), 206–7 and 230 for uses of *andres,* 'gentlemen', an address discussed in Further Reading.

212 Gomme and Sandbach (1973), 364. Socrates has a *daimonion*, but there is controversy about what this means. See further Bussanich and Smith (eds), (2013), 284–93: it is a divinity or a voice (whether external or internal is disputed) which warns against certain actions. Here in *Epitrepontes*, it tells Charisios what he has done wrong; there may be humour, or perhaps the meaning of the word is different or has changed, to being now a kind of conscience. But it may be used again about punishment at 927 (see Arnott (1997 with corr.), although Gomme and Sandbach (1973), 365 do not include this as a reading. (In the New Testament, the word can, but need not have negative nuances). The idea (as *phrourarchon*, 'guardian'), occurs again in Onesimos's 'philosophy' at 1093ff, there partly in relation to a man's character. See below. For more ancient references to these ideas, see Ireland in Menander (2010), 258.

213 'Editors disagree about where this starts' (Gomme and Sandbach (1973), 364).

214 For instance, Gomme and Sandbach (1973), 363 and 366.

215 See Bain (1977), 145ff. Bain argues his case from dialogue which ends Act IV. See also Blundell (1980), 13 n. 8. Frost (1988), 75 in particular agrees with Bain and notes that, if present, Onesimos lies about this to his master at lines 935–6.

216 Bain (1977), 146.

217 Dickey (1996), 170 collects references for its use in Menander, which is common by comparison with other authors, where it is apparently absent, apart from later prose. On insults generally, see 167ff. At 169, she notes that Menander tends to have characters of a higher social status use higher-register insults, and those of a lower level use lower insults, although there are exceptions to this.

218 Frost (1988), 76.

219 Gomme and Sandbach (1973), 366. Gomme objected that Onesimos would then know that all is well: why, then, is he still afraid? Sandbach assumes that he could nevertheless expect to be in trouble for telling the tales in the first place that led to Charisios's and Pamphile's separation.

220 Gomme and Sandbach (1973), 369–70; Ireland (1992), 79ff. On the likelihood that riotous endings were traditional, see Handley in Menander (1992), 284.

221 On the Greek phrase, see Ireland in Menander (2010), 234 on Onesimos's 'doubting response' to Habrotonon at 479, and Furley (2009), 181, where he comments on its sense depending on the context, with the possibility of irony.

222 Gomme and Sandbach (1973), 377.

223 See Hunter (1985), 147–8, and Webster (1970), 50ff and 110ff on philosophy in comedy.

224 Gomme and Sandbach (1973), 377–8; see ch. 3 here for Menander and Epicurus.

225 Perhaps Onesimos's words here about character being each man's 'guardian' or 'captain' remind the audience, unfavourably for Charisios, of chastisement by his 'Power' at 912ff. The Greek *phrourarchos*, as a natural word for the period, could also recall the Macedonian garrison that had power over Athens (Gomme and Sandbach (1973), 379).

226 Gomme and Sandbach (1973), 379. It may, they think, be going too far to think that Onesimos is evoking an Aristotelian distinction. See the rest of his note with Furley (2009) 250, which distinguishes 'pure chance' from 'chance', good or bad. See further ch. 3.

227 An unusual word in the Greek.

228 Gomme and Sandbach (1973), 381–2. See further 381 on the assignment of speeches in 1120ff.

229 Unless the speaker is Sophrone, as some have supposed. See Gomme and Sandbach (1973), 382.

230 Sandbach (Gomme and Sandbach (1973)) assigns the threat to recite a whole tragic speech to Onesimos as an integral part of his impertinence towards Smikrines. Furley (2009), 253 agrees that the ability to carry out his threat would make Onesimos the sort of slave who is capable of doing so: 'no run-of-the-mill slave', though Sandbach's actual words are 'a smattering of education' (381). Sandbach (1970), 134–5 remarks on how the slave has already used 'out of the way words' and so that he should deliver such a speech here is credible. Ireland in Menander (2010), 260 notes the irony that Smikrines, although freeborn, does not get the reference straightaway.

231 See Gomme and Sandbach (1973), 382: 'particularly apposite'. See above on the Arbitration for the slave Syros's allusions to tragedy and compare Daos at *Aspis* 427f.

232 It does not occur in the orators or elsewhere in comedy: Gomme and Sandbach (1973), 383. The choice of translation recalls the themes of chance and fortune in Menander to which Furley (2009), 250 refers on line 1108.

233 See Kathryn Stockett's quotation in her note on the writing of her novel *The Help* (2009), 450 from Howell Raines: he observes that in the American South world of black and white segregation every emotion was suspect; Stockett goes on, however (451), to wish she had had time to portray more of the love that existed between white families and their black maids.

Conclusion

1 Vividness of characterization is not, as we have seen, always to be measured in terms of time on stage. For example Knemon's daughter in the *Dyscolus* appears only briefly but is memorable. Nikeratos's wife in the *Samia* never appears but seems real enough from others' references to her. Nikeratos's wife is an early version of the 'invisible missus' – a character often referred to in comedy but never seen. Compare Mrs Mainwaring in the television comedy series *Dad's Army*. The nurse in the *Samia* 'appears' solely through the marvellous vignette of Demeas's monologue in Act III. Sophrone, although she is mute, is referred to as if she were a character in her own right by Onesimos's words at 1117ff, and Smikrines' question to her at 1122. Compare the treatment of Syros's wife in Act II of *Epitrepontes* and the nurse at *Misoumenos* 612ff.

2 See Traill (2008), 223–5.

3 Traill (2008), 228ff. Note Habrotonon's use of the Greek word *nymphe* of Pamphile at *Epitr.* 872 although Pamphile has had a baby: see further Bathrellou (2009), 265 on how this term 'signals liminality', meaning a young girl who is of marriageable age or newly wed but has not yet borne a child, which would make her a proper *gyne*. Rangos (1995), 173–4 calls the word 'ambivalent' because it means both maiden (marriageable young girl is a better translation) and bride.

4 See Traill (2008), 225 on how Habrotonon reflects other characters' own preoccupations: Onesimos, for instance, assumes she is acting out of self-interest to get her freedom. Menander does ensure that she mentions money often enough for her motives to invite speculation, but she is a 'half-hearted gold-digger' (see Traill (2008), 230–1 and 238 on how she renders unpaid service).

5 Her sympathy for Pamphile seems to go beyond her own experience of men, and, as Traill notes (2008), 228, her admonishment to Onesimos in defence of the baby being raised a slave is 'a strong reaction for someone with no connection to the household'.

6 But not the powerful, prominent roles of some of their tragic counterparts, such as Clytemnestra or Medea or Lysistrata in Aristophanes. See Foley (1981a), 127–8.

7 Bathrellou (2012), 171.

8 Traill (2008), 229, who sees how the audience is invited to think of her too as a *parthenos* at *Epitr.* 517, when she anticipates her pretence to Charisios. She also notes (188) how Pamphile's relationship with Charisios when put in terms of dowry received, as Smikrines does, is a kind of 'reverse prostitution'.

9 Traill (2008), 232 is sceptical about repressed maternal instincts, but there is enough tenderness to make this a viable interpretation.

10 Traill (2008) notices how 'her motives are left unclear' (224), she is nosy (230), but she does seem to take an unselfish pleasure in bringing about the happiness of others.

11 Goldberg (1980), 64.

12 On women's presence at the theatre, see ch. 2.

13 Ireland (1992), 72 and 74.

14 Menander develops the *hetaira* type significantly: Traill (2008), 242. See also 236.

15 Gomme and Sandbach (1973), 330.

16 See Rangos (1995), 101ff, 103. The relationship is supported, he claims, by the similarity in the architecture of the temples (this is conjecture for Artemis Mounychia, however). See further Bathrellou (2012), 155ff on the archaeology of the Tauropolia and on Brauron.

17 The earth being associated with fertility. See Glossary.

18 Rangos (1995), 1 and 149. See further Sissa (1990a, 1990b).

19 So Rangos suggests (1995), 141 with notes 202–5: Pollux 2.173, Galen 14.706 (*LSJ*); Iphigeneia is called *atauros* because she has not experienced copulation at line 245 of Aeschylus's *Agamemnon*, Sophocles's *Ajax* 172–5 refers to lustfulness and Aristophanes *Lysistrata* lines 215–18 refer to sexual abstinence. Hesychius s.v. *taurinda* denotes a phallic game.

20 Found by Traill (2008), 240 towards Habrotonon.

21 The opposite conclusion from that ultimately reached by Traill (2008), 241.

22 As Traill (2008), 241 seems to suggest.

23 See Arnott (1975), 13ff, for example, for Euripides's influence on Menander. Euripides depicted all too vividly, for instance, in his *Trojan Women* the dangers of being enslaved that could face the freeborn, and in particular women (Hall (1997), 98).

24 Konstan (1995), 141, 146 and 152.

25 Heap (1998a), 124; Omitowoju (2002), 174ff; James (2014), 24.

26 Lape (2004), 25ff and 250.

27 Furley (2009), 237 and Omitowoju (2002), initially at least, 177.

28 A very negative analysis of Syros's character which parallels that of Daos's selfishness, but not one shared by most scholars, may be found in Iversen (2001). Furley (2009) does not agree, saying that two shifty servants are not necessary (161), but does draw attention to Syros as the name of a comic slave (142), one named as likely to steal from his master at *Bacchides* 649: the Plautus is based on the *Dis Exapaton* by Menander and this slave is the counterpart of Chrysalus in Plautus. So there may be further play with audience expectation.

29 Bathrellou (2014a), 52.

30 As, with a long speech, such a character does in the *Kolax* at E225ff in Arnott (1996b).

31 Bathrellou (2014a), in a good study of slaves outside the master–slave relationship in *Epitrepontes*, reaches a different conclusion: the plays are products of the élite, although they are useful sources for social history (52).

32 For a thorough and critical approach to the literary evidence, see Garlan (1988) 14ff with Tordoff (2013), 2.

33 Bathrellou (2014a) still takes this view in a study which looks at slaves in Menander as creating identities outside the master-slave relationship and networking, whilst allowing them to be useful sources for social historians. For Menander's status, see ch. 3 here.

34 Puzzling for this view of sympathy for slaves, however, is *Aspis* 54ff, where Daos guards other slaves. See the discussion in ch.5. The tragic language and metre appear to express Daos's sorrow at the loss of his master rather than at the fate of the captives.

35 Synodinou (1977): she argues (110) that, unlike in Aeschylus and Sophocles, slaves and slavery are so much a feature of his plays that Euripides appears to be revealed as an opponent of Aristotle's concept of slavery by nature. But slavery in tragedy has not received very much attention: Hall (1997), 126 (Bibliographical Note).

36 See further Tordoff (2013) in his introduction to Akrigg and Tordoff's volume on slaves in Greek comedy, 2–3.

37 See Fitzgerald (2000), 10.

38 Konstan (1995), 165, 167, citing Brenkman (1987), 108, 105.

39 Lape (2004), 247, 251–3.

40 See Proffitt (2011), 153ff. Her position is effectively argued, partly by reference to the insights about Shakespeare in Ryan (1989), which lend support to such an approach to drama. See further in particular Ryan (2009), at 23–24 and 38 in an essay on *The Taming of the Shrew*. Proffitt (2011) adopts independently a similar approach to Menander's slaves to the position taken here and in Heap's MPhil thesis (1998b), and draws on comments about babies in Heap (2002–3): Heap observed there (99) that slavery, and, by metaphorical extension, power, are themes in *Epitrepontes*, a discussion which is developed here.

41 So even Lape (2004), 252. Tordoff (2013), 42 certainly finds the ideology of slaveholders to be reinforced. Vester (2013), 227, n. 36 is right to point out that (against Proffitt's unsubstantiated claim for Onesimos (2011), 162 and n. 16) it is not known from what is extant whether Onesimos or Habrotonon achieve their freedom by the end of *Epitrepontes*.

42 It is worth remembering that women and slaves may have been in the audience at this period (see ch. 2 here).

43 For example, Karion's role, more major than usual for Aristophanes, in *Wealth*, Pseudolus in the Plautine play of that name and Geta in *Phormio*.

44 On Plautus's slaves, see McCarthy (2000) (discussed by Proffitt (2011), 159ff, especially at 161) and Segal (1987), ii. The fact that Menander survives only in part makes it difficult to be sure of the nature of his influence. But there is already great variety in the small proportion of Menander that survives. What sort of slaves might have been given life in the rest of his work?

45 See ch. 1.

46 The details of the ending of *Epitrepontes*, such as whether Habrotonon gained her freedom, are not known (yet), but it may be assumed that slavery is not abolished, any more than equality is achieved for women. But see also Traill (2008), 248ff, esp 248, arguing against Lape (2004), on how marriage in Menander is more about happiness than politics. Characters in Menander do not seem, nevertheless, to be changed by their experiences, to judge, for example, by Knemon in *Dyscolus* and Moschion in *Samia*.

47 Comedy with tragic elements but a basically happy ending, as opposed to the tragicomedy of, for example, Samuel Beckett's *Waiting for Godot*, which has comic features and some optimism, but ultimately an opposite, overall darker, effect. For humour in Euripides, see Michelini (1987): for example, 66 on how mixing genres requires a very 'adroit' touch.

Bibliography

Akrigg, B., and R. Tordoff (eds) (2013), *Slaves and Slavery in Ancient Greek Comic Drama*, Cambridge: Cambridge University Press.

Alston, R., E. Hall and L. Proffitt (eds) (2011), *Reading Ancient Slavery*, Bristol: Bristol Classical Press.

Anderson, W. S. (1970), 'A New Menandrian Prototype for the 'Servus Currens' of Roman Comedy', *Phoenix* 24, 229–36.

Apollodorus (1992), *Apollodoros Against Neaira (Demosthenes) 59* edited and translated by C. Carey, Warminster: Aris and Phillips.

Apollodorus (1999), *Apollodoros 'Against Neaira' [D.59]*, with introduction, translation and commentary by K. A. Kapparis, Berlin: de Gruyter.

Aristophanes (1994), *Thesmophoriazusae*, edited with translation and notes by A. H. Sommerstein, Oxford: Aris & Phillips.

Aristophanes (1996 with corr.), *Wasps*, edited with translation and notes by A. H. Sommerstein, Warminster: Aris & Phillips.

Aristophanes (1998), *Ecclesiazusae*, edited with translation and commentary by A. H. Sommerstein, Warminster: Aris & Phillips.

Aristophanes (2001), *Wealth*, edited with translation and commentary by A. H. Sommerstein, Warminster: Aris & Phillips.

Arnott, W. G. (1975), *Menander, Plautus, Terence*, G&R N.S. 9, Oxford: Clarendon.

Arnott, W. G. (1977), 'Four Notes on Menander's *Epitrepontes*', *ZPE* 24, 16–20.

Arnott, W. G. (1995), 'Menander's Manipulation of Language for the Individualisation of Character' in F. De Martino & A. H. Sommerstein (eds) (1995), *Lo Spettacolo delle Voci* Part 2, Bari, Levante, 147–64.

Arnott, W. G. (1996a), *Alexis: the Fragments: a Commentary*, Cambridge: Cambridge University Press.

Arnott, W. G. (ed.) (1996b), *Menander* edited and translated by W. G. Arnott, v.2, new ed., Loeb Classical Library, Cambridge, MA: Harvard University Press.

Arnott, W. G. (ed.) (1997 with corr.), *Menander* edited and translated by W. G. Arnott, v.1, new ed. with corr., Loeb Classical Library, Cambridge, Mass.: Harvard University Press.

Arnott, W. G. (ed.) (2000), *Menander* edited and translated by W. G. Arnott, v.3, new ed., Loeb Classical Library, Cambridge, MA: Harvard University Press.

Arnott, W. G. (2004a), 'New Menander from the 1990s' in G. Bastianini and A. Casanova (eds), *Menandro: Cent'Anni di Papiri: Atti del Convegno Internazionale di Studi*, Firenze, 12–13 Giugno 2003, Istituto Papirologico 'G. Vitelli', Studi e Testi di Papirologia, *N.S.* 5, Florence University Press, 35–53.

Arnott, W. G. (2004b), 'Menander's *Epitrepontes* in the Light of the New Papyri' in D. L. Cairns and R. A. Knox (eds) (2004), *Law, Rhetoric, and Comedy in Classical Athens: Essays in Honour of Douglas M. MacDowell*, Classical Press of Wales, 269–92.

Arnott, W. G. (2010), 'Middle Comedy' in G. W. Dobrov, *Brill's Companion to the Study of Greek Comedy*, Leiden and Boston: Brill, 279–31.

Ashmolean Museum (2011), *Heracles to Alexander the Great: Treasures from the Royal Capital of Macedon, an Hellenic Kingdom in the Age of Democracy: a Collaboration*

Between the Ashmolean Museum, University of Oxford, and the Hellenic Ministry of Culture and Tourism, 17th Ephorate of Prehistoric and Classical Antiquities, Oxford: Ashmolean Museum.

Ault, B. A., and L. C. Nevett (eds) (2005), *Ancient Greek Houses and Households: Chronological, Regional and Social Diversity*, Philadelphia: University of Pennsylvania.

Austin, C. (2006), 'My Daughter and her Dowry (Smikrines in Menander's *Epitrepontes*)' in D. Obbink and R. Rutherford (eds) (2011), *Culture in Pieces: Essays on Ancient Texts in Honour of Peter Parsons*, Oxford: Oxford University Press, 160–73.

Austin, C. (2008), 'Marriage on the Rocks: Pamphile in Menander's *Epitrepontes*' in *AAH* 48, 19–27.

Austin, M. M. (1981), *The Hellenistic World from Alexander to the Roman Conquest: a Selection of Ancient Sources in Translation*, Cambridge: Cambridge University Press.

Austin, M. M., and P. Vidal-Naquet (1977), *Economic and Social History of Ancient Greece: an Introduction*, 2nd ed., translated and revised by M. M. Austin, London: Batsford.

Bagnall, R. S. (ed.) (2009), *The Oxford Handbook of Papyrology*, Oxford: Oxford University Press.

Bain, D. M. (1977), *Actors and Audience: a Study of Asides and Related Conventions in Greek Drama*, Oxford: Oxford University Press.

Bain, D. M. (1984), 'Female Speech in Menander', *Antichthon* 18, 24–42.

Bain, D. M. (1998), Review of J. R. Green and A. Seeberg, *Monuments Illustrating New Comedy*, 2v., 3rd edn revised and enlarged, *BICS* Supplement 50 (1995) in *CR N.S.* 48, 547–8.

Barsby, J., ed. (2002), *Greek and Roman Drama: Translation and Performance*, Drama 12, Stuttgart: Metzler.

Bastianini, G., e A. Casanova (eds) (2004), *Menandro: Cent'Anni di Papiri: Atti del Convegno Internazionale di Studi, Firenze*, 12–13 Giugno 2003, Istituto Papirologico 'G. Vitelli', Studi e Testi di Papirologia, *N.S.* 5, Florence: Istituto Papirologico 'G. Vitelli'

Bate, J. (2007), Introduction to J. Bate and E. Rasmussen (eds), *William Shakespeare: Complete Works*, RSC Shakespeare, Basingstoke: Macmillan, 8–57.

Bathrellou, E. (2009), *Studies in the Epitrepontes of Menander*: Dissertation submitted for the Degree of PhD, University of Cambridge.

Bathrellou, E. (2012a), 'Menander's *Epitrepontes* and the Festival of the Tauropolia' in *Cl. Ant.* 31, 151–92.

Bathrellou, E. (2014a), 'Relationships Among Slaves in Menander' in A. H. Sommerstein, *Menander in Contexts*, London: Routledge, 40–57.

Bathrellou, E. (2014b), 'New Texts: Greek Comic Papyri 1973–2010', Appendix 1 to M. Fontaine and A. C. Scafuro (eds), *The Oxford Handbook of Greek and Roman Comedy*, Oxford: Oxford University Press, 803–70.

Baynham, E. (2003), 'The Ancient Evidence for Alexander the Great' in J. Roisman (ed.), *Brill's Companion to Alexander the Great*, Leiden and Boston: Brill, 3–29.

Berczelly, L. (1988), 'The Date and Significance of the Menander Mosaics at Mytilene', *BICS* 35, 119–26 with plates.

Bieber, M. (1961), *The History of the Greek and Roman Theater*, 2nd ed. revised and enlarged, Princeton, NJ: Princeton University Press.

Biles, Z. P. (2014), 'The Rivals of Aristophanes and Menander' in M. Revermann (ed.), *The Cambridge Companion to Greek Comedy*, 43–59.

Blackman, M. (2006–), *Noughts and Crosses* series, London: Corgi.

Blackman, M. (2007), *Unheard Voices: a Collection of Stories and Poems to Commemorate the 200th Anniversary of the Abolition of the Slave Trade Act*, London: Corgi.

Blanchard, A. (2014) 'Reconstructing Menander' in M. Fontaine and A.C. Scafuro (eds), *The Oxford Handbook of Greek and Roman Comedy*, 239–57.

Blundell, J. (1980), *Menander and the Monologue*, Hypomnemata, Heft 59, Göttingen: Vandenhoeck & Ruprecht, 1980.

Boardman, J. (1997), *The Great God Pan: the Survival of an Image*, London: Thames and Hudson.

Borgeaud, P. (1988), *The Cult of Pan in Ancient Greece*, translated by K. Atlass and J. Redfield, Chicago: Chicago University Press. Originally published in 1979 in French.

Boswell, J. (1988), *The Kindness of Strangers: the Abandonment of Children in Western Europe from Late Antiquity to the Renaissance*, London: Allen Lane.

Bowden, H. (2014), *Alexander the Great: a Very Short Introduction*, Oxford: Oxford Universisty Press.

Bowie, A. (2010), 'Myth and Ritual in Comedy' in G. W. Dobrov (ed.), *Brill's Companion to the Study of Greek Comedy*, Leiden and Boston: Brill, 143–76.

Bowman, A. K. (2002), 'Recolonising Egypt' in T. P. Wiseman (ed.), *Classics in Progress: Essays on Ancient Greece and Rome*, Oxford: Oxford University Press, 193–223.

Bradley, K. (2012), 'Slavery' in S. Hornblower, A. Spawforth and E. Eidinow (eds), *Oxford Classical Dictionary*, 4th ed., Oxford: Oxford University Press.

Bradley, K. and P. Cartledge (eds) (2011), *The Cambridge World History of Slavery* v.1: *The Ancient Mediterranean World*, Cambridge: Cambridge University Press.

Braund, D. (2011), 'The Slave Supply in Classical Greece' in K. Bradley and P. Cartledge (eds), *The Cambridge World History of Slavery* v.1: *The Ancient Mediterranean World*, Cambridge: Cambridge University Press, 112–33.

Brea, L. B. (1981), *Menandro e il Teatro Greco nelle Terracotte Liparesi*, Genova: Sagep Editrice.

Brea, L. B. (2001), *Maschere e Personaggi del Teatro Greco nelle Terracotte Liparesi*, con la collaborazione di M. Cavalier, Rome: 'L'Erma' di Bretschneider.

Brenkman, J. (1987), *Culture and Domination*, Ithaca: Cornell University Press.

Brown, P. G. McC. (1984), Review of L. B. Brea, *Menandro e il Teatro Greco nelle Terracotte Liparesi* in *LCM* 9, 108–12.

Brown, P. G. McC. (1990), 'Plots and Prostitutes in Greek New Comedy', in F. Cairns and M. Heath (eds), *Roman Poetry and Drama, Greek Epic, Comedy, Rhetoric*, Papers of the Leeds International Latin seminar 6, 241–66.

Brown, P. G. McC. (1991), 'Athenian Attitudes to Rape and Seduction: the Evidence of Menander's *Dyscolus* 28–93', *CQ* 41, 533–34.

Brown, P. G. McC. (1995), 'Aeschinus at the Door: Terence, *Adelphoe* 632–43 and the Traditions of Greco-Roman Comedy' in *Roman Comedy, Augustan Poetry, Historiography*, edited by R. Brock and A. J. Woodman, Papers of the Leeds International Latin Seminar 8, 71–89.

Bugh, G. R., ed. (2006), *The Cambridge Companion to the Hellenistic World*, Cambridge: Cambridge University Press.

Bussanick, J. and N. D. Smith (eds) (2013), *Bloomsbury Companion to Socrates*, London: Bloomsbury.

Buxton, R. G. A. (1982), *Persuasion in Greek Tragedy: a Study of Peitho*, Cambridge: Cambridge University Press.

Cairns, D. L. and R. A Knox (eds) (2004), *Law, Rhetoric, and Comedy in Classical Athens: Essays in Honour of Douglas M. MacDowell*, Classical Press of Wales.

Calame, C. (1986), 'Facing Otherness: the Tragic Mask in Ancient Greece', *History of Religions* 26, 125–42.

Cameron, A., and A. Kuhrt (eds) (1993), *Images of Women in Antiquity*, 2nd. ed. Croom Helm.

Camp, J. M. (2001) *The Archeology of Athens*, New Haven, CN: Yale University Press.

Cantarella, E. (2005), 'Gender, Sexuality and Law' in Gagarin, M. and D. Cohen (eds), *Cambridge Companion to Greek Law*, Cambridge: Cambridge University Press, 236–53.

Cantarella, E. (2011), 'Greek Law and the Family' in B. Rawson (ed.), *A Companion to Families in the Greek and Roman Worlds*, Hoboken, NJ: Wiley-Blackwell.

Carey, C. (1992), 'Return of the Radish *or* Just When You Thought It Was Safe To Go Back into the Kitchen', *LCM* 18, 53–5.

Carey, C. & R. A. Reid (eds) (1985), *Demosthenes: Selected Private Speeches*, Cambridge: Cambridge University Press.

Cartledge, P. (1985a), 'Rebels and Sambos in Classical Greece: a Comparative View' in P. Cartledge and F.D. Harvey (eds), *CRUX: Essays in Greek History Presented to G.E.M de Ste. Croix on his 75th birthday*, 16–46.

Cartledge, P. (1993), *The Greeks: a Portrait of Self and Others*, Opus, Oxford: Oxford University Press.

Cartledge, P. (2002), 'Greek Civilization and Slavery' in ed. T. P. Wiseman, *Classics in Progress: Essays on Ancient Greece and Rome*, Oxford: Oxford University Press, 247–62.

Cartledge, P. (2004), *Alexander the Great: the Hunt for a New Past*, Basingstoke: Macmillan.

Cartledge, P. (2011), 'The Helots: a Contemporary Review' in K. Bradley and P. Cartledge (eds), *The Cambridge World History of Slavery* v.1, 74–90.

Cartledge, P., P. Garnsey and E. Gruen (eds) (1997), *Hellenistic Constructs: Essays in Culture, History, and Historiography*, Berkeley: University of California.

Cartledge, P., & F. D. Harvey (eds) (1985), *Crux: Essays in Greek History Presented to G.E.M. de Ste Croix on his 75th Birthday*. Duckworth/Imprint Academic.

Cartledge, P., P. Millett & S. Todd (eds) (1990), *Nomos: Essays in Athenian Law, Politics and Society*, Cambridge: Cambridge University Press.

Casanova, A. (2014), 'Menander and the Peripatos: New Insights into an Old Question' in A. H. Sommerstein (ed.), *Menander in Contexts*, New York and London: Routledge, 137–51.

Casson, L. (1991), *The Ancient Mariners: Seafarers and Sea Fighters of the Mediterranean in Ancient Times*, 2nd ed., Princeton: Princeton University Press.

Casson, L. (2002), *Libraries in the Ancient World*, New Haven, CN: Yale Note Bene.

Cavalier, M. (1991), *Il Museo Eoliano di Lipari*, Milan: Oreste Ragusi Editore (with English, French, German and Italian text).

Chaniotis, A. (2007), 'Theatre Rituals' in P. Wilson (ed.), *The Greek Theatre and Festivals: Documentary Studies*, Oxford: Oxford University Press, 48–66.

Charitonidis, S., L. Kahil, and R. Ginouvès (1970), *Les Mosaïques de la Maison du Ménandre a Mytilène, Ant.K* 6, Bern.

Christodoulou, D. (1997), *The Hetaira in the Ancient Greek World*, PhD, University of Cambridge.

Cohen, A. (2011), 'Picturing Greek Families' in B. Rawson ed. (2011), *A Companion to Families in the Greek and Roman Worlds*, Chichester: Wiley-Blackwell, 465–87.

Cohen, D. (1989), 'Seclusion, Separation and the Status of Women in Classical Athens', *G&R* 36, 3–15.

Cohen, D. (1990), 'The Social Context of Adultery at Athens' in P. Cartledge, P. Millett & S. Todd (eds), *Nomos: Essays in Athenian Law, Politics and Society*, Cambridge: Cambridge University Press, 147–65.

Cohn-Haft, L. (1995), 'Divorce in Classical Athens', *JHS* 115, 1–14.

Cohoon, J. W. (1914), 'Rhetorical Studies in the Arbitration Scene of Menander's *Epitrepontes*', *TAPhA* 45, 141–230.

Cole, S. G. (1993), 'Procession and celebration at the Dionysia' in R. Scodel (ed.) *Theater and Society in the Classical World*, Ann Arbor, MI: University of Michigan Press, 25–38.

Compton-Engle, G. (2015), *Costume in the Comedies of Aristophanes*, Cambridge: Cambridge University Press.

Cox, C. (2011), 'Marriage in Ancient Athens' in B. Rawson (ed.), *A Companion to Families in the Greek and Roman Worlds*, Chichester: Wiley-Blackwell, 231–44.

Cox, C. (2013), 'Coping with Punishment: the Social Networking of Slaves in Menander' in B. Akrigg and R. Tordoff (eds), *Slaves and Slavery in Ancient Greek Comic Drama*, Cambridge: Cambridge University Press, 159–72.

Cropp, M., K. Lee and S. Sansone (eds) (2000), *Euripides and Tragic Theatre in the Late Fifth Century*, *Illinois Classical Studies* v. 24–5.

Csapo, E. (1997), 'Hellenistic Comedy in Art and Society: review of MNC3' in *JRA* 10, 336–40.

Csapo, E. (2000), 'From Aristophanes to Menander? Genre Transformation in Greek Comedy' in M. Depew and D. Obbink, *Matrices of Genre: Authors, Canons and Society*, Cambridge, MA: Harvard University Press, 115–33.

Csapo, E. (2007), 'The Men who Built the Theatres: *Theatropolai*, *Theatronai* and *Arkhitektones*' in P. Wilson ed., *The Greek Theatre and Festivals: Documentary Studies*, 87–115.

Csapo, E. (2010), *Actors and Icons of the Ancient Theater*, Chichester: Wiley-Blackwell.

Csapo, E. (2014), 'Performing Comedy in the Fifth through Early Third Centuries' in M. Fontaine and A. C. Scafuro (eds), *The Oxford Handbook of Greek and Roman Comedy*, Oxford: Oxford University Press, 50–69.

Csapo, E., and W. J. Slater (1994), *The Context of Ancient Drama*, Ann Arbor, MI: University of Michigan.

Csapo, E., R. Goette, J. R. Green and Wilson, P. (eds) (2014), *Greek Theatre in the Fourth Century BCE*, Berlin: De Gruyter.

Csapo, E. and P. Wilson (forthcoming), *Historical Documents for the Greek Theatre down to 300 BC*, 3v.

Cuddon, J. A. (1991), *A Dictionary of Literary Terms*, rev. ed., Oxford: Blackwell.

Dasen, V. (2011), 'Childbirth and Infancy in Greek and Roman Antiquity' in B. Rawson (ed.), *A Companion to Families in the Greek and Roman Worlds*, Chichester: Wiley-Blackwell, 291–314.

Davidson, J. (1997), *Courtesans and Fishcakes: the Consuming Passions of Classical Athens*, HarperCollins.

Deacy, S. and K. F. Pierce (eds) (1997), *Rape in Antiquity: Sexual Violence in the Greek and Roman Worlds*, Classical Press of Wales and Duckworth.

De Beauvoir, S. (1953), *The Second Sex*, translated and edited by H. M. Pashley, London: Jonathan Cape.

De Beauvoir, S. (2010), *The Second Sex*, new ed., translated from the French, London: Vintage.

De Martino, F. and A. H. Sommerstein (eds) (1995), *Lo Spettacolo delle Voci* Part 2, Bari, Levante.

Depew, M. and D. Obbink (eds) (2000), *Matrices of Genre: Authors, Canons and Society*, Cambridge, MA: Harvard University Press.

De Souza, P. (1995), 'Greek Piracy', in A. Powell (ed.), *The Greek World*, London: Routledge, 179–98.

De Souza, P. (1999), *Piracy in the Graeco-Roman World*, Cambridge: Cambridge University Press.

Dick, D. (1996), *Talking Heads: Notes*, Harlow: Longman.

Dickey, E. (1996), *Greek Forms of Address: from Herodotus to Lucian*, Oxford: Clarendon.

Dobrov, G. W. (ed.) (1995), *Beyond Aristophanes: Transition and Diversity in Greek Comedy*, American Philological Association, American Classical Studies 38, Atlanta, GA: Scholars Press.

Dobrov, G. W. (ed.) (1997), *The City as Comedy: Society and Representation in Athenian Drama*, Chapel Hill, NC: University of North Carolina Press.

Dobrov G. W. (ed.) (2010a), *Brill's Companion to the Study of Greek Comedy*, Leiden and Boston: Brill.

Dobrov, G. W. (2010b), 'Comedy and her Critics' in G. W. Dobrov, *Brill's Companion to the Study of Greek Comedy*, 3–33.

Douglass, F. (1845, 1986), *Narrative of the Life of Frederick Douglass, an American Slave, Written by Himself*, edited with an introduction by H. A. Baker Jr, first published in the USA by the Anti-Slavery Office, Penguin.

Dover, K. J. (1972), *Aristophanic Comedy*, Berkeley: University of California Press.

Dover, K. J. (1974), *Greek Popular Morality in the Time of Plato and Aristotle*, Oxford: Blackwell.

Dover, K. J. (1985), 'Some Types of Abnormal Word Order in Attic Comedy' *CQ NS* 35 (1985), 324–43. This article is reprinted in K. J. Dover (1987), *Greek and the Greeks: Collected Papers 1: Language, Poetry and Drama*, 43–66.

Dover, K. J. (1989), *Greek Homosexuality*, 2nd ed. Cambridge, MA: Harvard University Press.

Dover K. J. (2012) 'Parody, Greek' in S. Hornblower, A. Spawforth and E. Eidinow (eds), *Oxford Classical Dictionary*, 4th ed., 1083.

DuBois, P. (2008), *Slaves and Other Objects*, Chicago, IL: University of Chicago Press.

Duckworth, G. E. (1994), *The Nature of Roman Comedy: a Study in Popular Entertainment*, 2nd ed. with a foreword and bibliographical appendix by R. Hunter, Norman: University of Oklahoma Press.

Dugdale, E. (2008), *Greek Theatre in Contexts*, *G&R:* Texts and Contexts, Cambridge: Cambridge University Press.

Dupont, F. (2001), 'The Theatrical Significance of Duplication in Plautus's *Amphitruo*' in E. Segal ed., *Oxford Readings in Menander, Plautus and Terence*, New York and Oxford: Oxford University Press, 176–88.

Easterling, P. E. (1993), 'Tragedy and Ritual' in R. Scodel ed. (1993), *Theater and Society in the Classical World*, Ann Arbor, MI: University of Michigan Press, 7–23.

Easterling, P. E. (1995), 'Menander: Loss and Survival', in A. Griffiths, ed., *Stage Directions: Ancient Drama - Essays in Honour of E. W. Handley*, BICS Suppl. 66, 153–60.

Easterling, P. E. (ed.) (1997), *The Cambridge Companion to Greek Tragedy*, Cambridge: Cambridge University Press.

Easterling, P. E. (1999), 'Actors and Voices: Reading Between the Lines in Aeschines and Demosthenes' in S. Goldhill & R. Osborne (eds), *Performance, Culture and Athenian Democracy*, Cambridge: Cambridge University Press, 154–66.

Easterling, P. E. (2002), 'Actor as Icon' in P. E. Easterling and E. Hall (eds), *Greek and Roman Actors: Aspects of an Ancient Profession*, Cambridge: Cambridge University Press, 327–41.

Easterling, P. E., 'Messages and Messengers in Greek Tragedy' (an unpublished paper), 1–3.

Easterling, P. E. and E. Hall (eds) (2002), *Greek and Roman Actors: Aspects of an Ancient Profession*, Cambridge: Cambridge University Press.

Easterling, P. E., and B. M. W. Knox (eds) (1989), *The Cambridge History of Classical Literature*, v. 1, pt.2: *Greek Drama*, Cambridge: Cambridge University Press (reprint of chapters 10–12 of *The Cambridge History of Classical Literature* v.1 (1985), 258–425).

Edwards, M. (2015), 'Hyperides in the Archimedes Palimpsest' in R. Green and M. Edwards (eds), *Images and Texts: Papers in Honour of Professor Eric Handley, CBE, FBA, BICS* Suppl. 129, 81–6.

Ehrenberg, V. (1962), *The People of Aristophanes: a Sociology of Old Attic Comedy*, 3rd ed., New York: Schocken Books.

El-Abbadi, M. (1990), *The Life of the Ancient Library of Alexandria*, Paris: Unesco.

Engels, J. (2010), 'Macedonians and Greeks' in J. Roisman and I. Worthington (eds), *A Companion to Ancient Macedonia*, Chichester: Wiley-Blackwell, 81–98.

Epicurus (1994), *The Epicurus Reader: Selected Writings and Testimonia* edited and translated by B. Inwood and L. P. Gerson, introduction by D. S. Hutchinson, Indianapolis and Cambridge: Hackett.

Equiano, Olaudah (1789, 2003), *The Interesting Narrative and Other Writings*, edited with an introduction (and notes) by Vincent Carretta, rev. ed., Harmondsworth: Penguin.

Erskine, A., ed. (2009), *A Companion to Ancient History*, Oxford: Blackwell.

Eubulus (1983), *Eubulus: the Fragments*, edited with a commentary by R. L. Hunter, Cambridge: Cambridge University Press.

Fantham, E., H. P. Foley, N. B. Kampen, S. B. Pomeroy and H. A. Shapiro (1994), *Women in the Classical World: Image and Text*, Oxford: Oxford University Press.

Ferrari, G. (2003 with corr.), *Figures of Speech: Men and Maidens in Ancient Greece*, Chicago, IL: University of Chicago Press.

Finley, M. I. (1981), *Economy and Society in Ancient Greece*, edited with an introduction by B. D. Shaw and R. P. Saller, London: Chatto & Windus.

Fisher, N. R. E. (1992), *Hybris: a Study of the Values of Honour and Shame in Ancient Greece*, Oxford: Aris and Phillips.

Fisher, N. R. E. (2001), *Slavery in Classical Greece*, 2nd ed., London: Bristol Classical Press.

Fittschen, K. (1991), 'Zur Rekonstruktion Griechischer Dichterstatuen 1. Teil: Die Statue des Menander,' *AM* 106, 243–79.

Fitzgerald, W. (2000), *Slavery and the Roman Literary Imagination*, Cambridge: Cambridge University Press.

Foley, H. P. (1981a), 'The Conception of Women in Athenian Drama' in H. P. Foley (ed.), *Reflections of Women in Antiquity*, New York: Gordon and Breach Science, 127–68.

Foley, H. P., ed. (1981b), *Reflections of Women in Antiquity*, New York: Gordon and Breach Science.

Fontaine, M. and A. C. Scafuro (eds) (2014), *The Oxford Handbook of Greek and Roman Comedy*, Oxford: Oxford University Press.

Fortenbaugh, W. W. (1974), 'Menander's *Perikeiromene*: Misfortune, Vehemence, and Polemon,' *Phoenix* 28, 430–43.

Fortenbaugh, W. and others (eds) (1992), *Theophrastus of Eresus: Sources for his Life, Writings, Thought and Influence*, Part One, Philosophia Antiqua v.54.1, Leiden, New York and Cologne: Brill.

Fortenbaugh, W. W. and E. Schütrumpf (eds) (2000), *Demetrius of Phalerum: Text, Translation and Discussion*, Rutgers University Studies in Classical Humanities 9, New Brunswick, NJ: Transaction.

Foucault, M. (1985), *The History of Sexuality*, translated from the French by R. Hurley, v.2: *The Uses of Pleasure*, Harmondsworth: Penguin.

Foxhall, L. (2003), 'Pandora Unbound: the Feminist Critique of Foucault's *History of Sexuality*' in M. Golden and P. Toohey (eds), *Sex and Difference in Ancient Greece and Rome*, Edinburgh: Edinburgh University Press, 67–82.

Foxhall, L. (2013), *Studying Gender in Classical Antiquity*, Key Themes in Ancient History, Cambridge: Cambridge University Press.

Foxhall, L. and G. Neher (eds) (2011), *Gender and the City Before Modernity*, *Gender & History* v. 23, no. 3 *Special Issue*.

Foxhall, L., and J. Salmon (eds) (1998), *Thinking Men: Masculinity and Its Self Representation in the Classical Tradition* v.1, *When Men Were Men: Masculinity, Power and Identity in Classical Antiquity* and v.2, *Thinking Men: Masculinity and its Self Representation in the Classical Tradition*, Leicester-Nottingham Studies in Ancient Society, London: Routledge.

Fraenkel, E. (2007), *Plautine Elements in Plautus (Plautinisches im Plautus)*, translated by T. Drevikovsky and Frances Muecke, Oxford: Oxford University Press.

Frederiksen, R. (2002), 'The Greek Theatre. A Typical Building in the Urban Centre of the Polis' in T. H. Nielsen (ed.), *Even More Studies in the Ancient Greek Polis*. Papers from the Copenhagen Polis Centre 6 Historia Einzelschriften 162, 65–124.

Fredricksmeyer, E. (2003), 'Alexander's Religion and Divinity' in J. Roisman (ed.), *Brill's Companion to Alexander the Great*, Leiden and Boston: Brill, 253–78.

Frost, K. B. (1988), *Exits and Entrances in Menander*, Oxford: Clarendon.

Furley, W. D. (2009), *Menander Epitrepontes: Introduction, Translation and Commentary* by W. D. Furley, *BICS* Suppl. 106.

Furley, W. (2013), 'Pamphile Regains Her Voice: On the Newly Published Fragments of Menander's *Epitrepontes*, *ZPE* 185, 82–90.

Furley, W. (2014), 'Aspects of Recognition in *Perikeiromene* and Other Plays in A. H. Sommerstein (ed.), *Menander in Contexts*. London: Routledge, 106–15.

Furley, W. (2015), 'The Text and Staging of the Recognition Scene in Menander's *Perikeiromene*' in R. Green and M. Edwards (eds), *Images and Texts: Papers in Honour of Professor Eric Handley, CBE, FBA, BICS* Suppl. 129, 31–43.

Gagarin, M. (2000), 'The Legislation of Demetrius of Phalerum and the Transformation of Athenian Law' in W. W. Fortenbaugh and E. Schutrümpf, *Demetrius of Phalerum: Text, Translation and Discussion*, Rutgers University Studies in Classical Humanities 9, New Brunswick: Transaction, 347–65.

Gagarin, M. (2001), 'Women's Voices in Attic Oratory' in A. Lardinois & L. McClure (eds), *Making Silence Speak: Women's Voices in Greek Literature and Society*', Princeton: Princeton University Press, 161–76.

Gagarin, M. and D. Cohen (eds) (2005), *Cambridge Companion to Greek Law*, Cambridge: Cambridge University Press.

Gallo, I. (1986), *Greek and Latin Papyrology*, translated by M. R. Falivene and J. R. March, Institute of Classical Studies, University of London.

Gardner, J. (1989), 'Aristophanes and Male Anxiety: the Defence of the *Oikos*', *G&R* 36, 51–62.

Garlan, Y. (1988), *Slavery in Ancient Greece*, revised and expanded edition, translated by J. Lloyd, Ithaca, NY: Cornell University Press.

Garland, R. (1990), *The Greek Way of Life from Conception to Old Age*, London: Duckworth.

Garnsey, P. (1996), *Ideas of Slavery from Aristotle to Augustine*, Cambridge: Cambridge University Press.

Geddes-Brown, L. (1988), 'Isle of Fire', *Country Life* v.182 (4 August), 100–01.

Gerö, E. C. and H.-R. Johnsson (2001), 'Where Were the Women When the Men Laughed at "Lysistrata"? An Inquiry into the Question Whether the Audience of the Old Comedy Also Included Female Spectators', *Eranos* 99, 87–99.

Getty Museum (2002), *Handbook of the Antiquities Collection*, Los Angeles: Getty Museum.

Ghiron-Bistagne, P. (1976), *Recherches sur les Acteurs dans la Grèce Antique*, Paris: Société d'Édition 'Les Belles Lettres'.

Gill, C. (1996), *Personality in Greek Epic Tragedy and Philosophy: the Self in Dialogue*, Oxford: Clarendon.

Goette, H. R. (2007a), 'An Archaeological Appendix' to E. Csapo, 'The Men who Built the Theatres: *Theatropolai, Theatronai* and *Arkhitektones*' in P. Wilson (ed.), *The Greek Theatre and Festivals: Documentary Studies*, Oxford: Oxford University Press, 116–21.

Goette, H. R. (2007b), 'Choregic Monuments and the Athenian Democracy' in P. Wilson, ed., *The Greek Theatre and Festivals: Documentary Studies*, 122–49.

Goldberg, S. M. (1980), *The Making of Menander's Comedy*, London: Athlone Press.

Goldberg, S. M. (1986), *Understanding Terence*, Princeton, NJ: Princeton University Press.

Goldberg, S. M. (2007), 'Comedy and Society from Menander to Terence' in M. McDonald and J. M. Walton (eds), *The Cambridge Companion to Greek and Roman Theatre*, Cambridge: Cambridge University Press, 124–38.

Golden, M. (2015), *Children and Childhood in Classical Athens*, 2nd ed., Baltimore, MD: Johns Hopkins University Press.

Golden, M. (1995), 'Baby Talk and Child Language in Ancient Greece', in F. De Martino and A. H. Sommerstein (eds), *Lo Spettacolo Delle Voci* Part 2, 11–34.

Golden, M. (2011a), 'Other People's Children' in B. Rawson ed., *A Companion to Families in the Greek and Roman Worlds*, Chichester: Wiley-Blackwell, 262–75.

Golden, M. (2011b), 'Slavery and the Greek Family' in K. Bradley and P. Cartledge (eds), *The Cambridge World History of Slavery* v.1: *The Ancient Mediterranean World*, Cambridge: Cambridge University Press, 134–52.

Golden, M. (2015), *Children and Childhood in Classical Athens* 2nd ed., Baltimore, MD: Johns Hopkins University Press.

Golden, M. and P. Toohey (eds) (2003), *Sex and Difference in Ancient Greece and Rome*, Edinburgh: Edinburgh University Press.

Goldhill, S (1990), 'The Great Dionysia and Civic Ideology' in J. J. Winkler and F. I. Zeitlin (eds), *Nothing To Do With Dionysos?: Athenian Drama In Its Social Context*, 97–129.

Goldhill, S. (1991), *The Poet's Voice: Essays on Poetics and Greek Literature*, CUP.

Goldhill, S. (1994), 'Representing Democracy: Women at the Great Dionysia' in R. Osborne and S. Hornblower, *Ritual, Finance, Politics: Athenian Democratic Accounts Presented to D. Lewis*, 347–69.

Goldhill, S. (1997), 'The Audience of Athenian Tragedy' in Easterling, P. E. (ed.,), *The Cambridge Companion to Greek Tragedy*, Cambridge: Cambridge University Press, 54–68.

Goldhill, S. and R. Osborne (eds) (1999), *Performance Culture and Athenian Democracy*, Cambridge: Cambridge University Press.

Gomme, A. W. (1957), 'Interpretations of Some Poems of Alkaios and Sappho', *JHS* 77, 255–66.

Gomme, A. W. & F. H. Sandbach (1973), *Menander: a Commentary*, Oxford: Oxford University Press.

Graf, F. (2007), 'Religion and Drama' in M. McDonald and J.M. Walton (eds) (2007), *The Cambridge Companion to Greek and Roman Theatre*, Cambridge: Cambridge University Press, 55–71.

Green, J. R. (1994), *Theatre in Ancient Greek Society*, London: Routledge.

Green, J. R. and E. W. Handley (1995), *Images of the Greek Theatre*, London: British Museum.

Green, J. R. and A. Seeberg, A. (1995), *Monuments Illustrating New Comedy*, 2v., 3rd edn revised and enlarged, *BICS* Suppl. 50.

Green, J. R. and M. Edwards (eds) (2015), *Images and Texts: Papers in Honour of Professor Eric Handley, CBE, FBA, BICS* Suppl. 129.

Green, P. (1990), *Alexander to Actium: the Historical Evolution of the Hellenistic Age* Berkeley, CA: University of California Press.

Griffith, M. (2007), 'Telling the Tale: a Performing Tradition from Homer to Pantomime' in M. McDonald and J. M. Walton, *The Cambridge Companion to Greek and Roman Theatre*, Cambridge: Cambridge University Press, 13–35.

Gronewald, M. (1986), 'Menander, *Epitrepontes*: Neue Fragmente aus Akt III und IV', *ZPE* 66 (1986), 1–13.

Habicht, C. (1997), *Athens from Alexander to Antony*, translated by D. L. Schneider, Cambridge, Mass.: Harvard University Press. Originally published in 1995 in German.

Hall, E. (1991), *Inventing the Barbarian: Greek Self-Definition Through Tragedy*, Oxford: Clarendon.

Hall, E. (1997), 'The Sociology of Athenian Tragedy' in P. E. Easterling (ed.), *The Cambridge Companion to Greek Tragedy*, Cambridge: Cambridge University Press, 93–126.

Hall, E. (2002), 'The Singing Actors of Antiquity' in P. E. Easterling and E. Hall (eds), *Greek and Roman Actors: Aspects of an Ancient Profession*, 3–38.

Hall, E. (2006), *The Theatrical Cast of Athens: Interactions Between Ancient Greek Drama & Society*, Oxford: Oxford University Press.

Hall, E., R. Alston and J. McConnell (2011), *Ancient Slavery and Abolition: from Hobbes to Hollywood*, Classical Presences, Oxford: Oxford University Press.

Halperin, D. M. (1990), *One Hundred Years of Homosexuality and Other Essays on Greek Love*, London: Routledge.

Halperin, D. M., J. J. Winkler and F. I. Zeitlin (eds) (1990), *Before Sexuality: the Construction of Erotic Experience in the Ancient Greek World.* Princeton, NJ: Princeton University Press.

Hamel, D. (2003), *Trying Neaira: the True Story of a Courtesan's Scandalous Life in Ancient Greece*, New Haven, CN: Yale University Press.

Handley, E.W. et al. (1970), 'Ménandre: Sept Exposés Suivis de Discussions' in *Entretiens Sur L'Antiquité Classique* v.16, Vandoeuvres, Geneva: Fondation Hardt.

Handley, E. W. (1987), 'Acts and Scenes in the Comedy of Menander', *Dioniso* 57, 299–312.

Handley, E. W. (1989), 'Comedy' in P. E. Easterling and B. M. W. Knox (eds), *The Cambridge History of Classical Literature*, 1, Cambridge: Cambridge University Press.

Handley, E. W. (1990), 'The Bodmer Menander and the Comic Fragments' in E. W. Handley and A. Hurst (eds), *Relire Ménandre*, 123–48.

Handley, E. W. (2002), 'Acting, Action and Words in New Comedy' in P. E. Easterling and E. Hall (eds), *Greek and Roman Actors: Aspects of an Ancient Profession*, Cambridge: Cambridge University Press, 165–88.

Handley, E. W. (2009) on P Oxy. 4936 in *P Oxy.*, v.73.

Handley, E. W. (2011), 'The Rediscovery of Menander' in D. Obbink and R. Rutherford (eds), *Culture in Pieces: Essays on Ancient Texts in Honour of Peter Parsons*, 138–59.

Handley, E. W. and A. Hurst (eds) (1990), *Relire Ménandre*, Recherches et Rencontres; 2, Geneva: Librairie Droz.

Harding, P. (2008), *The Story of Athens: the Fragments of the Local Chronicles of Attika*, London: Routledge.

Harris, E. M. (1990), 'Did the Athenians Regard Seduction as a Worse Crime Than Rape?' *CQ* N. S. 40, 370–77.

Harrison, A. R. W. (1998), *The Law of Athens*, 2nd ed. v.1: *The Family and Property*, v.2: *Procedure*, foreword and bibliography by D. M. MacDowell, London: Duckworth.

Harvey, D. (1990), 'The Sykophant and Sykophancy: Vexatious Redefinition' in P. Cartledge, P. Millett & S. Todd (eds), *Nomos: Essays in Athenian Law, Politics and Society*, 103–21.

Harvey, D. and J. Wilkins (eds) (2000), *The Rivals of Aristophanes: Studies in Athenian Old Comedy* with a foreword by K. Dover, London: Duckworth.

Heap, A. M. (1992), 'Word order in Menander', *LCM* 17 no. 4, 56–58.

Heap, A. M. (1994), 'Lipari's secret', *Omnibus* no. 27, 7–8.

Heap, A. M. (1998a), 'Understanding the Men in Menander' in L. Foxhall and J. Salmon (eds), *Thinking Men: Masculinity and Its Self-Representation in the Classical Tradition.*, Leicester-Nottingham Studies in Ancient Society, London: Routledge, 115–29.

Heap, A. M. (1998b), *People in Menander: Social Norms and Characterization*, MPhil, University of London.

Heap, A. M. (2002–03), 'The Baby as Hero: the Role of the Infant in Menander', *BICS* 46, 77–129.

Heap, A. M. (2005), Review of Lape (2004) in *JACT* 3rd series, no. 5, 27.

Henderson, J. (1991), 'Women and the Athenian Dramatic Festivals', *TAPhA*, 133–47.

Henry, M. M. (1985), *Menander's Courtesans and the Greek Comic Tradition*, Studien zur Klassischen Philologie 20, Frankfurt and New York: Peter Lang.

Henry, M. M. (1995), *Prisoner of History: Aspasia of Miletus and her Biographical Tradition*, New York, Oxford: Oxford University Press.

Heubeck, A. and A. Hoekstra (1990), *A Commentary on Homer's Odyssey v.2, Books IX–XVI*, Oxford: Clarendon.

Hofmeister, T. P. (1997), 'Hai Pasai Poleis: Polis and Oikoumene in Menander' in G. W. Dobrov (ed.), *The City as Comedy: Society and Representation in Athenian Drama*, University of North Carolina Press, 289–342.

Hokenson, J. W. (2006), *The Idea of Comedy: History, Theory, Critique*, Madison: University of Farleigh Dickinson.

Holloway, R. R. (1967), Review of Brea/Cavalier Meligunìs-Lipára v.2, Museo Eoliano di Lipari, Palermo (1965) in *Gnomon* 39, 400–04.

Homer (1965), *The Odyssey of Homer*, translated with an introduction by Richmond Lattimore. New York: Harper & Row.

Homer (1993), *The Odyssey: translation and analysis* by R. D. Dawe, Lewes: Book Guild.

Hornblower, S. (1982), *Mausolus*, Oxford: Clarendon.

Hornblower, S., A. Spawforth and E. Eidinow (eds) (2012), *Oxford Classical Dictionary*, 4th ed., Oxford: Oxford University Press.

Horrocks, G. (2010), *Greek: a History of the Language and its Speakers*, Chichester: Wiley-Blackwell.

Hubbard, T. K. (ed.) (2014), *A Companion to Greek and Roman Sexualities*, Chichester: Wiley-Blackwell.

Hughes, A. (2012), *Performing Greek Comedy*, Cambridge: Cambridge University Press.

Humphreys, S. C. (1993), *The Family, Women and Death: Comparative Studies*, 2nd ed., Ann Arbor: University of Michigan.

Hunt, P. (1998), *Slaves, Warfare and Ideology in the Greek Historians*, Cambridge: Cambridge University Press.

Hunter, R. L. (1979), 'The Comic Chorus in the Fourth Century', *ZPE* 36, 23–38.

Hunter, R. L. (1985), *The New Comedy of Greece and Rome*, Cambridge: Cambridge University Press.

Hunter, R. L. (2002), 'Acting Down' in P. E. Easterling and E. Hall (eds) (2002), *Greek and Roman Actors: Aspects of an Ancient Profession*, Cambridge: Cambridge University Press, 182–206.

Hurst, A. (1990), 'Ménandre et la Tragédie' in E. W. Handley and A. Hurst (eds), *Relire Ménandre*, Recherches et Rencontres, Geneve: Droz, 93–122.

Hutchinson, G. O. (1988), *Hellenistic Poetry*, Oxford: Clarendon.

Huys, M. (1993), 'P.Oxy. LIII, 3705: A Line from Menander's *Perikeiromene* with Musical Notation', *ZPE* 99, 30–2.

Ireland, S. (1992), *Menander: Dyscolus, Samia and other plays; a Companion to the Penguin Translation of the Plays of Menander by N. Miller*, Bristol: Bristol Classical Press.

Ireland, S. (2010), 'New Comedy' in G. W. Dobrov, ed., *Brill's Companion to the Study of Greek Comedy*, 333–96.

Isager, S. (1981–82), 'The Marriage Pattern in Classical Athens: Men and Women in Isaios', *Class. Med.* 33, 81–96.

Isager, S., and M. H. Hansen (1975), *Aspects of Athenian Society in the Fourth Century BC: a Historical Introduction to and Commentary on the 'Paragraphe' – Speeches and the Speech Against Dionysodorus in the Corpus Demosthenicum (XXXII–XXXVIII and LVI)*, translated by J.H. Rosenmeier, Odense University Classical Studies v.5.

Iversen, P. A. (2001), 'Coal for Diamonds: Syriskos' Character in Menander's *Epitrepontes*', *AJPh.* 122, 381–403.

James, S. L. (2014), 'Reconsidering Rape in Menander's Comedy and Athenian Life: Modern Comparative Evidence' in A. H. Sommerstein, ed., *Menander in Contexts*. Routledge, 24–39.

Joshel, S. R. and S. Murnaghan (eds) (1998), *Women and Slaves in Greco-Roman Culture: Differential Equations*, London: Routledge.

Just, R. (1989), *Women in Athenian Law and Life*, London: Routledge.

Kapparis, K. A. (2002), *Abortion in the Ancient World*, London: Duckworth.

Kassel, R. (1973), 'Neuer und Alter Menander', *ZPE* 12, 1–13.

Kassel, R. (1996), 'Aus der Arbeit an der Poetae Comici Graeci', *ZPE* 114, 57–8.

Kassel, R. and C. Austin (eds) (1983–;), *Poetae Comici Graeci* v.1–, Berlin and New York: de Gruyter.

Katsouris, A. G. (1983), 'Menander's Techniques for Lowering Tension', *LCM* 8.2, 30–1.

Khan, H. A. (1993), 'Conflict and Solidarity in Menander's *Dyscolus*' in J. H. Molyneux, ed., *Literary Responses to Civil Discord*, with response by Arnott, Nottingham Classical Literature Studies v.1, 37–55.

Konstan, D. (1995), *Greek Comedy and Ideology*, Oxford: Oxford University Press. (Contains extensive revisions of previous essays.)

Konstan, D. (1997), *Friendship in the Classical World*, Cambridge: Cambridge University Press.

Konstan, D. (2003), 'Epicureanism' in *The Blackwell Guide to Ancient Philosophy*, ed. C. Shields, Oxford: Blackwell Publishing, 237–52.

Konstan, D. (2010), 'Menander and Cultural Studies' in A. K. Petrides and S. Papaioannou (eds), *New Perspectives on Postclassical Comedy*, 31–50.

Konstan, D. (2013), 'Menander's Slaves: the Banality of Violence' in B. Akrigg and R. Tordoff (eds), *Slaves and Slavery in Ancient Greek Comic Drama*, 144–58.

Konstan, D. (2014), 'Crossing Conceptual Worlds: Greek Comedy and Philosophy' in
M. Fontaine and A. C. Scafuro (eds) (2014), *The Oxford Handbook of Greek and
Roman Comedy*, Oxford: Oxford University Press, 278–94.

Lacey, W. K. (1980 with corr.), *The Family in Classical Greece*, Aspects of Greek and Roman
Life, New Zealand: University of Auckland.

Laes, C. (2011), 'Grieving for Lost Children, Pagan and Christian' in B. Rawson (ed.), *A
Companion to Families in the Greek and Roman Worlds*, Chichester: Wiley-Blackwell,
315–30.

Lane Fox, R. J. (1973), *Alexander the Great*, London: Allen Lane.

Lane Fox, R. J. (1996), 'Theophrastus' *Characters* and the Historian', *PCPS* 42, 127–70.

Lape, S. (2004), *Reproducing Athens: Menander's Comedy, Democratic Culture, and the
Hellenistic City*, Princeton, NJ: Princeton University Press.

Lape, S. (2006), 'The Poetics of the *Kômos*-Chorus in Menander's Comedy' *AJPh*. 127, 89–109.

Larson, J. (2007), *Ancient Greek Cults: a Guide*, London: Routledge.

Lee, M. M. (2015), *Body, Dress, and Identity in Ancient Greece*, Cambridge: Cambridge
University Press.

Lefkowitz, M. R. (1981a), *Heroines and Hysterics*, London: Duckworth.

Lefkowitz, M. R. (1981b), *The Lives of the Greek Poets*, London: Duckworth.

Lefkowitz, M. R. (1995), 'The Last Hours of the Parthenos' in E. D. Reeder (ed.), *Pandora:
Women in Classical Greece*, with essays by S. C. Humphreys [et al.], Princeton:
Princeton University Press, 33–38.

Lefkowitz, M. R., and M. B. Fant (1982), *Women's Life in Greece and Rome: a Sourcebook in
Translation*, London: Duckworth.

Le Guen, B. (2007), 'Kraton, Son of Zotichos: Artists' Associations and Monarchic Power in
the Hellenstic Period' in P. Wilson (ed.), *The Greek Theatre Theatre and Festivals:
Documentary Studies*, Oxford Studies in Ancient Documents, Oxford: Oxford
University Press, 246–78.

Le Guen, B. (2014), 'The Diffusion of Comedy from the Age of Alexander to the
Beginnings of the Roman Empire' in M. Fontaine and A. C. Scafuro (eds), *The Oxford
Handbook of Greek and Roman Comedy*, Oxford: Oxford University Press, 359–77.

Levi, P. (1984), *Atlas of the Greek World,* Oxford: Equinox.

Lewis, S. (2002), *The Athenian Woman: an Iconographic Handbook*, London: Routledge.

Lightfoot, J. (2002), 'Nothing to do with the *technîtai* of Dionysus?' in P. E. Easterling and
E. Hall (eds), *Greek and Roman Actors: Aspects of an Ancient Profession*, Cambridge:
Cambridge University Press, 209–24.

Ling, R. (1991), *Roman Painting*, Cambridge: Cambridge University Press.

Ling, R. (1998), *Ancient Mosaics*, London: British Museum.

Lord, C. (1977), 'Aristotle, Menander and the *Adelphoe* of Terence', *TAPhA* 107, 183–202.

Lowe, N. J. (2008), Comedy, *G&R N.S.*, no. 37, Cambridge: Cambridge University Press for
the Classical Association.

Lurie, A. (1981), *The Language of Clothes*, London: Heinemann.

MacCary, W. T. (1969), 'Menander's Slaves: their Names, Roles and Masks', *TAPhA* 100,
277–94.

McCarthy, K. (2000), *Slaves, Masters and the Art of Authority in Plautine Comedy*,
Princeton, NJ: Princeton University Press.

McClure, L. K. (2003), *Courtesans at Table: Gender and Greek Literary Culture in
Athenaeus*, New York and London: Routledge.

McDonald, M., and J. M. Walton (eds) (2007), *The Cambridge Companion to Greek and
Roman Theatre*, Cambridge: Cambridge University Press.

MacDowell, D. M. (1978), *The Law in Classical Athens*, Aspects of Greek and Roman Life, London: Thames and Hudson.

McKeown, N. (2007), *The Invention of Ancient Slavery?*, London: Duckworth.

Major, W. E. (1997), 'Menander in a Macedonian World', *GRBS* 38, 41–73.

Marshall, C. W. (2013), 'Sex Slaves in New Comedy' in B. Akrigg and R. Tordoff (eds), *Slaves and Slavery in Ancient Greek Comic Drama*, Cambridge: Cambridge University Press, 173–96.

Marshall, C. W., and G. Kovacs (eds) (2012), *No Laughing Matter: Studies in Athenian Comedy*, Bristol: Bristol Classical Press.

Menander (1985 with corr.), *Samia*, edited with translation and notes by D. M. Bain, Warminster: Aris & Phillips.

Menander (1987), *Plays and Fragments*, translated with an introduction by N. Miller. Harmondsworth: Penguin.

Menander (1992), *The Dyscolus*, ed. E. W. Handley, Bristol: Bristol Classical Press.

Menander (1995), *The Bad-Tempered Man (Dyscolus)*, edited with translation, introduction and commentary by S. Ireland, Warminster: Aris & Phillips.

Menander (1997–2000), *Menandri Epitrepontes* ed. A. Martin, 2v. (v.2.1 and 2), Rome: Kepos (in Italian).

Menander (2001), *Plays and Fragments*, translated with notes by M. Balme with an introduction by P. Brown. Harmondsworth: Penguin.

Menander (2009b), *Dyscolos* (DVD), University of Sydney.

Menander (2010), *The Shield (Aspis)* and *The Arbitration (Epitrepontes)*, edited and translated by Stanley Ireland, Oxford: Aris & Phillips.

Menander (2013), *Samia*, ed. A. H. Sommerstein, Cambridge Greek & Latin Classics, Cambridge: Cambridge University Press.

Menander (2015), *Perikeiromene or The Shorn Head*, edited with an introduction and commentary by W. Furley, *BICS* Suppl.127.

Menander (forthcoming), *Menandri Reliquiae Selectae* (forthcoming), formerly edited by F. H. Sandbach (1990), rev. edn with Appendix, Oxford Classical Texts, Oxford: Oxford University Press.

Merchant, M. (1972), *Comedy*, The Critical Idiom 21, London: Methuen.

Meritt, B. D. (1938), 'Greek Inscriptions' in *Hesperia* 7, 77–160.

Michelini, A. N. (1987), *Euripides and the Tragic Tradition*, Madison, WI: University of Wisconsin.

Mikalson, J. D. (1998), *Religion in Hellenistic Athens*, Hellenistic Culture and Society 29, Berkeley, CA: University of California Press.

Mikalson, J. D. (2010), *Ancient Greek Religion*, 2nd ed., Chichester: Wiley-Blackwell.

Miles, S. (2014), 'Staging and Constructing the Divine in Menander' in A. H. Sommerstein, ed., *Menander in Contexts*, London: Routledge, 75–89.

Millett, P. (2007), *Theophrastus and his World*, Cambridge Classical Journal: Proceedings of the Cambridge Philological Society, supplementary volume 33, Cambridge Philological Society.

Modrzejewski, J. M. (2005), 'Greek Law in the Hellenistic Period' in M. Gagarin and D. Cohen (eds), *Cambridge Companion to Greek Law*, Cambridge: Cambridge University Press, 328–54.

Moloney, E. (2014), '*Philippus in acie tutior quam in theatro fuit . . . (Curtius 9, 6, 25)*: The Macedonian Kings and Greek Theatre' in E. Csapo, R. Goette, J. R. Green and P. Wilson, eds (2014), *Greek Theatre in the Fourth Century BCE*. Berlin: De Gruyter, 231–48.

Molyneux, J. H. ed. (1993), *Literary Responses to Civil Discord*. Nottingham: University of Nottingham.

Morgan, G. (1982), 'Euphiletos' house: Lysias I', *TAPhA* 112, 115–24.

Morgan, J. (2010), *The Classical Greek House*, Exeter: Bristol Phoenix Press.

Nesselrath, H.-G. (1997), 'The Polis of Athens in Middle Comedy' in G. W. Dobrov (ed.), *The City as Comedy: Society and Representation in Athenian Drama*, 27–88.

Nesselrath, H.-G. (2011), 'Menander and his Rivals: New Light from the Comic Adespota?' in D. Obbink and R. Rutherford (eds), *Culture in Pieces: Essays on Ancient Texts in Honour of Peter Parsons*, Oxford: Oxford University Press, 119–37.

Nevett, L. C. (1992), *Variation in the Form and Use of Domestic Space in the Greek World in the Classical and Hellenistic Periods*, PhD dissertation, University of Cambridge.

Nevett, L. C. (1995), 'Gender Relations in the Classical Greek Household: the Archaeological Evidence', *ABSA* 90, 363–81.

Nevett, L. C. (1999), *House and Society in the Ancient Greek World*, New Studies in Archaeology, Cambridge: Cambridge University Press.

Nevett, L. C. (2010), *Domestic Space in Classical Antiquity*, Cambridge: Cambridge University Press.

Nielsen, T. H. (ed.) (2002), *Even More Studies in the Ancient Greek Polis. Papers from the Copenhagen Polis Centre*, 6, Historia Einzelschriften 162, Stuttgart: Franz Steiner.

Nünlist, R. (2004), 'The Beginning of *Epitrepontes* Act II' in G. Bastianini and A. Casanova (eds), *Menandro: Cent'Anni di Papiri: Atti del Convegno Internazionale di Studi, Firenze, 12–13 Giugno 2003* (2004), 95–106.

Oakley, J. H., and R. H. Sinos (1993), *The Wedding in Ancient Athens*, Madison, WI: University of Wisconsin.

Obbink, D. and R. Rutherford (eds) (2011), *Culture in Pieces: Essays on Ancient Texts in Honour of Peter Parsons*, Oxford: Oxford University Press.

Ogden, D. (1996), *Greek Bastardy in the Classical and Hellenistic Periods*, Oxford: Clarendon.

Ogden, D. (1997), 'Rape, Adultery and Protection of Bloodlines in Classical Athens', in S. Deacy and K. F. Pierce (eds), *Rape in Antiquity: Sexual Violence in the Greek and Roman Worlds*, Classical Press of Wales and Duckworth, 25–41.

Ogden, D. (ed.) (2002), *The Hellenistic World: New Perspectives*, Classical Press of Wales and Duckworth.

O'Higgins, L. (2003), *Women and Humor in Classical Greece*, Cambridge: Cambridge University Press.

Olson, S. D. (ed.) (2007), *Broken Laughter: Select Fragments of Greek Comedy*, edited with introduction, commentary and translation, Oxford: Oxford University Press.

Olson, S. D. (2010), 'Comedy, Politics and Society' in G. W. Dobrov, *Brill's Companion to the Study of Greek Comedy*, Leiden and Boston: Brill, 35–69.

Omitowoju, R. (2002), *Rape and the Politics of Consent in Classical Athens*, Cambridge Classical Studies, Cambridge: Cambridge University Press.

Omitowoju, R. (2010), 'Performing Traditions: Relations and Relationships in Menander and Tragedy' in A. K. Petrides & S. Papaioannou (eds), *New Perspectives on Postclassical Comedy*, Pierides Studies in Greek and Latin Literature v.2, Newcastle: Cambridge Scholars Publishing, 125–45.

O'Sullivan, L. (2009), *The Regime of Demetrius of Phalerum in Athens 317–307 BCE: A Philosopher in Politics,* Mnemosyne Supplements: History and Archaeology of Classical Antiquity, v. 318, Leiden: Brill.

Osborne, R. (1987), *Classical Landscapes with Figures: the Ancient Greek City and its Countryside*, London: George Philips.

Osborne, R., and S. Hornblower (eds) (1994), *Ritual, Finance, Politics: Athenian Democratic Accounts Presented to David Lewis*, Oxford: Clarendon.

Owen, J. (1997), *Disguise and Role-Playing in Drama with Particular Reference to Athenian Old Comedy*, M.Litt., University of Cambridge.

Owens, W. M. (2011), 'The Political Topicality of Menander's *Dyscolus*' in *AJPh*. 132, Special Issue: Classical Courts and Courtiers, 349–78.

Padel, R. (1990), 'Making Space Speak' in J. J. Winkler & F. I. Zeitlin (eds), *Nothing to do with Dionysos?: Athenian Drama in its Social Context*, Princeton, NJ: Princeton University Press, 336–65.

Parker, R. (2005), *Polytheism and Society at Athens*, Oxford: Oxford University Press.

Parsons, P. J. (2007), *City of the Sharp-Nosed Fish: Greek Papyri Beneath the Egyptian Sand Reveal a Long-Lost World*, edition with plates, London: Phoenix.

Parsons, P. J. (2015), 'A Few Letters More' in R. Green and M. Edwards (eds), *Images and Texts: Papers in Honour of Professor Eric Handley, CBE, FBA, BICS* Suppl. 129, 27–9.

Patterson, C. (1985), 'Not Worth the Rearing': the Causes of Infant Exposure in Ancient Greece' in *TAPhA* 115, 103–23.

Patterson, C. (1998) *The Family in Greek History*, Cambridge, MA: Harvard University Press.

Patterson, O. (1982), *Slavery and Social Death: a Comparative Study*, Cambridge, MA: Harvard University Press.

Patterson, O. (1991), *Freedom, v.1: Freedom in the Making of Western Culture*, I. B. Tauris.

Petrides, A. K. (2014), *Menander, New Comedy and the Visual*, Cambridge: Cambridge University Press.

Petrides, A. K., and S. Papaioannou (eds) (2010), *New Perspectives on Postclassical Comedy*, Pierides Studies in Greek and Latin Literature v.2, Newcastle: Cambridge Scholars Publishing.

Pickard-Cambridge, A. W. (1946), *The Theatre of Dionysus in Athens*, Oxford: Clarendon.

Pickard-Cambridge, A. W. (1988), *The Dramatic Festivals of Athens*, 2nd ed., revised by J. Gould and D. M. Lewis, reissued with supplement and corrections, Oxford: Clarendon. New edition forthcoming by E. Csapo and P. Wilson.

Pierce, K. (1998), 'Ideals of Masculinity in New Comedy' in L. Foxhall and J. Salmon (eds), *Thinking Men: Masculinity and its Self Representation in the Classical Tradition*, London: Routledge, 130–47.

Plautus (1986), *Bacchides,* edited with a translation and commentary by J. Barsby, Oxford: Aris & Phillips.

Plautus (2000), *Amphitruo*, ed. D. M. Christenson, Cambridge Greek & Latin Classics, Cambridge: Cambridge University Press.

Podlecki, A. J., 'Could Women Attend the Theater in Ancient Athens?', *AW* 21 (1990) 27–43.

Pomeroy, S. B. (1975), *Goddesses, Whores, Wives and Slaves: Women in Classical Antiquity*, New York: Schocken.

Pomeroy, S. B. (1993), 'Infanticide in Hellenistic Greece' in A. Cameron & A. Kuhrt (eds), *Images of Women in Antiquity*, rev. ed., London: Routledge, 207–22.

Pomeroy, S. B. (ed.) (1994), *Xenophon, Oeconomicus : a Social and Historical Commentary*, with a new English translation by S. B. Pomeroy, Oxford: Clarendon.

Pomeroy, S. B. (1997), *Families in Classical and Hellenistic Greece: Representations and Realities*, Oxford: Clarendon.

Porter, J. R. (2000), 'Euripides and Menander: *Epitrepontes*, act. IV' in M. Cropp, K. Lee and S. Sansone (eds), *Euripides and Tragic Theatre in the Late Fifth Century*, Illinois Classical Studies v. 24–25, Urbana. IL: University of Illinois Press, 157–73.

Post, L. A. (1939), 'Dramatic Infants in Greek', *CPhil.*, 34, 193–208.

Powell, A. (ed.) (1995), *The Greek World*, London: Routledge.

Proffitt, L. (2011), 'Family, Slavery and Subversion in Menander's *Epitrepontes*' in R. Alston, E. Hall and L. Proffitt, *Reading Ancient Slavery*, London: Bristol Classical Press, 152–74.

Purves, A. C. (2010), *Space and Time in Ancient Greek Narrative*, Cambridge: Cambridge University Press.

Rabinowitz, N. S. (1998), 'Slaves with Slaves: Women and Class in Euripidean Tragedy' in S. R. Joshel and S. Murnaghan (eds), *Women and Slaves in Greco-Roman Culture: Differential Equations*, London: Routledge, 56–68.

Rangos, S. (1995), *Cults of Artemis in Ancient Greece*: thesis submitted to the Faculty of Classics, University of Cambridge, for the PhD degree.

Rasmussen, T. and N. Spivey (eds) (1991), *Looking at Greek Vases*, Cambridge: Cambridge University Press.

Rawson, B. (ed.) (2011), *A Companion to Families in the Greek and Roman Worlds*, Chichester: Wiley-Blackwell.

Re, R. (2002), 'A Persisting Evil: the Global Problem of Slavery', *HIR* 23, 32–5.

Reeder, E. D. (ed.) (1995), *Pandora: Women in Classical Greece*, New Jersey: Trustees of the Walters Art Gallery in association with the University of Princeton.

Rehm, R. (2007), 'Festivals and Audiences in Athens and Rome' in M. McDonald and J. M. Walton (eds), *The Cambridge Companion to Greek and Roman Theatre*, Cambridge: Cambridge University Press, 184–201.

Revermann, M., ed. (2014), *The Cambridge Companion to Greek Comedy*, Cambridge: Cambridge University Press.

Richlin, A. (2009), 'Writing Women into History' in A. Erskine (ed.), *A Companion to Ancient History*, Oxford: Wiley-Blackwell, 146–53.

Richter, G. M. A. (1965), *The Portraits of the Greeks*, 3v., London: Phaidon.

Richter, G. M. A. (1984), *The Portraits of the Greeks*, abridged and revised by R. R. R. Smith, London: Phaidon.

Riddle, J. M. (1992), *Contraception and Abortion from the Ancient World to the Renaissance*, Cambridge, MA: Harvard University Press.

Riemer, P. and B. Zimmermann (eds) (1998), *Der Chor im Antiken und Modernen Drama* (Drama 7), Stuttgart: Metzler.

Roisman, J., ed. (2003), *Brill's Companion to Alexander the Great*, Leiden: Brill.

Roisman, J. and I. Worthington (eds) (2010), *A Companion to Ancient Macedonia*, Chichester: Wiley-Blackwell, 572–98.

Römer, C. (2012a), 'New Fragments of Act IV, *Epitrepontes* 786–823 Sandbach (P. Mich. 4752a, b and c)', *ZPE* 182, 112–202.

Römer, C. (2012b), 'A New Fragment of End of Act III, *Epitrepontes* 690–701 Sandbach (P. Mich. 4805)', *ZPE* 183, 33–6.

Roselli, D. K. (2011), *Theater of the People: Spectators and Society in Ancient Athens*, Austin: University of Texas.

Rosenbloom, D. (2014), 'The Politics of Comic Athens' in M. Fontaine and A. C. Scafuro (eds), *The Oxford Handbook of Greek and Roman Comedy*, Oxford: Oxford University Press, 297–320.

Rosivach, V. J. (1984), 'Aphairesis and Apoleipsis: a Study of the Sources' *RIDA* 31, 193–230.

Rosivach, V. J. (1998), *When a Young Man Falls in Love: the Sexual Exploitation of Women in New Comedy*, London: Routledge.

Rothwell, K. S. (1995), 'The Continuity of the Chorus in Fourth-Century Attic Comedy' in
    G. W. Dobrov (ed.), *Beyond Aristophanes: Transition and Diversity in Greek Comedy*,
    Atlanta, GA: Scholars Press, 99–118.
Ruffell, I. (2014), 'Character Types' in M. Revermann (ed.), *The Cambridge Companion to
    Greek Comedy*, Cambridge: Cambridge University Press, 147–67.
Rusten, J. (ed.) (2011), *The Birth of Comedy: Texts, Documents, and Art from Athenian
    Competitions, 48–280*, translated by J. Henderson and others, Baltimore: Johns Hopkins
    University Press.
Ryan, K. (1989), *Shakespeare*, London: Harvester Wheatsheaf.
Ryan, K. (2009) *Shakespeare's Comedies*, New York: Palgrave Macmillan.
Sandbach, F. H. (1970), 'Menander's Manipulation of Language for Dramatic Purposes', in
    E. G. Turner (ed.), *Entretiens Hardt 16: Ménandre*, 113–36, with discussion, 137–43.
Scafuro, A. C. (1997), *The Forensic Stage: Settling Disputes in Graeco-Roman New Comedy*,
    Cambridge: Cambridge University Press.
Scafuro, A. C. (2014), 'Comedy in the Late Fourth and early Third Centuries BCE' in M.
    Fontaine and A. C. Scafuro (eds), *The Oxford Handbook of Greek and Roman Comedy*,
    Oxford: Oxford University Press, 199–217.
Schaps, D. M. (1977), 'The Woman Least Mentioned: Etiquette and Women's Names' in
    CQ N.S. 27, 323–30.
Schaps, D. M. (1981), *Economic Rights of Women in Ancient Greece*, 2nd ed., Edinburgh:
    Edinburgh University Press.
Scheidel, W. (1995), 'The Most Silent Women of Greece and Rome: Rural Labour and
    Women's Life in the Ancient World I', *G&R* v.42, 202–17.
Scheidel, W. (1996), 'The Most Silent Women of Greece and Rome: Rural Labour and
    Women's Life in the Ancient World II', *G&R* v.43, 1–10.
Scodel, R. (ed.) (1993), *Theater and Society in the Classical World*, Ann Arbor, Mich.:
    University of Michigan Press.
Scott, M. (2009), *From Democrats to Kings: the Brutal Dawn of a New World from the
    Downfall of Athens to the Rise of Alexander the Great*, Thriplow: Icon Books.
Scott, M. (2013), *Ancient Greece: The Greatest Show on Earth* (3-part television series,
    updated 2017), Open University, https://www.open.edu/openlearn/tv-radio-events/tv/
    ancient-greece-the-greatest-show-on-earth
Scullion, S. (2014), 'Religion and the Gods in Greek Comedy' in M. Fontaine and
    A. C. Scafuro (eds), *The Oxford Handbook of Greek and Roman Comedy*, Oxford:
    Oxford University Press, 340–55.
Segal, E. (1987), *Roman Laughter: the Comedy of Plautus,* 2nd ed., Oxford: Oxford
    University Press.
Segal, E. (ed.) (2001), *Oxford Readings in Menander, Plautus and Terence*, Oxford: Oxford
    University Press.
Shapiro, H. A. (1993), *Personifications in Greek Art: the Representations of Abstract
    Concepts 600–400 BC*, Zurich: Akanthus.
Sharples, R. W. (2006), 'Philosophy for Life' in G. R. Bugh ed., *The Cambridge Companion to
    the Hellenistic World*, Cambridge: Cambridge University Press, 223–40.
Shields, C. (ed.) (2003), *The Blackwell Guide to Ancient Philsosophy*, Oxford: Blackwell.
Shipley, G. (2000), *The Greek World after Alexander 323–30 BC*, London: Routledge.
Shipley, G., J. Vanderspoel, D. Mattingly and L. Foxhall (2006), *The Cambridge Dictionary
    of Classical Civilization*, Cambridge: Cambridge University Press.
Sidwell, K. (2014), 'Fourth Century Comedy before Menander' in M. Revermann (ed.) (2014),
    The Cambridge Companion to Greek Comedy, Cambridge: Cambridge University Press.

Silk, M. (1998), 'Style, Voice and Authority in the Choruses of Greek Drama' in P. Riemer and B. Zimmermann (eds) *Der Chor im Antiken und Modernen Drama* (Drama 7) Stuttgart: Metzler.

Simon, E. (1982), *The Ancient Theatre*, translated by C. E. Vafopoulou-Richardson, rev. ed., London: Methuen (repr. London: Routledge, 1988).

Sissa, G. (1990a), *Greek Virginity*, translated by A. Goldhammer, Cambridge, MA: Harvard University Press.

Sissa, G. (1990b), 'Maidenhood without Maidenhead: the Female Body in Ancient Greece' in D. M. Halperin, J. J. Winkler and F. I. Zeitlin (eds), *Before Sexuality: the Construction of Erotic Experience in the Ancient Greek World*, Princeton, NJ: Princeton University Press, 339–64.

Sisti, F. (1991), *Epitrepontes*, Università di Genova (in Italian).

Skinner, M. B. (2005), *Sexuality in Greek and Roman Culture*, Ancient Cultures, Oxford: Blackwell.

Slater, N. W. (2001), '*Amphitruo, Bacchae*, and Metatheatre' in E. Segal, ed., *Oxford Readings in Menander, Plautus and Terence*, Oxford: Oxford University Press, 189–202.

Slater, N. W. (2002), *Spectator Politics: Metatheatre and Performance in Aristophanes*, Philadelphia, PA: University of Pennsylvania Press.

Sommerstein, A. H. (1980), 'The Naming of Women in Greek and Roman Comedy' in *Quaderni di Storia* 6 (11), 393–418.

Sommerstein, A. H. (1995), 'The Language of Athenian Women' in F. De Martino & A. H. Sommerstein (eds), *Lo Spettacolo delle Voci,* Bari, Levanti, 61–85.

Sommerstein, A. H. (1998), 'Rape and Young Manhood in Athenian Comedy' in L. Foxhall and J. Salmon (eds), *Thinking Men: Masculinity and its Self Representation in the Classical Tradition*, 100–14.

Sommerstein, A. H. (2002), *Greek Drama and Dramatists*, London: Routledge.

Sommerstein, A. H. (ed.) (2014), *Menander in Contexts*, London: Routledge.

Sommerstein, A. H. (2014), 'Menander and the *Pallake*' in A. H. Sommerstein, ed. (2014), *Menander in Contexts*, London: Routledge, 11–23.

Soskice, J. (2010), *Sisters of Sinai: How Two Lady Adventurers Found the Hidden Gospels*, Vintage.

Sourvinou-Inwood, C. (2003), *Tragedy and Athenian Religion*, Greek Studies: Interdisciplinary Approaches, Lanham, MD: Lexington Books.

Stafford, E.J. (1998), 'Masculine Values, Feminine Forms: on the Genre of Personified Abstractions' in L. Foxhall and J. Salmon (eds) *Thinking Men: Masculinity and its Self Representation in the Classical Tradition*, London: Routledge, 43–56.

Stafford, E. (2000), *Worshipping Virtues: Personification and the Divine in Ancient Greece*, London: Duckworth.

Steel, C. (2009), 'Oratory' in A. Erskine (ed.), *A Companion to Ancient History*, 67–76.

Stevenson, H. (2009), *Jobs for the Boys: a Story of a Family in Britain's Imperial Heyday*, London: Dove Books.

Stockett, K. (2009), *The Help*, London: Fig Tree.

Storey, I. (2003), *Eupolis: Poet of Old Comedy*, Oxford: Oxford University Press.

Synodinou, I. (1977), *On the Concept of Slavery in Euripides,* Ioannina: Philosophike Schole Panepistemiou Ioanninon.

Taplin, O. (1993), *Comic Angels and Other Approaches to Greek Drama Through Vase-Paintings*, Oxford: Clarendon.

Taplin, O. (1999), 'Spreading the Word Through Performance' in S. Goldhill and R. Osborne (eds), *Performance Culture and Athenian Democracy,* 33–57.

Taylor, C. (2011), 'Women's Social Networks and Female Friendship in the Ancient Greek City' in L. Foxhall and G. Neher (eds) (2011), *Gender and the City Before Modernity, Gender & History* v. 23, no.3 Special Issue, 703–20.

Taylor, D. (1999), *The Greek and Roman Stage*, Bristol: Bristol Classical Press.

Theophrastus (1993), *Characters*; Herodas, *Mimes*, Cercidas and the Choliambic Poets, edited and translated by J. Rusten, I. C. Cunningham and A. D. Knox, 2nd edn, Loeb Classical Library, Cambridge, MA: Harvard University Press.

Theophrastus (2004), *Characters*, edited with introduction, translation and commentary by James Diggle, Cambridge: Cambridge University Press.

Tierney, M. (1935–37), 'Aristotle and Menander', *PRIA* 43, Sect. C. 241–54.

Todd, S. C. (1993), *The Shape of Athenian Law*, Oxford: Clarendon.

Todd, S. C. (2007), *Lysias: A Commentary . . . Speeches 1 –11*, Oxford: Oxford University Press.

Too, Y. L. (2001), 'The Economics of Pedagogy: Xenophon's Wifely Didactics' in *PCPS* 47, 65–80.

Tordoff, R. (2013), 'Introduction: Slaves and Slavery in Ancient Greek Comedy' in B. Akrigg and R. Tordoff (eds), *Slaves and Slavery in Ancient Greek Comic Drama*, Cambridge: Cambridge University Press, 1–62.

Traill, A. (2008), *Women and the Comic Plot in Menander*, Cambridge: Cambridge University Press.

Trendall, A. D. (1969), 'The Stevenson Collection from Lipari – Greek Vases', *SAR* 12, 1–5 and 28.

Trendall, A. D. (1989), *Red-Figure Vases of South Italy and Sicily: a Handbook*, London: Thames and Hudson.

Trendall, A. D. and T. B. L. Webster (1971), *Illustrations of Greek Drama*, London: Phaidon.

Trendall, A. D. (1991), 'Farce and Tragedy in South Italian Vase-Painting' in T. Rasmussen & N. Spivey (eds), *Looking at Greek Vases*, Cambridge: Cambridge University Press, 151–82.

Trümper, M. (2010), *Graeco-Roman Slave Markets: Fact or Fiction?*, Oxford: Oxbow.

Turner, E. G. (1980), *Greek Papyri: an Introduction*, rev. edn, Oxford: Clarendon.

Tusa, S. (1999), 'Obituary of Bernabò Brea', *ANT* 73 (1999), 255–8.

Urbainczyk, T. (2008), *Slave Revolts in Antiquity*, Acumen.

Ussher, R. G. (1977), 'Old Comedy and "Character": Some Comments', *G&R* N.S. 24, 71–9.

Ussher, R. G. (ed.) (1993), *The Characters of Theophrastus*, edited with introduction, commentary and index, rev. ed., Bristol: Bristol Classical Press.

Vester, C. (2013), 'Tokens of Identity in Menander's *Epitrepontes*' in B. Akrigg and R. Tordoff (eds), *Slaves and Slavery in Ancient Greek Comic Drama*, Cambridge: Cambridge University Press, 209–27.

Vidal-Naquet, P. (1986), *The Black Hunter: Forms of Thought and Forms of Society in the Greek World*, translated by A. Szegedy-Maszak, with a foreword by B. Knox, Baltimore, MD: Johns Hopkins University Press.

Vogt, J. (1974), *Ancient Slavery and the Ideal of Man*, translated by T. Wiedemann, Oxford: Blackwell.

Voigt, F. (1937), 'Peitho (Literatur)' in *RE* 19, 194–217.

Walton, J. M. and P. D. Arnott (1996), *Menander and the Making of Comedy*, Westport, CT: Praeger.

Webb, R. (2002), 'Female Entertainers in Late Antiquity' in P. E. Easterling and E. Hall (eds), *Greek and Roman Actors: Aspects of an Ancient Profession*, Cambridge: Cambridge University Press, 282–303.

Webster, T. B. L. (1969), 'The Stevenson Collection from Lipari' *SAR* 12 (1969) 6–7 and 28.

Webster, T. B. L. (1970a), *Greek Theatre Production*, 2nd edn, London: Methuen.

Webster, T. B. L. (1970b), *Studies in Later Greek Comedy*, 2nd edn, Manchester: Manchester University Press.

Webster, T. B. L. (1974), *An Introduction to Menander*, Manchester: Manchester University Press.

Weiler, I. (2002), 'Inverted *Kalokagathia*' in T. Wiedemann and J. Gardner (eds), *Representing the Body of the Slave*, London: Frank Cass, 11–28.

Wiedemann, T. (1981), *Greek and Roman Slavery*, London: Routledge.

Wiedemann, T. (1987), *Slavery, G&R N.S.* no. 19.

Wiedemann, T. and J. Gardner (eds) (2002), *Representing the Body of the Slave*, London: Frank Cass.

Wilamowitz-Moellendorff, U. v. (ed.) (1961), *Das Schiedsgericht (Epitrepontes)*, 3rd edn, Berlin: Weidmannsche (in German).

Wiles, D. (1989), 'Marriage and Prostitution in Classical New Comedy' in *Themes in Drama 11: Women in Theatre*, edited by J. Redmond, Cambridge: Cambridge University Press, 31–48.

Wiles, D. (1991), *The Masks of Menander: Sign and Meaning in Greek and Roman Performance*, Cambridge: Cambridge University Press, 1991.

Wiles, D. (2000), *Greek Theatre Performance: an Introduction*, Cambridge: Cambridge University Press.

Wiles, D. (2007), *Mask and Performance in Greek Tragedy: From Ancient Festival to Modern Experimentation*, Cambridge: Cambridge University Press.

Williams, R. (1983), *Writing in Society*, London: Verso.

Williams, R. (2002), 'Performance and Dramatic Discourse in New Comedy' in J. Barsby ed., *Greek and Roman Drama: Translation and Performance*, Stuttgart: Metzler, 12, 125–45.

Williams, R. (2004), 'Digital Resources for Practice-Based Research: the New Comedy Masks Project', *Literary and Linguistic Computing* 19, 415–25.

Wilson, N. (1996), *Scholars of Byzantium*, rev. edn, London: Duckworth.

Wilson, N. (2014a), 'The Transmission of Comic Texts' in M. Revermann (ed.), *The Cambridge Companion to Greek Comedy*, Cambridge: Cambridge University Press, 424–32.

Wilson, N. (2014b), 'The Transmission of Aristophanes' in M. Fontaine and A. C. Scafuro (eds), *The Oxford Handbook of Greek and Roman Comedy*, Oxford: Oxford University Press, 655–6.

Wilson, P. (2000), *The Athenian Institution of the Khoregia: the Chorus, the City and the Stage*, Cambridge: Cambridge University Press.

Wilson, P. (2002), 'The Musicians Among the Actors' in P. E. Easterling and E. Hall (eds), *Greek and Roman Actors: Aspects of an Ancient Profession*, Cambridge: Cambridge University Press, 39–68.

Wilson, P. (ed.) (2007), *The Greek Theatre and Festivals: Documentary Studies*, Oxford Studies in Ancient Documents, Oxford: Oxford University Press.

Winkler, J. J., and F. I. Zeitlin (eds) (1990), *Nothing To Do With Dionysos?: Athenian Drama In Its Social Context*, Princeton, NJ: Princeton University Press.

Winnington-Ingram, R. P. (1989), 'Aeschylus,' in Easterling, P. E. and B. M. W. Knox (eds) (1989), *The Cambridge History of Classical Literature*, v. 1, pt.2: *Greek Drama*, Cambridge: Cambridge University Press, 29–43.

Wiseman, T. P. (ed.) (2002), *Classics in Progress: Essays on Ancient Greece and Rome*, Oxford: Oxford University Press for the British Academy.

Witzke, S. (2014), 'An Ideal Reception: Oscar Wilde, Menander's Comedy and the Context of Victorian Classical Studies' in A. H. Sommerstein (ed.) (2014), *Menander in Contexts*, London: Routledge, 215–32.

Wood, M. (1998), 'In the Footsteps of Alexander the Great: a Journey from Greece to Asia' (DVD), Maryland Public Television for the BBC.

Wrenhaven, K. L. (2011), 'Greek Representations of the Slave Body: a Conflict of Ideas?' in R. Alston, E. Hall and L. Proffitt (eds), *Reading Ancient Slavery*, Bristol: Bristol Classical Press, 97–120.

Wrenhaven, K. L. (2012), *Reconstructing the Slave: the Image of the Slave in Ancient Greece*, Bristol: Bristol Classical Press.

Wyles, R. (2011), *Costume in Greek Tragedy*, Bristol: Bristol Classical Press.

Xanthakis-Karamanos, G. (1980), *Studies in Fourth-Century Tragedy*, Athens: Akademia Athenon.

Zagagi, N. (1994), *The Comedy of Menander: Convention, Variation & Originality*, London: Duckworth. (Includes abridged, revised versions of some previous papers.)

Zanker, P. (1995), *The Mask of Socrates: the Image of the Intellectual in Antiquity*, translated by A. Shapiro, Berkeley, CA: University of California Press.

Index

9 781350 190696